Yale Romanic Studies, Second Series, 22

TOWARD DRAMATIC ILLUSION:

THEATRICAL TECHNIQUE AND MEANING

FROM HARDY TO *HORACE*

BY T. J. REISS

New Haven and London, Yale University Press

1971

Published with assistance from
the Louis Effingham deForest Memorial Fund.
Copyright © 1971 by Yale University.
All rights reserved. This book may not be
reproduced, in whole or in part, in any form
(except by reviewers for the public press),
without written permission from the publishers.
Library of Congress catalog card number: 77–115376
International standard book number: 0–300–01328–0
Designed by John O. C. McCrillis
and set in Press Roman type.
Printed in the United States of America by
The Carl Purington Rollins Printing-Office
of the Yale University Press.
Distributed in Great Britain, Europe, and Africa by
Yale University Press, Ltd., London; in Canada by
McGill-Queen's University Press, Montreal; in Mexico
by Centro Interamericano de Libros Académicos,
Mexico City; in Central and South America by
Kaiman & Polon, Inc., New York City; in Australasia
by Australia and New Zealand Book Co., Pty., Ltd.,
Artarmon, New South Wales; in India by UBS Publishers'
Distributors Pvt., Ltd., Delhi; in Japan
by John Weatherhill, Inc., Tokyo.

To Jean
and to my parents

Contents

Introduction

From the Renaissance to the present day literary creativity in France has been accompanied by innumerable sage theories (some more valuable than others) as to what the creator should really be doing. At times the artist and the theorist are one and the same, as in most prefaces and many *Examens* and *Notes.* More often the latter is a critic, himself not directly involved in the creative labor, or at most a mediocre artist—particularly in the seventeenth century—which leads one to suspect that the connection between theory and practice is less close than is generally claimed. There are, indeed, very good reasons why theory and practice should differ somewhat, since their roots are quite distinct.

Taking into account that the classical theater is no more than a rather impressive wave in an always rolling sea, it is my intention here to attempt an examination of the specific currents which contributed to it by a close study of the works themselves, rather than the various comments upon them. Since theater is the object of this study, it seems to me that, as far as possible, all theatrical elements—*mise en scène,* acting, the spoken language in conjunction with visual effect, the spectator—should be considered, as it is apparent that the ostensible themes of the theater often become just one more of these elements. It will become equally clear, I hope, that the classical theater did not arise out of a previously formless and unchanging mass.

Of all these elements the most important is the spectator, and it is precisely he who is never taken into account in current explanations of the "sudden" change in the direction of the French theater around 1640. Some indication is needed of the spectator's effect on a play, and vice versa: a view of the spectator not as the recipient of a play's moral or entertaining effects, but as an integral part of what Sartre and others call the theatrical "ritual."[1]

---

1. See, e.g., Jean-Paul Sartre, "Forgers of Myths. The Young Playwrights of France," *Theatre Arts,* XXX, 6 (June 1946), 324-35.

In order to undertake a study toward this end, one must somehow
compensate for lack of first-hand reports on how spectators reacted
to specific plays during this period. It is impossible to compile a cata-
logue such as that of Pierre Mélèse for the period prior to 1659. One
can, however, make certain inferences, based on authors' remarks and
comments by later critics, like those of D'Aubignac on Théophile's
Pyrame et Thisbé. These inferences are the subject of Chapter 4,
which follows my examination of the early theater, thus enabling a
comparison between critical remarks and actual practice. It is hoped
that this comparison will illuminate the problem of the spectator's
perception.

I do believe that a close analysis of certain plays will reveal a distinct
difference in the kind of responses demanded of the spectator, even
over the relatively short period between 1600 and 1640 or so. The
text itself will be considered here as simply another element of the
total production, thus shifting a certain degree of emphasis to the
spectator. While he is no more important than any other single factor,
this focus may clarify the balance playwrights sought to achieve among
all the factors involved, and so define a style of theater.

In the following discussion, the concept of "psychical distance" as
formulated by Edward Bullough[2] will prove helpful toward understanding the different relationships evolving between the stage and the spectator. This term implies that separation of two parts of the mind—the
one objective, the other subjective—which allows a spectator on the one
hand to make an intellectual, moral and aesthetic judgement, and on
the other to absorb himself emotionally in the spell of the theatrical
action. While the subjective mind seems involved in the stage action,
the objective looks on from a distance, and judges not only the action
but also the viewer's emotion, its effect and significance; this division
is the essence of "psychical distance." How far these two parts are actually separated—the precise "distance," that is—must depend on the
audience in question, and the play as well. A more cerebral audience
will succumb less readily to the stage action; a more emotional audience
will be less likely to appreciate the play aesthetically or morally. Brecht,
for example, would seem to need (if not demand) a more intellectual

2. In his article "'Psychical Distance' as a Factor in Art and an Esthetic Principal," *British Journal of Psychology*, V (1913), 87-118.

audience to obtain the *Verfremdungseffekt* which he envisaged as the most appropriate means for achieving social instruction. Total distancing, as Brecht's experience illustrates, is just as rare as the reduction of distance to zero, when the spectator is entirely given over to the action, when he can make no kind of judgment because his "attitude est uniquement commandée par la force dramatique de l'événement."[3]

This distance between stage and spectator may remain at one level throughout a performance, or fluctuate as the drama progresses; and the spectator's reaction, both affective and intellectual, will be determined accordingly. Thus, an understanding of psychical distance will perhaps enable a clearer comprehension of what a theater is trying to communicate. I do not mean to suggest that there is a simple choice between "fluctuation" and "stability"—the condition created by the stage will alter the effect, and the combinations are probably endless. What I wish to do here is trace the changes in reaction and communication over the years between 1600 and about 1640: changes which constitute a steady development.

Despite the wide currency of the "adaptations" of Aristotle's *Poetics* by Castelvetro, Scaliger, and the rest during the sixteenth century, their effect on theatrical output was immediate only in certain cases and in the very restricted milieu of the schools. The theory was poetic rather than dramatic, in fact, and had little theatrical application for the very good reason that it was formulated virtually in a void. As far as the public it could reach was concerned, the theory preceded the practice, and since for the most part it did not stress theatricality, it led to the production of versified dialogue or monologue which the actor orated on stage. The output of Jodelle, Mellin de Sainct-Gelais, Antoine de Baïf, and even Grévin, whatever their individual merits and whether or not they approached a less static theater, was presented by scholars and poets to an audience composed of the same. This limited audience, untouched by the mysteries, the miracle plays, the farces and *sotties,* tended to isolate a highly-specialized theater, and had little interest in drawing in a wider public. The theorists were at once highly refined and highly restricted; it is scarcely surprising that their views

3. Henri Gouhier, *L'Essence du théâtre* (Paris, 1943), p. 163.

should not affect the entertainment of their more "vulgar" contemporaries.

The reasons for the sharply divided theater audience during this period are difficult to adduce. It is certain, however, that in the mid-1590s an Alexandre Hardy could start producing relatively sophisticated plays which enjoyed sufficient success in the provinces to keep an entire theater troupe on the road. Perhaps he, and others now largely unknown, were forced in this direction to make a living, for the religious wars had deprived them of many wealthy patrons.[4] Economic success would naturally entail less concern with high-sounding theories and more for the simpler tastes of the general, and paying, public.

Between the turn of the century and the mid-1620s, writers for a nonpaying public produced little except the semi-dramatized poetry of Montchrestien and Billard, whose acceptance depended on the awareness of their small aristocratic audiences of a dramatic action in language itself. In any case, the type of prospective patron and audience returning from the wars was doubtless somewhat rougher than its predecessor, and interested in sport more lusty or spectacular than that provided by this scholarly theater. While one or two might read Montchrestien or Billard, it was hardly likely that several would gather together and sit peacefully through a performance of a poetic play. This enlivened audience may explain why the more spectacular ballets (which also gave the nobles parts more suited to their temperaments) had such a vogue at court from a time which roughly coincided with Hardy's appearance to the early 1620s. Paris proved singularly inhospitable to Hardy and Valleran, and one can only speculate that the ballets maintained sufficient interest at court to keep most of the nobility away from the performance of Tabarin or the *farceurs* at the Hôtel de Bourgogne.

Within the capital, then, the audiences remained separate for the time being. In the provinces, on the other hand, there was no ballet; and while some country noble might present an entertainment in his chateau (even then, as often as not, using itinerant players), those who wanted to see a play—or simply be entertained—had to go where the general populace went. It was this mixed audience that supported the

---

4. Maurice Descotes, *Le Public du théâtre et son histoire* (Paris, 1964), p. 27.

theater of Alexandre Hardy (supplemented by works of Garnier and others).[5]

In Paris there were few changes on the theater scene until the early 1620s, with the appearance of Mairet and Théophile (who may or may not have written for the boards before *Pyrame et Thisbé* [circa 1621]), and of Racan with *Les Bergeries* (circa 1623). The immense success of *Sylvie* (1626) doubtless stemmed from more causes than can be imagined here. Certainly Hardy's influence cannot be underestimated, and that the French theater burgeoned when it did must be credited in part to him. In 1621 the standard of the *ballets de cour* dropped sharply with the death of De Luynes, the man chiefly responsible for these events. In 1623 Hardy's *Theagene et Cariclée* appeared in print. At the same time, too, it is possible that the lure of the farce was weakening. Mairet, in *Sylvie,* managed to appeal both to the pastoral vogue at court and the less "elevated" demands of the public. At once spectacular and occasionally indecent, the play is made up of components very similar to those in the works of Hardy. Mairet's approach, however, was very different from Hardy's; one of the purposes of this study is to examine that approach. Finally, between 1628 and 1630, a whole new group of dramatists made a firm and sparkling debut: Du Ryer, Rotrou, Corneille, Scudéry, Auvray, all started their writing careers, and Paris now became the center of theatrical activity. It had always the advantage of a permanent theater, and with the addition of a heterogeneous audience the critics had to give it their attention.

The wider, less-sophisticated public still remained, at least in the playwrights' eyes, the most important. Hardy noted in the *Epitre* addressed to Payen before *Theagene et Cariclée:* "Mais que ceux là [the critics] se representent que tout ce qu'aprouue l'usage et qui plait au public deuient plus que legitime."[6] The same feeling is reflected in Ogier's later claim in his preface to Schélandre's *Tyr et Sidon* (1628) that a play should be written entirely "pour le plaisir et le divertisse-

---

5. See two articles by Raymond Lebègue, "Le répertoire d'une troupe française à la fin du xvie siècle," *Revue d'Histoire du Théâtre,* I–II (1948), 9–24; and "Unité et pluralité de lieu dans le théâtre français (1450–1600)," in *Le Lieu théâtral à la Renaissance,* éd. Jean Jacquot (Paris, 1964), pp. 347–55.

6. Alexandre Hardy, *Les Chastes et loyalles amours de Theagene et Cariclée* (Paris, 1623), ã iij.

ment." The controversy on the proper aim of the theater—pleasure or social and moral utility—was to continue throughout the century. The Aristotelian and Horatian theories from Chapelain to Boileau were to come into conflict with the practice, as represented in Ogier's famous preface, in Scudéry's prefaces to *Ligdamon et Lidias* (1631) and *Andromire* (1641) (but not his *Apologie* [1641] or his remarks on *Le Cid*), and similar discussions.

With the appearance of Mairet's *Sophonisbe* in 1634, practice seemed to approach the theories, but this play was no more than a successful model. Despite the later claims made for *Le Cid*, it is hard to see how that play can really be said to have adopted the unities and other "necessities" of the classical stage (which is what enabled Scudéry, with scant regard for his own record, to attack it), since at the time its success was entirely popular, not critical. Few plays of the period reveal much concern for the theories. Later, Corneille was to follow most of the rules most of the time, like Racine in his secular plays. But playwrights who observed the rules were, on the whole, no more successful than those who ignored them: indeed, the younger Corneille's *Timocrate* (1656), the greatest success of the century, harks back more to the Scudérys and the Mairets than to his brother's *Horace*.

This résumé is intended to suggest that despite the commonly-held view that seventeenth-century drama is entirely classical—in the confining sense of abiding by the unities and *bienséances* as formulated by Chapelain and Sarasin, by the abbe D'Aubignac and La Mesnardière—the true state of affairs is otherwise. Lough has pointed out that dramatists of that period seemed to have "a greater freedom and range" than those of the next century.[7] Borgerhoff has confirmed this by showing how much of a struggle it was for dramatists of the first half of the eighteenth century to break away from certain fixed ideas they held about the theater, based upon the practice of Racine and the theories of Boileau alone.[8] By far the greatest proportion of the seventeenth-century dramatic output is by authors other than Pierre Corneille and Racine, and their obedience to the theoreticians

7. John Lough, *Paris Theatre Audiences in the Seventeenth and Eighteenth Centuries* (London, 1957), p. 162.
8. E. B. O. Borgerhoff, *The Evolution of Liberal Theory and Practice in the French Theater 1680-1757* (Princeton, 1936).

is wavering, to say the least. Moreover, the very economics of the theater oblige them to heed the demands of a wider public.

This is not to say that the authors ignore the critics. Most of them are well aware of the theorists' desires, and take pains to indicate this awareness. A preface may suggest how well the author has maintained unity in the play which follows, or, when that unity is less obvious, describe his product at some length to prove its unity. In his preface to *Esther* (1644), Du Ryer explains,

> Au reste j'ai crû qu'il estoit besoin de dire que la Delivrance des Iuifs est la fin & le but que se propose cét ouurage, afin de satisfaire ceux qui me pourroient demander où est l'vnité d'action.

Five years later, in his introduction to *Annibal,* de Prade, as he justifies his use of a fictional episode in Hannibal's life, demonstrates his knowledge of Aristotle's recent interpreters: [L]e Poete paruient mieux à se fin, qui est de mouuoir les passions pour en laisser en suitte vne juste mediocrité." De Brosse does the same in his preface to the comedy, *Les Innocens coupables* (1645), while Benserade defends at length the apparent lack of unity in his tragedy *La Mort d'Achille* (1636) and remarks with pride before *Meleagre* (1641) that "au moins n'est-il point embarassé, les reigles [sic] du temps & du lieu y sont dans leur seuerité toute entiere."

If he does not nod to the critics in his preface, an author may do so in the text of his play whenever possible. His comment then becomes an aside whose intention is to deflect possible criticism. Examples justifying the completing of an action within twenty-four hours are, of course, widespread. In his *Illustre comedien* (1645), Desfontaines writes into Genest's role an observation on the unity of place:

> Nous pouvons sans sortir nous concerter icy,
> Et sans qu'il soit besoin d'aprests ny de theatre.
>
> (I.3)

De Brosse finds another way of making a similar kind of appeal to the critics when, in his *Curieux impertinent* (1645), he adds a note to a stage direction: "Lotaire paraist pour lier la Scene" (III.5).

Despite their avowed acceptance of the critics' advice—most vehement during the mid-1640s, though the theater supposedly changed direction some 10 years earlier—very few of these authors (Du Ryer excepted) truly gave their allegiance to their artistic advisers. It is not

only Corneille who interprets their demands "à sa guise." Most of
them do no more than occasionally accept the letter of the *règles;*
the spirit is quite absent. Yet if the basic style of the theater seems
to change little during the century, it nonetheless answered a certain
need of the public, and so has its significance. More important for
this study, however, is that from this basic style, at a certain moment
in time, evolved the so-called "classical" theater.

It is not a matter of judging (if one can) by the standards of one's
own time whether a play is "great," or even good. This one is certainly justified in doing as a critic, so long as the view is clearly a
subjective interpretation of a contemporary entertainment (whatever the date of the work of art). The historian's task is to try to understand why a certain type of play—not necessarily "good" or "bad"
—was written during a given period in history. If a play is known to
have been particularly popular—Mairet's *Sylvie,* Corneille's *Cid,* his
brother's *Timocrate*—one may suppose that it struck a strong chord
in the public's emotions; this conclusion aids the understanding, but
does not answer the main questions. Why did playwrights employ a
given form of theatrical writing? What are the differences between it
and a previous or a successive style? To what public or private im-
pulses do these forms seem to correspond? Only by considering
these matters can we begin to understand an author's intention in a
given play, and what kind of pleasure the spectator may have received
from it. Dramatic style is perhaps one of the clearest indications of a
public's sensibilities.

René Bray touched on a drawback to this type of study when he ex-
plained his use of critics rather than plays in his *Formation de la doctrine classique:* it demands the analysis of a considerable number of
plays. A series of explications of two or three hundred plays of distinctly varying merit would scarcely hold any reader's interest for
long. A choice must be made, not to limit the extent of one's own
reading and examination, but to limit what will be presented.

Strictly speaking there is a continuity in the French theater from
the indigenous theater of the Middle Ages and the "borrowed" theater of the Renaissance, but some restrictions are needed. My study
covers a period when the change in the theater seemed to stem primarily from the theater itself (not that there were no other influences),
rather than from any number of external causes.

Insofar as the stage prior to 1625 is concerned, the choice to be made does not really pose a problem, since we possess only a part of Hardy's output, and that of such playwrights as Chrestien des Croix, Pierre Mathieu, Nicolas de Montreux, and Jean Prevost. Other playwrights of this period whose theatrical output was not inconsiderable —Garnier, Montchrestien and Billard—were evidently writing for a very different audience than the one I am concerned with here, and the success of their plays as theater would seem to depend on their very particular attitude toward language. In choosing among Hardy's plays, I started at random and discussed as few as I thought necessary to illustrate a style and its intentions. The choice of *Mariamne* and *Panthée*, however, obviously reflects the opportunity they provide for comparison with Tristan's treatment of the same subjects.

After reading many plays of the period following Hardy's, it became clear to me that at least two very different types of theater were involved, needing separate discussion. These I will call here the second and third moments. The sizeable number of extant plays of the time, by many authors, entailed a random choice. If my ideas concerning the theater of the second movement were accurate, a discussion of almost any play would validate them. Thus, close examination of a few and mention of many more, combined with insights resulting from a knowledge of still more, seemed the best means of working out the problems involved. The basic mold of this theater may be gauged just as well from a look at two little-known plays as a study of two better-known ones, with the advantage of illuminating some undeservedly neglected authors.

On this basis, I decided not to discuss at greater length Mairet's *Sylvie* (1626), Théophile's *Pyrame* (c. 1621), Desmarets' *Visionnaires* (1637), or some play of Rotrou, but instead made the perhaps somewhat whimsical choice of Scudéry's *Ligdamon et Lidias* (1631) and Monléon's *Amphytrite* (1630). As it happened, these two plays turned out to be particularly rich in those elements that appear characteristic of the period, although neither is by any means unique. Even so, these discussions may appear rather longer than necessary: my intention is to guide the reader through the play in his imagination as I suppose the spectator experienced it in the theater. My only regret is that it would have been repetitious to pursue a similar line with plays by such authors as de Brosse, Baro, or Benserade. In

view of the numerous studies which have recently appeared on Rotrou, I have curtailed my examination of that playwright.[9]

Having arrived at some definite conclusions concerning the development of theatrical style from Hardy to the period between 1625 and
1640, it will be helpful to examine a play typical of the third moment,
which saw an end to the development (although the style of the second did not die out). Since the essentially illusionistic nature of this
end result is well known, one representative play will suffice as an example.

Sophonisbe strikes me as more accidental than deliberate, a prophecy, a larger and more impressive ripple than most, but no more.
Médée (1635) still scorns the *bienséances* too much (I suggest later
how this affected the spectator's attention) to represent a very great
development. *Le Cid* (1636) is even less suitable. Rotrou gradually
approached a more unified concept of character through such plays
as *Hercule mourant* (1634), *Crisante* (1635), *Antigone* (1637) and
Laure persecutée (1637), but failed to remove other barriers to identification; despite the magnificence of some figures out of context,
the production as a whole would detract from the spectator's ability
to identify with them.

Horace, for reasons I will explain fully in Chapter 5, settles firmly
at the "end" of both this development and a fascinating parallel development within Corneille's own theater. Thus my discussion of
Corneille includes, in addition to *Horace,* a number of his plays from
the second moment which illustrate a variation of the progression
whose firmness seems peculiar to Corneille.

I would like to make two further notes here. The first is simply
a technical explanation: all references to plays will be given by act,
scene and line where possible from the editions given in the bibliography. Where an edition does not indicate line numbers, references
will be given by act and scene. References to Hardy will be by act
and line, since division into scenes in his plays is quite inconsistent.

9. See particularly Jacques Morel's recent volume, *Jean Rotrou, dramaturge de l'ambiguité* (Paris, 1968), which I have had in my hands too late to
do more than indicate in a footnote the areas where his magnificent discussion of Rotrou coincides with my more general concerns. But see my own
review of the volume in *Esprit créateur*, IX, 1 (Spring 1969): 67-68.

Unless otherwise stated, dates given after plays are those of first performances, except in cases where reference is clearly to an author's published preface. In the cases of *Mélite, La Veuve, La Place royalle, L'Illusion comique* and *Le Cid,* all references are to the modern critical reprints of the first editions, while I have used for Rotrou the edition of Viollet-le-Duc.

My second desire is to thank all those who have helped see this work through. My deepest gratitude goes to Professor Judd Hubert who guided the thesis which has become this volume; I would further thank him and Professor Stanley Gray, to whom I owe my interest in these aspects of the theater, for their painstaking corrections of an often irksome style and suggestions for improving certain ideas or their expression. In the labor of reworking the text into its present form, I owe particular thanks to Professors Georges May and Jacques Guicharnaud for their interest and most valuable criticisms, given freely despite the heavy demands on their time; to Professor Henri Peyre, whose joy is an inspiration; to Professor Victor Brombert and Mr. Wayland Schmitt who saw the book to the Press; most particularly the latter and Mrs. Jennifer Alkire, without whose enthusiasm and labors the present volume would have been very different. I should also like to thank the staffs of the various libraries who have facilitated my work: at the University of Illinois, the Bibliothèque Nationale and Yale University; as also the Department of French of the University of Illinois whose subsidies twice enabled me to consult works I could not otherwise have examined. My greatest debt is to my wife, who had to put up with a great deal. I thank her.

1. Alexandre Hardy: The Spectator and the
Theater of Destiny

> Captif du labyrinthe aux inconus détours,
> Où l'infernale nuit se rencontre toujours,
> Où l'implacable faim d'vne horreur de nature,
> Dans son ventre deuoit faire sa sépulture,
> Où rien ne paroissoit qu'vne image de mort,
> Où le courage estoit inutile, & l'effort.
>
> *(Ariadne*, I.11-16)

It is important to judge Hardy by some measure other than that of
the classical theater which followed him a generation or two later.
For to take his measure in the light of standards unfamiliar to him
and to which he by no means aspired is to see him fall short of those
standards. If one looks only at Hardy, ignoring what is basic to his
own theater, he appears no more than a precursor of a theater to
come. Thus Rigal, suggesting that Hardy disliked the solution of
simply filling his plays with complications of one kind or another,
and was incapable of creating "la tragédie psychologique," of conceiving "l'intérêt de la lutte des passions," concluded that the playwright was left with "un système mixte et mal défini, où une action
plus animée, un commencement d'intrigue, quelque étude des caractères et des passions vinssent renforcer ceux des éléments tradition-
nels de la tragédie qui se pouvaient maintenir encore."[1] Much of
this is undoubtedly true, but when Rigal comments that if Hardy
had attempted to inaugurate the psychological tragedy, "un public
ignorant et grossier se fut mal prêté à l'innovation," he seems to approach a more fruitful examination of Hardy's theater, which might
enable a comparison with the classical theater in terms other than
those of subordination. For if the audience could not be held in the
kind of relationship necessitated by a "psychological theater," what
other kind of rapport would hold it? One cannot find an answer by
studying the plays in the light of a theater which came into being a
generation later.

1. Eugène Rigal, *Alexandre Hardy et le théâtre français à la fin du xviie et
au commencement du xviie siècle* (Paris, 1889), p. 254.

If the action in Hardy's plays seems more animated than in Garnier or Montchrestien, in Jodelle or de Baïf (but not than in Jean de la Taille or the popular theater), in the tragedies at least this animation stems not from more physical movement on stage, but rather from a change in the use of language. Garnier's language appears to be divided up among the characters to satisfy certain metaphorical exigencies, as does Montchrestien's, whereas Hardy's projects characters who come alive and struggle to escape the web of the language in which they are caught. The language becomes the echo of their destiny and the symbol of the life they must see through to the end. The characters struggle, not internally, not even simply against one another, but against the fatality of their natures, against fatality itself. This opposing force becomes almost tangible in an oppressive atmosphere, created by the language, which weighs on character and spectator alike. Within such a frame the "commencement d'intrigue" to which Rigal refers, like the "quelque étude des caractères et des passions," can clearly be no more than a "beginning" and a "slight study"; for plot and characters may extend only to the bounds laid down by this fatality, and to those permitted by the language which creates this fatality, whose presence is confirmed by their very limitations.

In the following discussion of three plays by Hardy, it must be borne in mind that his audience could not be satisfied by a dry revelation of the condition of humanity. For this revelation to impress the audience, it had to be founded in something more interesting and entertaining: things had to happen, there had to be movement to some degree, the playwright had to "contenter les yeux." It is equally apparent that in any theater the nature of the rapport is never altogether constant. The point is not, of course, to analyze the reactions of a particular spectator; it is to attempt to discover what was, or seems to have been, the principal relationship sought by the author between this stage and its spectator.

Didon se sacrifiant: **Liturgy and the spectator; problems of performance**

Didon opens with a long speech delivered by Aenée which, more than anything else, serves to set the atmosphere of the play. This atmosphere reflects Hardy's desire to achieve a sense of fatality, a sense peculiar to the Greek and Roman theaters as well as the mystery

plays, and crucial to their view of man as subject to the divine
power. The speech takes the form of a prayer:

> Grands Dieux, qui disposez des Empires du monde,
> Toy qui portes en main ce tonnerre qui gronde . . .

(I.1-2)

And the rhetoric of the entire discourse is conceived as a prayer. Yet
at the same time it is a prophecy; it becomes apparent to the spectator that the ultimate end of the Trojans' voyage is the founding of
Rome, and that Aenée regards this end as inevitable:

> Mais d'ailleurs le destin de prudence infinie
> Traisne ce beau dessein iusqu'au bord d'Ausonie,
> Là se doit restaurer le mur Dardanien,
> Là s'appaiser la soeur du grand Saturnien,
> Là, le Tybre coulant d'vne douce entresuite,
> Arrester des Troyens la vagabonde fuite,
> Là mon espoir Ascaigne, Ascaigne mon soucy,
> Redoutable, regner sous vn ciel adoucy,
> Laissant de race en race, vne splendeur d'Empire
> Sur tout où le Soleil fait ses flammes reluire.

(41-50)

The spectator is not given an introduction to the play simply in terms
of historical background and knowledge of present circumstances; he
is also enveloped in a mood. Character, as conceived by Racine or
even Corneille, is here quite irrelevant, for man is to be shown in relation to the universe and as controlled by that universe. The atmosphere
of the play will place the spectator in a situation analogous to that of
Aenée. This is made clear in the next few lines: Aenée's reactions as
a personality occur only within the framework set by the will of the
gods, whose past actions he already knows and whose future intentions
he has been informed of by oracle:

> Entre l'obscurité de ce Dédale ombreux:
> Entre le souuenir de nos maux encombreux,
> Et la comparaison de la presente joye
> Mon esprit agité s'esgare, se fourvoye.

(51-54)

He complains to the gods of this uncertainty, for he knows the joyful present cannot continue against their wish; yet he does not know what will happen before the voyage ends. He knows the goal and he knows the gods desire its achievement, but the rest is concealed from him. This situation explains his response to Achate when the latter asks why he appears so anxious:

> La crainte du futur, du futur, que les Dieux,
> Sous l'ombre d'vn repos dérobent à nos yeux.
>
> (71-72)

Acnée, thus placed in a position not unlike that of the Senecan hero, is oppressed by the will of the gods, against whom he is powerless to do much more than bear the pain, despite all his struggles. The "volonté" of which Palinure speaks (82) in fact is not the voyagers', but that of the gods, and on that basis he criticizes Aenée for succumbing to his love for Didon:

> . . . un fils de Deesse, vn heros indompté,
> Vn, qui sçait des destins le sacre volonté,
> Vn, qui doit rebastir dans le sein de l'Itale
> Notre seconde Troye, à la premiere égale,
> Qui tient notre salut enchaisné dans le sien,
> Cedant aux passions, d'excusable n'a rien.
>
> (107-12)

Achate, however, goes further and suggests that even this passion, which might seem an exercise of Aenée's will, actually served to save them all; and Jupiter will pardon an infidelity to Didon insofar as it was perpetrated in accordance with his will. Their present situation is thus revealed as no more than another stage of their voyage, in which everything is planned beforehand by the divinity. None of their actions is actually the result of their own free will.

The examples already quoted suggest the liturgical tone of Hardy's language, which often rises to a level of considerable exaltation, evoking an atmosphere that comes to dominate the stage activity. The actions of the characters in their entirety are at all times shadowed by this atmosphere. The spectator must feel the weight of fatality upon him as he watches the vain struggles of the characters. With character subordinated to the rhetorical expression of man's situation, there is nothing with which the spectator may continuously identify, so that he does not feel himself in the emotional position of those on stage. Rather, watching the actors from a distance, he senses the pervading fatality of their condition. To achieve this link between actor and spectator, the playwright must avoid changing the atmosphere through the action of a character: his plays cannot start in a mood of happiness and end in grief, or vice versa, for the mood of destiny does not change with the fortunes of man. Aenée and his nobles exit to allow the entrance of Didon and Anne, but the speech and actions of these women must function to develop the mood rather than reveal them as individuals. If Didon came in happy in Aenée's love, the mood of the first scene would be broken and the audience would respond to the feelings of a particular character in a given situation instead of the pervasive atmosphere. In fact, the mood of the second scene is as somber as that of the first, and since it follows with no delay it allows the audience no fluctuation in reaction.

As the nobles depart on Aenée's order to prepare the ships, the sisters enter on Anne's plea that Didon tell her what grief

> Vous semble repousser le bon-heur qui vous suit,
> Et de votre beau iour faire vne sombre nuit.

(151-52)

Since it was impossible for Didon to know of Aenée's decision, it is apparent that her grief cannot be caused by certain knowledge. What the spectator does learn is that she suffers from a feeling of guilt, believing that she is committing adultery against her dead husband, Sichée. She says he recently appeared to her in a dream, warning her that she would be punished and that in any case Aenée is bound to leave her. Replying to Anne's objections, she adds that Aenée has spoken of Italy and of the "illustre renom" he must win there for himself (11. 198-200) in terms which only reinforce her dream. When her sister further suggests that Aenée's words are intended only to fortify the spirit of his son, who must continue the journey when he grows up, Didon, doubting still, goes to consult Juno. Thus Hardy continues to develop this idea of human submission to the divine authority, an idea reiterated in all his tragedies.

But the scene acquires even greater significance because the cause of Didon's grief is given immediately, not as suspicion of Aenée's imminent departure, but as guilt. Thus her reactions maintain the crucial atmosphere, while at the same time she is not forced to react to something of which she must still be ignorant. Although Hardy is not always careful about such details, he usually tries to achieve a certain logic even within patterns of coincidence.

Hardy may now introduce the further suspicions of Aenée's departure with less obviousness. Didon's guilty conscience serves as a useful bridge, hiding the coincidence while it maintains the mood. Hardy is not creating a specific theatrical atmosphere by simply suiting his characters' reactions to it regardless of logic. Rather, he determines the mood of his theater by revealing the reaction to a situation, likely enough, but subordinated in purpose to that mood.

At this point the chorus makes its initial appearance, and it is noteworthy that its first speech takes the form, not of a comment on the play's action, but again of a prayer. The Phoenician women beg the gods to allow Didon and Aenée to marry and live happily ever after (231-54, 267-84), pausing briefly to advise one another to dress suitably for the occasion.

The chorus maintains the atmosphere of divine control and of the lack of human freedom, but without the dolorous tone. Once the grave nature of human activity has been set forth, once the spectator has sensed the exalted pain of life within the divine pattern, Hardy allows the atmosphere to be lightened. This change is deceptive, however, since the tone speedily becomes ferocious in the scene that follows, when the slighted Iarbe calls on Jupiter to avenge the crime committed by Didon, adding that he will do it himself if necessary to fulfill the god's desire.

There is some question as to whether the choruses were actually performed. Rigal has said they were not, basing his opinion on Troterel, who claimed in the preface to his *Sainte Agnès* (pub. 1615) that he had seen over a thousand plays performed without a chorus.[2] Hardy, in his *Au lecteur,* commented that "Les Choeurs y sont obmis, comme superflus à la representation, & de trop de fatigue à refondre."[3] If this is the case, one may argue, why did he write any in the first place? Hardy was a *poète à gages;* his time and ink were valuable.

---

2. Ibid., p. 255. This claim in any case may not be too reliable, since Troterel is using it merely to justify his own omission of the device.

3. Alexandre Hardy, *Théâtre,* ed. E. Stengel, 5 vols. (Marburg and Paris, 1883), I, 5.

There are two possible conclusions: either Valleran (as leader of the troupe) cut them out after Hardy had written them, or Hardy's original view of the spectators' desires had altered by 1624. Actually, as should be evident, there are good reasons for their inclusion. If, as it appears, the major impact of this theater stems from atmosphere, here is an excellent way to sustain it. The chorus is by no means an imposition on the play, but seems an extension of the liturgical and fateful atmosphere created by Hardy. When the chorus prays, it seems to duplicate the prayers uttered by the heroes; when it comments on the condition of humanity, it echoes the spectator. There is no sudden creation of distance, since the spectator is already removed from the action as such.

Yet there is a further justification for the choral presence. Hardy's career began in the provinces, and he returned there continually when Paris failed to offer a living or when the *Confrères de la Passion* decided to dislike him and the troupe he accompanied.[4] In the provinces the mystery plays were performed regularly for years after Royal edict ended them in Paris,[5] so that audience would be quite familiar with the idea of the chorus. Besides, even the audience of the Hôtel de Bourgogne itself, well into the century at least, was still "le petit peuple qui se pressait pour assister à la représentation des mystères sur le parvis des églises; c'est la foule turbulente qui entourait les tréteaux des théâtres en plein air.[6] It is still, adds Descotes,[7] that audience stirred by and included in the atmosphere of the mystery play—a dramatic system which depends on an audience to help create its meaning. For the grandeur of the relationship between God and Man, taking all time and the world as its arena, can only be fully developed in the presence of a moving audience that continues its everyday activity while the play is being performed, much as the spectators to a series of Nō plays will bring their meals

4. Rigal, op. cit.; and S. Wilma Deierkauf-Holsboer, "Vie d'Alexandre Hardy, Poète du Roi," in *Proceedings of the American Philosophical Society,* XCIV, 4 (Oct. 24, 1947), 328-404.

5. See, for example, Raymond Lebègue, "Quelques survivances de la mise en scène médiévale," in *Melanges d'histoire du théâtre du moyen-âge et de la renaissance, offerts à Gustave Cohen,* (Paris, 1950), pp. 219-26. Also L. Petit de Julleville, *Les Mystères* (Paris, 1880), I, 451-53.

6. S. Wilma Deierkauf-Holsboer, *L'Histoire de la mise en scène dans le théâtre francais à Paris de 1600 à 1673* (Paris, 1960), p. 19.

7. Maurice Descotes, *Le Public de théâtre et son histoire* (Paris, 1960), p.25.

and games along. The theater, it would seem, cannot reach the spectator only by making him feel the emotions of certain characters: rather, he must be made to feel an atmosphere.

Thus the apparently random nature of some of Hardy's plays—particularly the pastorals and some of the tragi-comedies—appears more the result of an instinctive feeling for the needs of his spectators than the outcome of a careless haste; the multiple actions, the movement, the enforced use of a multiple set, correspond very much to the babble that, by all reports, was virtually continuous in the audience. Given the conditions prevalent in the auditorium, it would be impossible to hold the attention of the spectators long enough for them to identify with a character as they might at a Racinian play. A different kind of theater was indicated: one that would engulf its audience in the atmosphere created on the stage.

One way to achieve this overflowing atmosphere is to present sufficient movement and variety on stage to correspond with that of the audience (possible, naturally, only with the right kind of audience). These words of Rayssiguier need not be interpreted as a criticism:

> La plus grande part de ceux qui portent la teston à l'Hotel de Bourgogne veulent que l'on contente leurs yeux par la diuersité et le changement de la face du théâtre, et que le grand nombre des accidents et aventures extraordinaires leur ôtent la connaissance du sujet.[8]

Rather, this observation defines the situation that made possible, as it necessitated, a certain type of theater. In most cases the plot, whether one actually loses sight of it or not, is subordinated to that movement criticized by Rayssiguier, and the real intention of the plays is to be found in that motion. Solemnity is derived, not from the plots, but from the rhetoric which is imposed on the movement to create the atmosphere permeating the whole.

There seems to be no overwhelming argument either for or against the performance of the choruses, except in certain situations (discussed later) where a dialogue is in question. My own feeling would be that

---

8. Préface to *L'Aminte du Tasse* (Paris, 1632), quoted by René Bray, *La Formation de la doctrine classique en France* (Paris, 1927), p. 268.

they were probably included, at some times, but not at others.[9] They
would not in any case break the mood of the theater. Any attempt
to explain the presence or absence of choruses on the basis of *vraisemblance* is irrelevant here. At least one of the choruses in *Didon*,
however, that of the Troyens (II.557-616), may provide a better understanding of the concerns of this theater.

This chorus comments at once on the play's action and on the
wider significance of this action, already revealed to some extent by
Aenée's fear of the immediate future in spite of his knowledge of the
divine will (I.42). Man is doomed to be the prey of the "monstre
carnaciere" *(Meleagre,* I. 98), of the minotaur within the labyrinth
(Ariadne), until his death—the only certainty in life:

> L'etrange changement des affaires mondaines
> Ne ressemble rien plus,
> Que les courses des mers qui décroissent soudaines,
> Puis croissent d'vn reflus.
> Or la prosperité chez cetuy-cy seiourne,
> Tantost l'autre à son tour,
> Au favorable vent que fortune luy tourne,
> Iouït de son seiour.
> 'L'homme n'a de certain parmy l'incertitude,
> Que l'horreur du tombeau
> Tout le reste suiet à la vicissitude,
> Est vne ampoule d'eau'.
>
> (557-68)

9. In the preface (1631) to his *Amaranthe,* Gombauld makes the following
remark, which seems to suggest that the chorus was not an unusual part of a
play: "Ie passe des Scenes aux Choeurs qui n'ont pas les moindres beautez de
l'action, sinon en l'opinion de ceux qui ne font rien qu'à demy, & qui les tiennent pour choses vaines, pour ce qu'ils en ignorent l'usage. C'est là que les
loüanges, les plaintes, les descriptions, les Fleurs de Retorique, & les belles
pensées peuuent aller en foule; & qu'il faut recueillir les iugemens, les resolu-
tions, & les meilleurs sentimens qui peuuent inspirer les personnes & les choses
qui ont esté representées. Ainsi la Beauté, l'Amour & la Ialousie des Nymphes,
sont les trois sujets de mes premiers Choeurs [in *L'Amaranthe*]." For some
fuller comments, concerning not only the problem of the chorus but the whole
question of performance, see Jules Haraszti, êd., Jean de Schélandre, *Tyr et
Sidon ou les funestes amours de Belcar et Meliane, Tragedie* (Paris, 1908), pp.
xxxiii-vi.

Typically, this cliché is eventually applied more narrowly to Aenée himself, then modified into yet another cliché, as the chorus envies the lot of the common man:

> Hélas! combien au pris, combien est souhaitable
> Ceste condition;
> Qui remenant au soir les boeufs dedans l'estable,
> Nuë d'ambition,
> Ne pense au lendemain qu'à refendre les plaines.
>
> (597-601)

By carrying the cliché through to its traditional end, the chorus introduces here an ironical note:

> Ains contens de leur peu, dans vne maisonnette
> Attendent que la mort
> Les prenne apres cent ans la conscience nette
> De rapine et de tort.
>
> (613-16)

We will see the lie given to this particular hope when we come to glance at *Scédase;* here it illustrates the particular concern of Hardy, a concern whose revelation is one object of this form of theater.

These choruses, like the Homeric similes and extended metaphors they tend to contain, are only possible in a theater which replaces character realism with a stylized ballet of words and movement. As the spectator follows the story, it becomes a reflection of and a comment upon the nature of the human condition. Thus the spectator is not taken by surprise when Didon, for example, begins her lament of Act III, Scene 1, with an extended simile:

> Anne c'est fait de moy, ce corsair effronté
> Enleve impunément mon honneur affronté
> Ses mats sont couronnez, sa brigande cohorte,
> Nos viures dans les naux amasse de la sorte,
> Qu'vn troupeau picoreur de fourmis épandus,
> Aussi tost qu'en Iuillet les épics sont tondus:
> Il comble preuoyant, la froideur voisine,
> De quelque chesne vsé la profonde racine,
> Les chemins en sont noirs, & au labeur ardent,
> Il ne va qu'au trépas le butin démordant.
>
> (617-26)

This kind of semi-oracular discourse has the same effect as the frequent calls upon the divine authority and maintains the same solemn yet tense mood which unifies the play. Yet despite the solemn quasi-religious tone, or perhaps because it allows him to create a fury of language, Hardy is able to produce moments of terrible realism. Didon tries to prevent Aenée's departure with a plea—at first furious, then piteous—which is effective because it includes allusions forbidden in a later (and more "realistic") theater, where they would in any case appear outrageous. This speech increases Didon's complexity, for she is made eminently real as the wronged and unfortunate woman. Her plea is full of contraditions. She is by turns accusing, sorrowing, conciliatory, begging, dominated by a pride which throws the blame onto Aenée as she accepts her fault but insists that he repair it. Then finally she prays to him, forgetting her pride in her desire to have him stay. Her emotion must surely move the spectator, despite the grandiose nature of the rhetoric which formulates her plea.

The distance is not allowed to remain closed, and in contrast to the emotional Didon, Aenée continues to appear as the pale, cold instrument of the gods that he is. When the interest returns to him, the spectator once again assumes his original distance:

> N'accuse que le Ciel, ie ne suis plus à moy,
> Pressé du partement par sa seuere loy!

(785-86)

So Aenée shrugs off Didon's prayer with an excuse the spectator recognizes as true, for throughout her tirade the answer has been inevitable: it is impossible that he remain. The viewer is also aware that he may not reveal the excess of sorrow which realism might demand; he cannot stay, nor can Didon accept his explanations, for such is the order of things. Their confrontation parallels the dispute between reason and emotion later to characterize an era; here it is externalized as an argument between two people, in future dramas it will occur in the mind of a single character with whom the spectator will be forced to identify. Here the spectator's attitude is dictated by his knowledge of the divine inevitability weighing upon the situation, knowledge which is translated into feeling.

Hardy never allows the atmosphere to be dispelled. Once he has created the grandiose, liturgical tone he wants, he maintains it. Didon's lament rings out like some biblical cry in the wilderness:

Cherches-tu du repos, misérable insensée
L'âme de tant de soins ça, & là balancée?
Incertaine de viure encores vn moment,
Ores que l'infidelle est sur son partement,
Ores que le barbare, apres l'Adieu funeste,
Te fuit, ne plus ne moins, qu'vne effroyable peste,
Ores que retiré dans le creux d'vn vaisseau,
Possible il n'attendra le iour à fendre l'eau.
      Anne, où és-tu ma soeur? aproche ma chere âme,
Si tu veux renoüer le long fil de ma trâme,
Va trouuer le Troyen, va, non point à demy,
Coniurer la pitié de mon traitre ennemy.

(III.939-49)

She concludes with a prayer to Juno, and a foreboding of the future:

Las! vnc tristc horreur me presage, me dit,
Que ie ne fléchiray ce corsair maudit:
Qu'Anne perdra ses pas, & ses prières vaines,
Deia l'affreuse mort chemine par mes veines.

(1013-16)

From this point on, the role of the gods, of omens and visions, becomes the principal base of the action. Immediately following Didon's prayer, the Trojan chorus is seen praying for Neptune's help with their voyage, and soon after occurs the only physical divine intervention in the play (although Aenée considers it as a dream, since he sleeps through Mercury's visit and wakes only with his departure). The winged messenger appears to tell Aenée to fly before Didon can reach him in her "rage iniurieuse" (IIII.1080). The voyagers decide to leave, and when Anne attempts to sway Aenée one last time, reply only that it is the will of the gods.

The spectator is then returned to Didon as Anne goes to tell her what has happened, and Didon describes an evil omen: while making her annual sacrifice to the spirit of her husband, she was spattered with blood and the sacred wine turned to blood and became black. She interprets this omen as a sign to instruct her subjects to follow Aenée to the port and destroy him and his fleet. At this point Anne reflects, in an aside, on Didon's imprecations against herself and Aenée:

Comme vn flot se grossit de l'autre qui le suit,
Touiours de mal en pis sa plainte elle poursuit,
En imprecations aiguise sa colere,
Il vaut mieux l'interrompre, à peine de déplaire;
Toutefois ce venin rentré dedans le coeur,
La pourroit suffoquer à l'acces du rancoeur,
Plus discrette, attendons qu'elle vomisse à l'aise,
Qu'vn nuage de pleurs cette tourmente appaise.

(IIII.1381-88)

Spoken half to herself and half to the audience, Anne's commentary
has the same effect as that of a chorus. Since there is no character
with whom the spectator can identify, the speech simply supports the
distance that already exists between the stage character and the audience. This kind of device is relatively common, and seems to strength-
en the liturgical quality of the atmosphere.

Hardy formulates the final scene, which includes the death of Didon,
as a kind of litany between the chorus and Didon, then between the
chorus and Barce:

BARCE: Au meurtre, elle se tuë,
CHOEVR: ô prodige effroyable!
        Courons, pour retenir sa dextre impitoyable.
BARCE: Helas! il n'est plus tems, ce beau sein trauersé,
        L'ame fuit dans le sang à gros boüillons versé
CHOEVR: O ville desolée!
BARCE: ô chetiue vieillesse!
CHOEVR: He! d'où vient que sa soeur, à son besoin la laisse?
BARCE: La cruelle luy a expres commis le soin
        De sacrifice, afin de la tenir plus loin.
CHOEVR: O rage furieuse! ô maudite iournée!
BARCE: O celeste rancune, à nous nuire ostinée!

(V.1851-60)

Finally, the litany slows, as Anne, Barce, and the chorus reiterate the
themes already mentioned, bewailing the plight of humanity. The
play ends with the semi-ironic epilogue of Iarbe's messenger (finally
arrived in Carthage), who laments that had Didon married Iarbe this
catastrophe would have been averted, thus offering in effect a final
tribute to the fatal power of the gods.

The tone of this play is similar to that of Jodelle's *Didon se sacrifiant* (1560), a play which merits a brief glance. Very different from his earlier *Cléopâtre captive* (1552), Jodelle's *Didon* already seems to approach Hardy's style. In *Cléopâtre,* two "prologues" (I include here the monologue of Antoine's ghost) eliminate any possibility of the characters' escaping their destiny. In *Didon* this device is replaced with a monologue by a participant in the drama: Achate. His horror at the situation seems to come from within: that, at least, is how it appears to the spectator. The presentiment of an inescapable destiny evolves in the imagination of the character, not from some external pressure. The use of language to create this feeling seems to herald Hardy. Achate speaks of the "songes ambigus," the "redoutez oracles," the "monstrueux miracles" which are forcing the Trojans to leave Carthage. He would have his companions, Palinure and Ascaigne, consider Didon's grief when she hears of the decision, and he suggests they envisage the possibility of its resulting in her death: a suggestion reinforced by his insistence on the many reasons for her enormous grief.

To some extent, all the stylistic elements central to Hardy's *Didon* are already present here: the mythological references, the bold similes, the long and often contorted sentences (one, for example, of fourteen lines, reveals a part of Didon's grief via nine inversions of subject/verb/object), the force and the color, the dreams, the omens. These qualities reflect, to be sure, the poet's awareness of Seneca—perhaps, too, of some Italian model—but the parallels with Hardy in Jodelle's work should not be lightly dismissed.

There are differences. Jodelle's characters seem less awed by the feeling of some doom imposed from the outside. They continually insist that the fearfulness is generated not by an external force but by the personality of Achate. When Palinure and Ascaigne are discussing the power of the gods and the necessity of leaving Carthage to keep from growing fat there, Achate tells the latter that "sa jeunesse bouillante" could not entertain the same fears as his own old age, basing his thoughts in a very personal context. The old man's introductory lament itself remains at a human level. Unlike the lament Hardy gives Aenée, it does not become a plea to the gods. Rather, Achate skirts the idea of some universal control: the gods are responsible, he suggests, but it is the human spirit which interprets and reacts. There is a definite belief—on the part of the characters, if not the spectators—in individual responsibility. But as with Hardy's characters, their movements come to resemble those of a captive bird, and Palinure remarks:

> Jamais aux bas mortels les Immortels ne rendent
> Une asseurance entiere, et tousjours ceux qui tendent
> A la gloire plus haute ont leurs ames esteintes
> Aux soucis, aux travaux, aux songes, et aux craintes.
>
> (I.141-44)

In Jodelle's play Enee and Didon seem at similar emotional levels. The Trojan chief, like Octavien in *Cléopâtre*, becomes virtually an instrument of the gods, acting upon Didon. Her death is inescapable because he is a tool of fate, but he suffers far more than his counterpart in Hardy.

There is one difference more important than all these, of course: the audience. Jodelle's audience (so far as is known) was composed of humanists and scholars whose preoccupation with improving the French language enabled them to sympathize with the author's usages as Hardy's audience could not. Judging Jodelle's language as an instrument, his audience would be less susceptible to its emotional force. The aesthetic tension in Jodelle's theater must have been very different from that in Hardy's, primarily because the latter's audience was different. The atmosphere of his dramas incorporates both the characters, struggling against it in semi-ignorance, and the spectator, feeling it yet able to watch the characters with a certain detachment, to sense the irony of their position.

Scédase: Life as prison; problems of mise en scène

A favorite device of Hardy's, one I have already examined with regard to *Didon,* is to begin his play—whether tragedy, tragi-comedy or pastoral—with a kind of prologue, voiced either by a character who will not appear again or by one of the main characters. The prologue is not usually a plea to the audience, as it would be in the Elizabethan theater. Rather, it offers a commentary on man, and, indirectly, on the situation contained in the drama. *Scédase* begins with a kind of rhetorical prayer by Archidame, who expresses his hope that Sparta will not decline into luxury, and concludes, predictably, with a prayer to Juno. That the style and tone of this prologue should be so similar to that of *Didon* is of considerable significance, for whereas

Didon is concerned with a subject whose grandeur alone seemed to impose an oracular atmosphere, *Scédase* deals with a subject of an apparently far less lofty nature. *Didon* involved the kings, queens and demigods of ancient mythology; in *Scédase*, Hardy presents people of lowly status. Scédase himself is but a poor villager, and if Charilas and Evribiade are aristocrats, they are a long way from being princes.

The opening scene introduces us to two of the protagonists: Charilas and Evribiade, who enter with their governor, Iphicrate. Immediately the spectator grasps the import of the prologue; the two youths, sighing after "deux pucelles soeurs" (I. 52), are being opposed by Iphicrate, who holds up before them the decadence of this lust. Since the prologue has created in the spectator's mind certain expectations of what is to come, the argument is for him both ironic and prophetic:

> IPHICRATE: Ilion sans l'amour, & son vainqueur Achille,
> N'eussent seruy d'example, à quiconque facile
> Donne dans les gluaux de ce caut oyseleur,
> Et qui semble fatal aux hommes de valeur.
> CHARILAS: Ne t'imagine pas, que telle frenaisie
> Incurable domine en nostre fantaisie,
> L'vn & l'autre demeure amplement satisfait,
> Des faueurs du regard qui neglige l'effet.
> IPHICRATE: Les yeux premiers atteins, communiquent à l'ame
> Cette contagion qui la luxure enflame,
> De suite la raison abandonne son fort,
> Cede au vice ennemy, qui le chasse plus fort.
> (I.117-28)

The implied prophecy is soon made explicit:

> IPHICRATE: Certain sinistre augure agite ma poitrine,
> Tel que le Nort croissant, qui les ondes mutine,
> Augure auant-coureur du desastre auenir.
> (141-43)

As in *Didon,* the rhetoric itself seems to create a mood from which the characters cannot escape. Any argument seems to bring them headlong against the barrier created by the language, against the atmosphere of divine authority. The simile of the stormy north wind in the mouth of Iphicrate is used to increase the feeling of the oracular. Beneath this it will appear obvious to the spectator that the

youths' protestations that they are going only to seek hospitality
(149-60), if not actually untrue, are certainly vain.

The second act brings us to the home of the two beauties and their
father. It is filled with a certain rather horrible irony which perpetu-
ates the threatening atmosphere. The spectator sees Scédase busy
thanking his gods for his family's fortunate life (II.222-58) and for
the gracious organization of the world—a world in which the philosophy of Pangloss could surely have been justified:

> ... De sorte que parmy ces peuples que la terre
> Dans le cercle infiny de sa rondeur enserre
> Chacun, ou vit, ou peut viure content du sort,
> Que tu luy prescris iuge en suprême ressort.

(225-28)

But above all, the lowly villager should be content [10]

> Pour ne pâlir d'envie, & dans vn double coeur
> Loger la trahison, l'assacine rancoeur,
> Pour auoir la parole ainsy que le courage,
> Pour ne faire innocens à personne d'outrage.

(243-46)

With the irony of this passage already making its impression, Scédase
goes on to voice his one regret: he has no son, a lack compensated
for by his two beautiful and witty daughters, whom he wishes to see
married before his death. Hardy clearly intends the juxtaposition of
the two thoughts as an ironic prophecy. He delights in this kind of
intervention, and it furthers the creation and preservation of a fearful
atmosphere like that in *Didon*. Here, as in *Didon,* the spectator cannot identify with any character, for none is presented to him. All the
characters speak in general terms; they are created by rhetoric and
they act only in accordance with that rhetoric. And this stylized language is supported, as I will shortly demonstrate, by the sets at their
disposal.

With each new event of the plot, the spectator becomes more
aware of the atmosphere. Indeed, as with the characters, the plot
situations are created to intensify that atmosphere of fearfulness and
terror, of oracular dignity and occasionally ironic humor. Scédase,
before leaving for three days, gives his daughters advice whose gravity,

10. Compare *Didon se sacrifiant,* 11. 597-616 (see above, p. 21).

considering the length of his absence and the peaceful nature of the
region in which they live (according to him), seems excessive. But the
question of realism, in Hardy's plays, must be subordinate to the question of tone. Scédase, then, exhorts his daughters (II.267-96) to avoid
being tricked by one of these "ames fraudulentes," for

> En ce siècle peruers les vices déchainez
> Ne se trouuent que trop de supposts forçenez,
> Capables d'ébranler vn courage pudique.
>
> (283-85)

Here is a reversal of his previous position that can only detract from
his believability as a character. It is justified, however, in the context
of the atmosphere being sustained. Having thus committed "ce joyau
passant les perles Indiennes" (310) to the care of their possessors,
Scédase takes his farewell, leaving them overcome by a feeling of dread:

> EVEXIPE: Hé! Cieux, vne frayeur m'apprehende subite,
> Les cheueux herissez, tout le sein me palpite,
> L'aueugle euenement d'vn presage mortel,
> Me tient comme l'aigneau qu'on destine à l'Autel,
> Me dit que ce départ pour iamais nous sépare,
> THÉANE: Pareil augure à coup de mon âme s'empare,
> Hélas! cher geniteur de grace differez
> Ce voyage entrepris sous les Dieux colerez.
>
> (325-32)

The sudden "presage mortel," the feeling of being "l'aigneau qu'on
destine à l'Autel," the sentiment of the "Dieux colerez" and the def-
erence to the atmosphere of the oracle sustain the mood already communicated to the spectator:

> As flies to wanton boys, are we to the Gods;
> They kill us for their sport.
>
> *(King Lear)*

The spectator can now predict the course of the play. The plot
serves only to link situations, it no longer produces a tension through
arousing expectation and hope as a play by Racine might; there can
be no surprise, for the spectator is aware of the outcome. Hardy's
power lies in maintaining a play's atmosphere rather than construct-
ing a suspenseful plot.

It was not only Hardy's language that assured a close relationship between the spectator and the stage, but also the sets that were at the
disposal of the players. If the language were supported by an elabo-
rately realistic set the result would be an unacceptable anachronism;
Hardy's elaborate rhetoric would be reduced to an exercise in poetry.
If, on the other hand, the set were eliminated, a different kind of relationship would have to be devised with an audience that made no
visual demands: an audience quite unlike Hardy's. Another alternative might be an extremely simple set, all in one piece, as in the theater of Racine. This is not to suggest that there was any lack of luxury
in these later sets: "Mouvement et Pompe, tels sont les deux caractères du décor de théâtre, étudiés aprés 1640."[11] But, as Vanuxem
points out in the same article, this luxuriousness of scenery was continuous from the auditorium, thus reinforcing a language whose intention is to make the spectator forget he is in a theater. In Hardy's
theater the sets were of a very different nature:

> There was an unbroken tradition of productions with simulta-
> neous sets in France even though it was on its way out when
> Torelli came to Paris in 1645. With this convention the set was
> not regarded as an illusionary milieu. It was made up of a con-
> glomeration of localities clearly if symbolically defined but
> amounting to little more than signs. When this tradition died
> out it was superseded by sets that gave a stronger atmosphere
> of probability.[12]

Within these sets, as Bjurström suggests here, "il ne pouvait y
avoir ni illusion ni vraisemblance,"[13] but there can be little doubt
that they would please the eye. One who doubts the luxuriousness
of these sets need only glance at the illustrations in Le Mémoire de

11. Jacques Vanuxem, "Le décor du théâtre sous Louis XIV," XVIIe
Siècle, XXXIX (1958):197.

12. Per Bjurström, Giacomo Torelli and Baroque Stage Design (Stockholm,
1961), p. 196. See also George R. Kernodle, From Art to Theatre: Form
and Convention in the Renaissance (Chicago, 1944), passim, and T. E. Lawrenson, The French Stage in the xvii[th.] Century: A Study in the Advent of
the Italian Order (Manchester, 1957), chaps. II and V.

13. M. J. Moynet, L'Envers du théâtre, machines et décorations (Paris,
1888), p. 17.

Mahelot.[14] In addition, the traditional notion that the Hôtel de Bourgogne's stage was narrow to begin with, and would have been crowded with simultaneous sets, has been at least partially disproved. While Mme. Deierkauf-Holsboer's estimate of an immense stage has been corrected by Donald Roy, his calculation of its dimensions prior to 1647 nonetheless shows the stage to have been relatively large: 28½ feet deep and 31 feet 8 inches wide (i.e. 4½ *toises* × 5 *toises*).[15] All in all it seems safe to assume that the quantity of scenery and its appearance were sufficient to remind the spectator that he was inside a theater.[16] It must be kept in mind, of course, that elaborate sets were impractical for a travelling company, whose actors probably performed on a nearly empty stage; under such circumstances, the success of a play would depend even more on its language.

The rich, solid language of Hardy never attempts to alter this awareness. Rather, it recreates for the spectator the mythological Cretan maze, the order of life, than which

> Oncques de labyrinthe, ouurage Dedalique,
> N'eut vne obscurité de detours plus oblique.
>
> *(Scédase,* IV.949-50)

If the spectator is given to reflection, his thoughts will not interrupt the mood created by Hardy, for in any case that distance between audience and characters remains virtually constant in Hardy's theater. If he is not (as the major part of Hardy's audience was not), the

---

14. *Le Mémoire de Mahelot, Laurent et d'autres décorateurs de l'Hôtel de Bourgogne et de la Comédie-Française au xviie siècle,* éd. Henry Carrington Lancaster (Paris, 1920).

15. See Deierkauf-Holsboer, *Mise en scène,* pp. 18 and 49-50; Donald H. Roy, "La Scène de l'Hôtel de Bourgogne," *Revue d'Histoire du Théâtre* (1962), pp. 227-35, and T. E. Lawrenson, Donald Roy and Richard Southern, "Le *Mémoire* de Mahelot et l'*Agarite* de Durval: vers une réconstitution pratique," in *Le Lieu théâtral à la Renaissance,* éd. Jean Jacquot (Paris, 1964), pp. 363-76.

16. If one may believe anything found in laudatory verses, Lamy gives a hint of this effect when he speaks of reaction in a verse to Hardy (*Théâtre,* II):

> Plus souuent on se sent toucher,
> Si faut-il pourtant qu'on en rie,
> Puis qu'on ne sçauroit se fascher
> D'vne si iuste tromperie.

[p. 5]

relationship will parallel that imposed by the melodrama in contemporary theater. What is perhaps remarkable, and characteristic of
Hardy (if not of those who followed him) is that while utilizing most
features of the melodrama at one level—a simple spectacle of disguises,
murders, rapes, heroes and villains—he could at the same time inspire
awe with his oracular mood,[17] communicating a philosophy of life in
accordance with the essentially harsh existence of the men who were
present as spectators. Who knows? Perhaps the fate of Evexipe and
Théane, and of their father Scédase, raised in many minds a spectre
of the recent wars, not easily extinguished. Certainly, the violence of
this theater, its elation often bordering on the mystical, its repeated
prayers for tranquillity and happiness, the delusions of its characters
about the real nature of things (Charilas' and Evribiade's misconcep-
tion of their powers, or Scédase's naïve belief in a righteous world),
the final inevitable tragedy compounded on occasion by added injury
(Scédase's inability to obtain justice)—all these elements contribute
to a tone not unlike that of D'Aubigné's *Tragiques* or other semi-
polemical works which came out of the wars.

Hardy belongs, in a sense, to an earlier generation than Montaigne.
Or perhaps it is simply that his mood is nearer to that of the people
and slower to change. To him the notion of revealing the human
situation through a deep study of the individual seems quite alien.
Man is a creature caught up in a confusion he cannot pierce in a
system he cannot understand; within it his imagination is constantly
dismayed and his will must remain ineffective. Thus Hardy's characters turn about in an atmosphere representing a foreordained system
which leaves them powerless. If they act to their own advantage,
they realize too late that they have deprived themselves of shelter on
their way through the labyrinth:

> Fuyons, hé! Dieu, fuyons, iaçoit que désormais
> Nul azile assez seur ie n'espere jamais.
>
> (Scédase, III.831-32)

If, on the other hand, they feel assured of a resting place, their fate
is that of Didon, of Scédase and his daughters, of Panthée, Meleagre
and Atalante, Procris, and so many others, a fate from which there

17. Awe is one of the attitudes most often expressed in the laudatory verses
dedicated to Hardy.

is no retreat. Scédase cannot obtain justice from Agesilas and his
council, who remain indifferent to his woes. Those who escape do so
through accident rather than their own efforts (as in *Ariadne,* Dom
Jean in *La Belle Egyptienne,* or in *Gésippe).* In *Scédase,* the quasi-
legal objections of Androclide, Leonide and Xantippe to the pleas of
the bereaved father only reflect the indifference of the gods:

> Depuis que l'homme vient au monde,
> Iusqu'à l'heure de son trépas,
> Mille malheurs lâchent la bonde,
> Inseparables de ses pas:
> Il n'a felicité qui dure,
> Et celuy ce [sic] peut dire heureux,
> A qui la fortune moins dure,
> Ne montre vn front trop rigoureux.
>
> (V.1253-60)

In such a situation man can only break the bounds of his prison and
flee from the labyrinth in which he suffers, as Evandre comments:

> Depuis que le malheur étoufe l'esperance,
> L'homme doit courageux se tirer de souffrance:
> L'homme doit courageux, malgré l'inique sort,
> Ce qu'il ne peut icy le trouuer chez la mort.
>
> (V.1349-52)

Mariamne: The human theater—Hardy and Tristan

There is no sign of irony in the prologue to Hardy's *Mariamne:* only
a violent hatred and a prophecy, a curse brought down upon Herode
by the ghost of Mariamne's brother, Aristobule, himself slain by Herode.

> Monstre le plus cruel qui respire la vie,
> Tyran bouffi d'orgueil, & forcené d'enuie,
> Fleau de l'innocence, horreur du genre humain,
> Que fait si longuement ocieuse ta main?
> Comment peut reposer ta dextre carnassiere?
> Ta soif, qu'oncques le sang rebeu ne desaltere?
>
> (I.1-6)

Already the spectator may see rising before him the shadow of some
revolting ogre, an ogre created in a rhetorical world of fantasy—and

the more simple-minded spectator may tremble, as the lines evoke
some devil incarnate from the lurid tales of his childhood. Whatever
the case, it is this first passage, as always with Hardy, that begins to
set the mood of the spectator and auditorium. Once again the play
will depict a series of characters turning about one another under the
umbrella of a preordained fate:

> . . . ce destin moteur de l'vniuers,
> A de pires tourmens te reserve (peruers)
> Te donne mille morts de troubles domestiques,
> Outre vne fin tragique entre les plus tragiques,
> Deuoré de vermine en chaque part du corps,
> Au lieu d'vne, souffrant vn siecle mille morts.
> > Poursuy donc, poursuy donc, ô scelerat infame,
> Ta haine, ta fureur contre ta propre femme.
> Priue, ennemy commun, de la clarté du jour
> Celle qui te brûloit d'vn idolatre amour.

                                                        (I.27-36)

The notion of the cage of fate, the labyrinth, formulated as a prophecy,
takes its shape from the language rising up in a solid mass. The atmosphere of Hardy's theater (as distinct from the spectator's relationship
to it) is created entirely in this rhetoric, aided probably by the psalmo-
dic chant which appears to have been the normal mode of stage declama-
tion for tragedy in the period.

   This creation—a literary invention first and foremost—is artificial by
nature, like the non-illusionary sets then in use. Thus the spectator,
even if he gave all his attention to the performance on stage, must have
been kept constantly aware of *watching*, of being in a theater. Up to a
point, also, the contrast between the quasi-religious tone of the language and the romanesque sets would reinforce the impression of distance. In a theater such as Racine's the tone more nearly matches the
luxurious sets, which, being immobile, offer less of a visual obstacle
than earlier designs. And, since no doors or windows in the sets open
to admit passage or sight of a new character, the spectator may be
readily convinced by a language more easily comprehensible, less ob-
scure and *touffu* than Hardy's.[18]

   18. See p. 30, above.

With Hardy, however, the awe of the spectator under the oppressive atmosphere is dependent on his conscious *watching* of the stage action. The atmosphere permeates audience and stage with almost equal force. Although the spectator must feel it through the agency of a stage character, he approaches it as a product of the language rather than any tension within the character. After a while, indeed, the nature of the characters seems to derive from the language itself: they talk in a futile effort to understand and to act upon this pressure, the fatality of the divine will.

Their situation seems to become the spectator's own; or at least the latter's relationship to the atmosphere echoes that of the character to destiny. Indeed, the analogy works in reverse, and Hardy occasionally likens the situation of a character to that of the spectator who is watching him; or he may view the situation of the theater, of being part of an act, as the human situation. Salome reproaches Herode for his love toward Mariamne:

> Maistrise des boüillons d'vne jeunesse folle,
> Sur le theatre humain joüant vn moindre rolle
> On vous excuseroit.
>
> (I.209-211)

In *Panthée*, Araspe comments on the idea of a nation in decadence, pointing out that

> Notre theatre humain
> Spectacle plus fréquent sur soy ne represente.
>
> (I.64-65)

Elsewhere the world is seen as a "theatre miserable" (*Scédase*, V.1286), and the gods as "spectateurs immobiles" (*Didon*, V.1721). This, of course, is a common metaphor for the condition of humanity, but in a theatrical situation it acquires a unique significance.

It is impossible to estimate how far this relationship might go: this would naturally depend on each individual performance. The central point to bear in mind is that theatrical identification, if it interests the playwright at all, is far less important than the creation of an atmosphere that urges the spectator to a certain frame of mind, a certain manner of envisioning human action as the play runs its course. And this course holds no surprises, since the spectator is aware of its direction almost from the first line of the play. He is not affected as he

will be in the later theater by an emotional relation to the characters;
which emotion, according to Bullough, invites an absence of intellectual reflection (not on the development of the play but on its
meaning *at the time of performance).* He would be under the influence of the atmosphere, placed at a distance from the character yet
feeling equal to him: not necessarily in social status, but as a human
being caught up in the maelstrom of the universal system.

He knows then that whatever Herode does is futile; his actions are
bound to end with the death of Mariamne, and he will be unable
even to say that he has decided his own fate as may the Hérode of
Tristan.[19] Language, which creates Hardy's characters, and in whose
terms alone they may operate, becomes an insurmountable barrier between them and freedom. While these characters may realize the
nature of their relationship with one another, they cannot escape
from the thread of their destinies.

The ghost of Aristobule has prepared the spectator for the Herode
who boasts of his bloody ascent to the throne with Machiavellian
conviction:

> En matière d'estat les preceptes meilleurs,
> Gardons la piété, hormis ce point ailleurs,
> Preuoyans n'espargnons amis ny parentelle,
> Qui sa part auec nous du Royaume querelle.

$$(I.99-102)$$

Later in the same monologue, Herode, regretting Mariamne's lack of
affection for him (Mariamne, whose father and brother he has slain
because they tried to prevent him from usurping their kingdom),
cries out:

> O Mariamne ingrate! o farouche rebelle!
> Que n'es-tu plus benigne, ou moins chaste, ou moins belle?

$$(117-18)$$

The credibility of his reproach is irrelevant; this is the Herode for
whom the audience has been prepared. The spectator knows he can-

---

19. See, for example, the discussion by Claude K. Abraham, *The Strangers:
The Tragic World of Tristan l'Hermite,* University of Florida Monographs,
Humanities no. 23 (Gainesville, 1966).

not change, and he too seems already to know where this course must
lead him, to know that he is powerless to do anything about it:

> Ah! peruerse nature, ah! courage rebours,
> Les yeux clos furieuse à ta perte tu cours.

$$(123-24)$$

He appears to know as well as the spectator that Mariamne must die
at his hands, and to suspect its impact on himself. Any delays he
creates will be totally ineffective, for the rhetoric has already created
Mariamne's death, as it has created an atmosphere in which anything
but that death is inconceivable. The varying of an atmosphere within a single play is not a device of Hardy's, for he is not interested in
the endless possibilities of changing rhetoric or forms: his attitude is
simply that man is part of a massive and generally cruel system, whose
walls he may beat upon but never break down. It is this attitude which
pervades the theater of Hardy.

Thus the figures of poetic rhetoric abound in Hardy's theater. Most
apparent to the listener and most obviously "unrealistic" is the simile.
Herode at one point compares himself to Hercules (77ff) and Pherore
later likens him to a helmsman at sea:

> Le pilote asseuré du courroux de Neptune,
> Iouit telle qu'elle est de sa bonne fortune,
> N'a sans cesse ses yeux dans les astres fichez,
> Où ses robustes bras sur le timon panchez:
> Ainsi d'oresnauant les guerres étouffées,
> Par vos braves labeurs terminez en trophées.

$$(129-34)$$

And it is by way of metaphor rather than actual facts that Pherore
reaches the conclusion that Herode has calmed the people, that he is
the "bienfaiteur . . . enuers le commun" (144).

The character seems to run headlong into these solid figures of
speech, from which he draws conclusions that place him in the appropriate relationship to the other characters. Never does he give the
impression of playing with language, never does he rejoice in it as do
the characters of Rotrou's *Diane* or *Les Occasions Perdues*.[20] He cannot use it toward his own ends, or as a release from his anxieties:

20. See Chapter 3.

> Fauorisé de Mars autant qu'homme du monde,
> Ma grandeur affermie à peu d'autres seconde,
> Affluant de richesse, vn point d'aduersité
> Obscurcit le Soleil de ma felicité,
> Rembarre d'vn fleau domestique ma joye,
> De sorte que par tout vn tourment me costoye,
> De sorte que frustré de mon principal bien,
> Cuidant tout posseder ie ne possede rien.

                                                        (149-56)

Both points made here are contained in Aristobule's speech introducing us to the present and the future. The role of Herode is already created, as are those of the characters who surround him. They boast, regret, hate, only in accordance with lines already familiar to the spectator. The character feels, but these feelings can do nothing to help him evade the walls which surround him. As Rigal has said, there is "quelque étude des caractères et des passions,"[21] but of character and passion trapped. With Tristan they will be freed to act upon one another outside the oppression which weighs on them in Hardy's theater, and the spectator's attitude will be changed accordingly.

So Pherore rages against Mariamne just as she is obliged to rage against him. His allegiance has been revealed as Aristobule has created the language of Mariamne (37-56):

> Mariamne possible, ensuiuant sa coustume,
> D'vne rage d'orgueil encontre vous s'allume,
> Abusant du pouuoir que ce charme d'Amour
> Luy concede sur vous.

                                                        (157-60)

All this provides the spectator with no new information; he already knows how Herode and his associates will react once Aristobule, the harbinger, has come and gone. He knows too what his attitude must be toward each side.

Herode's efforts to reshape the character created for him are bound to fail, but they add an emotional liveliness to the scheme absent from the more static theater of Hardy's theoretically-minded predecessors.[22]

21. Rigal, *Alexandre Hardy*, p. 254.
22. See above, p. 13.

For example, when Pherore urges that he take Mariamne by force, he protests:

> L'éfort incompatible à sa beauté divine,
> A ce miracle issu de Royalle origine,
> N'aigriroit que ma playe au lieu de l'adoucir,
> Prolongeroit ma peine au lieu de l'acourcir.
> Sa haine, ses dédains, son mépris ordinaire
> Ie prefere aux faueurs d'vne amitié vulgaire.
>
> (165-70)

Soon, in another lively scene, Pherore and Salome try to convince Herode to kill Mariamne to foil her so-called plot against his life and throne. For although their essential behavior is ordained under the stifling atmosphere, within these bounds the characters (like Aenée) may sustain the illusion that their actions affect others. The spectator, not sharing this illusion, recognizes that Herode's eventual condemnation of Mariamne (Act III) stems from a situation created by the rhetoric as much as the plotting of his brother and sister.

While Hardy thus maintains a degree of distance between the spectator and the stage action, he also attempts to parallel the attitudes of character and spectator toward the atmosphere which determines that action.[23] Beneath the mood he has created Hardy can have his characters comment on a given situation as the spectator might, through employing various aphorisms and maxims (a common device among French Renaissance tragedians, particularly Montchrestien and Garnier):

> Rarement le Tyran paisible s'éjoüit,
> De son rapt execrable, & longuement joüit.
>
> (*Mariamne*, 479-80)

> Celuy triomphe plus, qui triomphe du vice.
>
> (*Panthée*, I.189)

> Le remors est l'éclair auant-coureur du vice.
>
> (*Panthée*, II.305)

> Il faut que la raison nos actions tempere.
>
> (*Panthée*, III.515)

23. See above, pp. 34-35.

Later, as Salome plots with the *Eschanson* to have Mariamne accused
of trying to poison Herode (II.529-704), the latter comes up with a
piece of social commentary:

> Eschanson: De nos conditions la disparité grande
> Dissout assez le noeud de semblable demande,
> Vous exempte du joug redoutable des loix,
> Moy prest de succomber si ie m'en préualois.
> Salome: Conjoints en ce dessein de gloire & de fortune,
> Presumez du surplus toute chose commune.
> Eschanson: L'vsage journalier apprend que les petits
> Demeurent impuissans du malheur engloutis,
> Portent seuls opprimez la peine temeraire
> Des projets suggerez.
>
> (609-18)

(I have already examined in *Scédase* the idea expressed here as a
maxim.) One could readily produce numerous examples to illustrate
Hardy's use of this device in order to place the character in a relationship to the overall atmosphere similar to the spectator's. The characters
often seem to withdraw from their own actions to comment upon them.
Yet, if they are capable of such abstraction upon occasion, as even
Herode may be, they soon return to the blind condition on which their
actions are based, drawn on as before by the power of the language
which envelops them:

> Serpent enflé d'orgueil, fere ingrate sortie
> Des antres Caspiens, ou des rocs de Scythie,
> Tigresse qui d'humain ne retiens que le front,
> Crois-tu qu'impunément ie porte cest affront?
> Cuides-tu me brassant injure sur injure,
> Qu'insensible d'honneur, sans cesse ie l'endure?
>
> (III.705-10)

Herode cries out against Mariamne when she refuses him her favors.
Unable to see the justice in her rejection or the parity between his
usurpation and her supposed attempts on his life, he can only rage
against her and his fate:

> Du prodige entendu le poil me herissonne,
> Vne stupide horreur mes membres enuironne,

O Cieux! ô Terre! ô Mer! hé! comment souffrez-vous
Des execrations si grandes entre nous?

(897-908)

A later dialogue between Herode and Mariamne reveals the full extent
of their captivity:

MARIAMNE: Libre ie veux mourir ainsi que ie fus née.
HERODE: Hé! quelle liberté ne t'ay-je pas donnée,
Maistresse de mon ame & de mes volontez,
Parauent les desseins de ce meurtre tentez?

(1017-20)

Whether or not these two are responsible for their present situation, it
is certain that they no longer have any power over it. They strive help-
lessly, like moths beating vainly against the windows of a lighted room.
Mariamne is prisoner of Herode's desires, desires over which he has no
control, and her attempts to free herself are under the control of another agent. The achievement of her death has little to do with her.
Herode, confronted in the trial scene by the eunuch, is unable to conceive of Mariamne as other than adulterous, so that he may confirm
an accusation which now expresses for him her very essence. Yet his
very notion of her guilty love for Soesme, which ultimately destroys
her (rather than the false rumors of her attempts on his life), has no
reality beyond that created for it in the dispute between Mariamne,
Herode and Soesme (Act III). In the end, Mariamne is condemned by
rhetoric.

In the final act, after the messenger has announced Mariamne's execution, Herode's first reaction is to reproach the gods, not himself, as
though he suddenly feels that responsibility for the situation lies with
them rather than with humanity:

Qu'à ton chef-d'oeuure, ô Ciel! n'as-tu presté secours?
Que n'as-tu retardé l'effect de ma colère?

(1450-51)

When the messenger continues to relate how Mariamne's mother cursed
her as she passed on her way to the headsman's block, Herode exclaims:

O grande cruauté! que le Ciel & la terre,
Ensemble t'ont liuré vne cruelle guerre.

(1519-20)

Heaven and earth together are the rulers of man's fate, not man himself. Yet again Herode cries out in despair and dismay:

> O astres inclemens!
> O Ciel! injuste Ciel, parfides Elements,
> Et ne pouuiez-vous pas resister à ma haine?
> Et ne deuiez-vous pas me repandre sa peine?
> Mariamne défaite!

(1565-69)

Finally Herode relinquishes all effort of will and gives himself up to the rule of the heavens in a kind of madness, a visionary exaltation. As Hardy presents it, this madness seems less an aberration than an exaggeration of the habitual state of mind of his heroes:

> Las! Helas! ie n'attens de reuoir que son ombre
> Cruelle épouuantable, en la demeure sombre,
> Armée de flambeaux, de tortures, de fers,
> Que dis-je ja déja hors du sueil des Enfers,
> Suiuie d'vne bande affreuse elle s'élance,
> Pardonne à mon outrage, & à ma violence,
> Pardonne moy ma vie, à grands coups redoublez
> Ie m'en vay satisfaire à tes Manes troublez,
> Plomber ce sein caduc, me déchirer la face,
> Arracher ces cheueux, me meurtrir sur la place,
> Ha cruel! ha bourreau, quelle punition
> Feroit de ton forfait digne expiation?

(1611-22)

As I have noted, there is no paradox in the last part of this lament, for acceptance of responsibility does not mean the act has been the result of the exercise of a free will. The will is free only within the bounds allowed by fatality. Further, Herode will not recieve his punishment at his own hands: Aristobule has already promised "vne fin tragique entre les plus tragiques" (30).

This punishment, however, bears no immediate relation to the idea of inescapable destiny; as in *Scédase,* as in *Didon,* as, to some extent, in *Panthée* (Araspe), the guilty parties will not be stigmatized in terms of social morality. It is not Hardy's purpose to preach morality. In the later theater, the guilty will normally be punished along with the innocent (Tristan, for example, was obliged to change the ending of his *Panthée* so that Araspe also died;[24] *Venceslas* is one exception), but for Hardy the exigencies of moral instruction are of no importance, and he is free to portray the sufferings of the human condition.

Jacques Madeleine, discussing Tristan's *Mariane* as an improvement over Hardy's version, made a remark on Tristan's development of his characters which may help to clarify the difference between these plays (and which, incidentally, demonstrates many of the dangers inherent in judging the products of one generation through comparison with those of another):

> Ainsi Mariamne, en sa chambre, confie à sa vieille nourrice les sang-lants griefs qu'elle a contre Hérode. Elle hait ce tyran au point que, si elle pouvait se défaire de luy, elle n'hésiterait pas. C'est un grand tort qu'elle aille jusqu'à dire cela. Du fait de cet aveu, la calomnie que l'on ourdira contre elle aura moins d'invraisemblance, en tout cas nous choquera moins. Josèphe ne parlant de rien de tel, Hardy a été mal inspiré d'ajouter ce trait malencontreux.[25]

As I have tried to show, at some length, Hardy is not interested in the kind of shock that concerns Tristan and his spectator. Rather, it is the portrayal of the inescapable nature of things that characterizes Hardy's theater, and the element of shock is out of place in this atmosphere. If the audience fails to recognize Hardy's concern, the prologue of Aristobule and the repetitive scenes of Pherore, Salome and Mariamne become quite incomprehensible. If Hardy sought to shock his spectator, he would produce a completely different kind of relationship between the stage and the audience: one which demanded a close interest in the characters themselves rather than in their situation. The same logic applies to the motivation of Herode's fury toward Mariamne.[26] Her refusal to grant him her favors, her supposed attempts on his life, her supposed adultery, or simply his desire to "faire plier Mariamne devant lui"—all these "motives" are important not as a revelation of character or the relationships between characters, but only as stages in the accomplishment of their destinies. If reality is the problem, there is surely no less

24. Abraham, *Strangers,* p. 62.
25. Jacques Madeleine, Introduction to *La Mariane* by François Tristan l'Hermite (Paris, 1917), pp. xiv-xv.
26. Ibid.

reality, if less *vraisemblance,* in a fluctuation between motives than in
the single-minded attention to one.

However, it is not simply in the degree of attention paid to the
characters that the play has been changed. Tristan has done away with
the ghost of Aristobule. The exposition is now achieved through a
dream, as Hérode wakes abruptly at the start of the play: "Fantosme
injurieux qui troubles mon repos." Immediately the spectator receives the shock of which I have been speaking: he experiences a
direct confrontation with a character's sensibility. Instead of being
faced with the ghost, and thus enabled to judge the various reactions
of the characters in the context of a familiar situation, the spectator
must consider the unfolding of the plot through the eyes and the
sensibilities of Hérode. Hardy's overshadowing atmosphere disappears, to be replaced by the spectator's anxiety.

To retain audience attention under these circumstances, a certain
vraisemblance is required. For Hardy, this problem was secondary;
for Tristan, it was central. Hence the logical progression of his scenes:
Pherore and the Captain of the Guard come running in response to
the same anxiety felt by the spectator as Hérode cries out for help.

> Mais quoy? le front me suë, & ie suis hors d'haleine,
> Mon ame en ce repos a trouué tant de peine
> A se desabuser d'vne fascheuse erreur,
> Que i'en suis tout émeu de colere & d'horreur.
> Hola.

(I.1.11-15)

According to Jacques Morel, the *mise en scène* here would also be
more "realistic" than in Hardy's play. Reasoning from Scudéry's
Mort de César (1635) and Tristan's own *Osman* (1646), he suggests
that the Marais in 1636 used a curtain or a door to conceal a room
in which Hérode would be lying on a bed. At the end of the scene
the king would step out onto the stage and the door would be
closed. The set would not include various compartments visible at
all times, but would represent "diverses parties d'un palais, qu'une
série de rideaux cachaient et découvraient tour à tour."[27]

27. Jacques Morel, "La Présentation scénique du songe dans les tragédies
françaises au xviie siècle," *Revue d'Histoire du Théâtre,* II (1951), 157.

The following scene confirms the personal nature of the new play. The manner of consolation, the discourse on the physiological causes of dreams (11.48-74), seem designed to make both Pherore and Hérode into recognizable characters. Unlike the semi-biblical figures Hardy created, they are—as characters—close to the spectator; thus he may readily feel their emotions. This relationship is strengthened in such scenes as the one Tristan has added between Mariane and Salome, in which they confront one another in a bitterly gentle attack (II.2), or in the new trial scenes (Act III).

The language, too, contributes to the total effect. As Hérode relates his dream (1.3), a new fantasy world is created, a world of language, as with Hardy. But there is a sharp difference: since the audience may feel with a character, seeing his reactions before knowing what has provoked them and thus sensing his emotions without the need of language, the language itself becomes "transparent," at least to a degree, although it may not remain so throughout. That is to say, the spectator sees through the language to the dream which is the result of Hérode's worries, and which is presented as such. Here, the spectator, no longer cut off from the character by a solid mass of language, is placed as it were *behind* the language with Hérode:

> Ne m'interromps donc pas quand i'auray commencé.
> La lumiere & le bruit s'espandoient par le monde:
> Et lors que le Soleil qui se leue de l'onde
> Esleuant au ceruleau de legeres vapeurs.
>
> (I.3.86-89)

Tristan seems well aware that a long unbroken *récit* of the dream might well produce the very barrier he wishes to avoid,[28] and takes

---

28. Tristan's *Avertissement* to *La Mariane* reads as follows: "Voy ceste peinture en son iour, & n'y cherche pas des finissemens qui pourroient affoiblir en quelque sorte la hardiesse du dessein: Ie ne me suis pas proposé de remplir cét ouurage d'imitations Italiennes, & de pointes recherchées; i'ai seulement voulu descrire auec vn peu de bienséance, les diuers sentimens d'vn Tyran courageux & spirituel, les artifices d'vne femme enuieuse & vindicatiue, & la constance d'vne Reine dont la vertu meritoit vn plus fauorable destin. Et i'ay dépeint cela de la maniere que i'ay creu pouuoir reussir dans la perspectiue du Theatre; sans m'attacher mal à propos à des finesses trop estudiées; & qui font paroistre vne trop grande affectation, en vn temps où l'on fait plus d'estat des beautez qui sont naturelles, que de celles qui sont fardées."

care first to justify its length (1. 86), and then to break it where possible (11. 107-09). Finally, when the dream is completed, a series of quick responses returns the viewer to the characters:

HÉRODE: Salome, qu'en dis-tu?
SALOME: Moy? ie dis que i'en tremble.
PHERORE: Ie ne celeray pas que i'en suis effrayé.
SALOME: C'est quelque auis du Ciel qui vous est envoyé.
HÉRODE: L'auis à déchifrer est si fort difficile
                Qu'il n'eust pû m'obliger d'vn soin plus inutile.
SALOME: L'Estat, d'vn changement peut estre menacé.

                                                        (140-45)

Thus, in a totally different tone and context, the idea of prophecy is once again introduced: not through an oracle, in accordance with which all the characters must act, or with whose utterances their actions are continually compared, but as information presented by the character most directly affected. The effect of the prophecy is, of course, colored for the spectator by the character in question. Man is still ruled by an all-seeing fate, but this fate is not revealed; the character presents his destiny as though it originated within him, not as something imposed from without.

Ce qu'escrit le Destin ne peut estre effacé.
Il faut bon-gré, mal-gré, que l'ame resoluë
Suiue ce qu'a marqué sa puissance absoluë:
De ses pieges secrets on ne peut s'afranchir,
Nous y courons plus droit en pensant les gauchir.

                                                        (146-50)

The hubris of Hérode's next utterance is confined to his defiance of a particular destiny, rather than a necessary fate imposed on all:

Mais qui me peut choquer? & qu'ay-je plus à craindre
Au faiste du bon-heur où l'on me voit atteindre?
Rien n'est assez puissant pour me perdre auiourd'huy,
Si le Ciel en tombant ne m'accable sous luy:
Ie ne puis succomber que par vne auanture
Dont le coup soit fatal à toute la Nature.

                                                        (155-60)

As, in the world, man no longer seems the plaything of nature,
so in the theater he is not submerged under an all-embracing atmosphere; he is a reflection of nature, he is the microcosm, and if the
one collapses, then so does the other. As Dalla Valle puts it, from
corrupt nature, man as microcosm "non può che derivarne la certezza
della propria misera, non può che dedurne la fatale fragilità e corrupti-
bilità dell'essere umano, 'qui se mine à toute heure et se destruit sans
cesse.'"[29] To echo this feeling in the theater the character himself
must become the center of all things. Through him, through his emotions and sensibilities, the spectator must be made aware of man's
relationship with the universe.

In his translation of *La Mariane* (1793), Compagnoni remarked:
"La verità tragica non soffre similitudini. Queste tradiscono il grande
interesse della illusionè, poicuè lo spettatore vede per esse facilmente
il poeta, e il poeta non deve vedersi mai."[30] This may be true up to a
point, but his notion of the tragic does not apply to Tristan. For the
artist of Tristan's period, it is not simply a matter of revealing a universe which carries within it the seeds of its own destruction by showing the psychology of an individual, or, rather, by enabling the spectator to feel the emotions of that individual. Tristan, like his contemporaries, is less sure of himself than the artist of a later (or for
that matter an earlier) generation. His view has been thrown off
balance, and he is not yet in a position to readjust it. He must find
a new base quite dissimilar from the old, but in the meantime he is
without support and no longer feels sure of man's position in the
universe. He is not simply a minute part overshadowed by an immense whole, nor is he free to stand up and shout at the universe
with impunity. He begins to conceive of the universe as something
carried within him, but is still not sure what this universe consists
of or what his own powers are. In his plays, therefore, he cannot
depict the universe as directed by a mind, or echoed in a mind,
since he is stumbling toward the portrayal of something he does not
yet know. His mind is wavering.

29. Daniela Dalla Valle, *Il Teatro di Tristan l'Hermite: Saggio storico e
critico*, Università di Torino. Pubblicazioni della Facoltà di Lettere e Filosofia, XV, Fasc. 2 (Turin, 1964), 146. The quotation is from *La Folie du
Sage*, IV.1.
30. Compagnoni, quoted by Dalla Valle, *Tristan l'Hermite*, p. 134.

This philosophical uncertainty (not resolved until the classical period) emerged for Tristan in a tendency toward verbal extravagance:
his use of *pointes, concetti,* similes and the rest, dismissed by Dalla
Valle as the "aspetto deteriore e marginale del barocchismo di Tristan."[31] This is why the spectator does not "identify" at all times
with a character; for at times the character disappears entirely, to be
replaced by the poet, through a kind of maxim:

> L'Homme à qui la Fortune a fait des auantages,
> Est comme le vaisseau sauué de cent orages;
> Qui subiet toutefois aux caprices du sort,
> Peut se perdre à la rade, ou perir dans le port.

(I.3.151-54)

through simple conceits:

> Aueugles Deïtez, egalez mieux les choses,
> Meslez moins de lauriers auecque plus de roses.

(219-20)

and through extended metaphors, as Hérode's description of Mariane:

> Si le diuin objet dont ie suis idolatre
> Passe pour vn rocher, c'est vn rocher d'albastre,
> Vn escueil agreable, où l'on voit esclater
> Tout ce que la Nature a fait pour me tenter.
> Il n'est point de rubis vermeils comme sa bouche,
> Qui mesle vn esprit d'ambre à tout ce qu'elle touche,
> Et l'esclat de ses yeux veut que mes sentimens
> Les mettent pour le moins au rang des diamans.

(271-78)

Dina, addressing Mariane, echoes these sentiments in a different context:

> Votre teint composé des plus aimables fleurs,
> Sert trop long-temps de lit à des ruisseaux de pleurs.

(II.1.437-38)[32]

---

31. Ibid., p. 138.
32. Dalla Valle quotes two other examples: 11. 1448-50 and 11. 1470-74. It
need scarcely be added that this does not exhaust the possibilities.

One could cite many more examples. Their effect is to prevent continuous identification; they set up a kind of fluctuating distance whereby the spectator is at one moment feeling with the character, at another watching him as a poetic creation—and, perhaps, creator. This fluctuation seems indicative of the general uncertainty often portrayed through metamorphosis as demonstrated by Rousset.[33] As I have suggested, the spectator may not yet see the universe through a character, since the artist is not yet convinced of certain logical relationships and effects; nor may a character appear to struggle against a solid wall, since his relationship to that wall is unclear. Hardy's labyrinth, with its blank walls, its turns and its frustrations, has suddenly become a hall of distorting mirrors in which every figure but one's own is no more than a reflection. The spectator can only be sure of his own mind; and though he knows that it perceives, he has not yet determined what it perceives.

By its very nature, the theater must deal with these problems of reality and illusion which concerned the artists of this period, and it is scarcely surprising that their philosophical explorations led eventually to an examination of the theater itself. This development (and the sudden growth of interest in the theater which it reflects) occurred partly because the philosophical problems in question inevitably go arm in arm with aesthetic and social concerns. One must not forget that, at precisely this period, the composition of the audience was changing:

> L'évolution est rapide: les spectateurs qui, en 1626, assurent le succès de *La Sylvie* de Mairet sont déjà très différents de ceux qui applaudissaient *Scédase* ou *Phraarte*. En 1656 avec le *Timocrate* de Thomas Corneille, l'évolution est achevée: un public à peu près homogène est désormais constitué.[34]

The aristocrat remains, but now his wife or mistress comes to the theater without danger of a slur on her reputation. More important, however, are the bourgeois, the nouveaux riches, those aspiring to raise their social rank—they come to the theater as men on the move, as men improving, or eager to improve, their relative social position.

33. Jean Rousset, *La Littérature de l'âge baroque en France: Circé et le paon* (Paris, 1954).
34. Descotes, *Public du Théâtre*, p. 23.

Before long, Richelieu and his successors will be elevating these men to important positions in the government bureaucracy. At all levels, except perhaps the highest and the lowest, society is in a state of flux, the old certainties of rank and position suddenly replaced by doubts. The aesthetic change, the mirror of metaphysical doubt, reflects the social situation. It is impossible, I believe, for this analogy to be overextended; the two areas are inextricably tangled, and a study of one cannot ignore the other.

The *Mariane* of Tristan, then, falls somewhere between Hardy and the "classical" ideal, perhaps nearer to the latter. At the end of the play Hérode's character remains ambivalent, and the spectator is uncertain how much a man's actions reveal either of himself or of the universe in which he lives. As Narbal says:

> Tu sçais donner des loix à tant de Nations,
> Et ne sçais pas regner dessus tes passions.
> Mais les meilleurs esprits font des fautes extrémes,
> Et les Rois bien souvent sont esclaves d'eux-mesmes.
>
> (V.3.1809-12)

Man is still the microcosm of the imperfect. His will remains an unreliable instrument. He has lost the certainty of his relationship with the macrocosm, and he has yet to replace it with the certainty of his own reason.

The subject of *Panthée* receives similarly differing treatments at the hands of Hardy and Tristan, and reflects the same difference of intent evident in their versions of the story of Herod and his queen. As with other plays, Hardy begins his *Panthée* with a prologue, here an exchange of praise between Cirus and Araspe, followed by the moving dialogue between Cirus and Panthée herself. Again tone is created with great blocks of majestic language, then fragmented as the characters are presented. Again the characters continually exalt their miseries, finding themselves the butts of fate within the majestic vault of their universe. Araspe falls in love with Panthée:

> Agité du flambeau d'vne aueugle furie,
> Perclus de mouuemens, ma conscience perie:
> Réduit à n'esperer qu'vn honteux desespoir,
> Réduit à desirer ma ruyne, & la voir;

Fut-il onc vn desastre, vn malheur memorable,
A la fiere rigueur de mon sort comparable?

(II.209-14)

Once more the fate of the characters is prophesied beforehand; and
throughout the play, prayers and imprecations guide them while the
language shuts them in.

As with *La Mariane*, Tristan quickly shows his concern with provid-
ing a *vraisemblable* motivation for his characters. He carefully prepares for the arrival of Abradate: Panthée has sent him a letter asking
him to come and fight for Cirus in return for the latter's magnanimity
toward her. Thus her own magnanimity is established, and Araspe's
crime will seem the more deplorable. The idea that Abradate should
fight for Cirus originates with her (she is ignorant of the hope Cirus
expressed in I.1),[35] and she takes the first step toward accomplishing
it. She and Cirus are thus equated in terms of heroic stature, and
further motivation is supplied for her suicide in the final act. Tristan,
sensing no doubt that Abradate's change in allegiance would detract
from his stature in the eyes of the spectator, creates an evil liege for
him:

[PANTHÉE:] . . . ce nouveau Tyran, lâche et cruel ensemble,

. . . .

Il est impie, injuste, insolent, & trompeur,
Il ne se fait servir qu'en donnant de la peur;
Son âme dans le crime est toûjours occupée,
Ce n'est que de la boüe en du sang détrempée,
On ne peut l'assister sans quelque lâcheté,
Et l'on peut le quitter par générosité.

(I.4)

This monster, Panthée goes on to say, has already tried to separate
her from Abradate. Her information not only contributes to the effect of *vraisemblance*, but also prepares the spectator for what is to
come, without being a prophecy as it would have in Hardy. The last

35. The version in *Théâtre François ou Recueil des meilleures pièces du
théâtre,* (Paris, 1737), from which I have quoted, has I.4 twice, which puts
the succeeding scenes of the first act off their numbering. I have readjusted
this numbering in my references.

detail of this motivation is filled in when Cirus questions whether Abradate would have so "legere" a spirit as to change sides (even given his
tyrannical liege); and when these doubts as to his merit are dispelled
by Hidaspe (I.5). The direction of Tristan's adjustment is clear: the
spectator learns of the character's motivation before the occurrence,
so he will not stop to wonder at the character's behavior and lose the
thread of his emotions in the process. Another important change
parallels his treatment of *Mariane:* the love interest is strengthened
and he adds a scene (II.3) in which Araspe pretends to be writing a
poem for a friend and recites it as such to Panthée, thus avowing his
love to her (he has already confessed once to Charis, her companion
[I.7]). Later (V.1) Araspe rejoices in Abradate's death, supposing
that he is free to win Panthée, and finally kills himself to rejoin her
in death (V.9).[36] This strengthening of the love theme greatly increases Tristan's opportunities for poetic conceits, which he employs
with effects similar to those noted in *Mariane.*

   The difference between the two playwrights, then, seems to be clear.
In Hardy's theater, the spectator's eye meets that of the character
under a stifling atmosphere created by the language. Above all, the
spectator must see this character move, he must watch him struggle
against this atmosphere. And perhaps it is this relationship which
accounts both for Hardy's success and his importance: his plays may
stimulate a spectator to reflect on their deeper significance, and at
the same time evoke audience response at the level of simple entertainment. It is noteworthy that during the period of Hardy's decreas-
ing popularity, the public's desire for entertainment was linked to a
growing belief that man was perhaps after all the possessor of a strong
and free will, or was at least something more than a plaything of the
gods. At this time, people began to feel that man alone was responsible
for his accomplishments, thus affirming the concept of individual
strength which Hardy's theater could not express. The creation of
atmosphere is a major concern for Hardy whether it be tragic, tragi-
comic (which, although lighter, may still convey a sense of tragic

   36. I must confess that I do not understand how Lancaster E. Dabney can
put the role of Araspe in Tristan and Hardy on a par, when he suggests the
love interest in both to be minor: in Hardy it covers only Act II and Act III,
Scene 1, but in Tristan it is considerable. See Dabney, *French Dramatic Literature in the Reign of Henri IV. A Study in the Extant Plays composed in French
between 1589 and 1610* (Austin, Texas, 1952), p. 181.

exaltation), or pastoral. In the last the tone is light, happy, and
humorous throughout; the spectator is inspired with joy rather than
fear; yet the atmosphere continues to influence the characters, as in
darker plays.[37] Through this atmosphere, then, Hardy is able to make
his spectator feel before he gets to know the character in any sense.

The literary consequence of a belief in free will is that language
may take on an infinite number of meanings according to the whim
of the individual mind; and these meanings, in turn, may enable an
understanding of the universe not attainable through direct perception. Language experiments with form, but is guided by the person
who wields it. This principle will become the basis of a later theater,
one that continues to rely largely upon language, but whose characters control that language. The period of philosophical and artistic
questioning described above led artists to question the theater itself,
and to write such plays as the *Comédie des comédiens* of Gougenot
(1633) and Scudéry (1633), *L'Illusion comique* (1636), *Les Visionnaires* (1637), *L'Hopital des fous* (1635). This same questioning
produced systematic portrayals of madness on the stage, as in *Les
Folies de Cardenio* (1629), *La Folie du Sage* (1642), *L'Hypocondriaque* (1628); in these works, deception becomes a chief stock-in-
trade, while devices such as metamorphosis and illusion raise doubts
on the nature of both the divine system and the theater which echoes
that system.

This theater has little in common with that of Hardy, which strove
to relate the spectator to the situation of the character by means of
atmosphere. Henri Gouhier recently commented on the quality of
the tragic:

37. Tristan makes a comment on this changing atmosphere in some *Stances*
dedicated to Hardy (*Théâtre*, III):

> S'il découure vne jeune ardeur;
> Où s'il exprime vne pudevr,
> Sa veine est toute douce, où bien toute innocente;
> Mais lors que le sujet l'oblige à s'irriter,
> On trouue que sa Scene est aussy menaçante
> Que les foudres de Jupiter.

[p. 6]

Le tragique . . . est une dimension de l'existence réelle. La tragédie est de l'ordre de la littérature et du théâtre, mais le tragique est de l'ordre de la vie.[38]

Hardy, it seems to me, tried to place his spectator in the order of the tragic.

38. Henri Gouhier, "Tragique et transcendance: Introduction à un débat général," in *Le Théâtre tragique*, éd. Jean Jacquot (Paris, 1962), p. 479.

2. 1625-1635: The Spectator and the Theater of Doubt

> O pauvre comédie, objet de tant de veines,
> Si tu n'es qu'un portrait des actions humaines,
> On te tire souvent sur un original
> A qui, pour dire vrai, tu ressembles fort mal!
> (Corneille, *La Galerie du Palais,* I.7)

> Que souvent notre esprit trompé de l'apparence
> Règle ses mouvements avec peu d'asseurance!
> Qu'il est peu de lumière en nos entendements,
> Et que d'incertitude en nos raisonnements!
> Qui voudra désormais se fie aux impostures
> Qu'en notre jugement forment les conjectures,
> Tu suffis pour apprendre à la postérité
> Combien la vraisemblance a peu de vérité.
> (Corneille, *Clitandre,* V.4)

In the years immediately following the era of Hardy, the theater became increasingly self-conscious. At first this new direction was apparent only in occasional references by playwrights, but they soon undertook a complete re-examination of the nature of the theater. In the anonymous comedy *Les Ramonneurs* (c. 1624),[1] Galaffre tells his master, Scanderbec, that he should speak more softly because of "ce peuple Badaut qui s'assemble, et s'imagine qu'en vertu de quelques charmes vous allez métamorphoser ce miserable Toict à pourceaux en quelqu'autre Luxembourg" (I.1). Later on Martin mocks Bonarsius, telling him his disciples will be able to go and see performed "l'histoire de ces belles amours dans un hotel de Bourgogne" (IV.10),[2] while Scanderbec himself, sending for provisions for the proposed feast at the end of the play, addresses the audience:

1. Discovered in manuscript and published by Austin Gill: *Les Ramonneurs, comédie anonyme en prose,* éd. Austin Gill (Paris, 1957).
2. Cf. Corneille, *La Galerie du Palais; le mercier* to *la lingère:*

> Là, là, criez bien haut, faites bien l'étourdie,
> Et puis on vous jouera dedans la comédie.
> (IV.12. 1397-98)

Je me doute bien que vous autres Spectateurs attendez qu'on vous
convie à ce festin, mais l'incommodité du lieu . . . me dispense de
vous en prier davantage; chacun donc se retire chez soy au petit
pas. (V.8)

In Rotrou's *La Bague d l'oubly* (1628-29), Mélite remarks of Liliane's
failure to recognize the King:

> Bons Dieux! comme elle ment d'une façon hardie!
> On diroit que ces jeux sont une comédie.
>
> (III.5)

Dorimant, in *La Galerie du Palais* (1632 or 1633), turns to Aronte to
ask him: "C'est donc en ce Marais que finit ton voyage?" (IV.2.1085),
while Chrysante, in the same play, comments that a suggested marriage
between herself and Pleirante "sentirait trop sa fin de comédie" (V.2.
1794).[3] D'Ouville's Lucidor in *Les Morts vivants* (1644) turns to his
friend Adraste to speak of Florante, whom he loves but believes to be
dead (she is disguised as one Dorise, unable to reveal her true identity):

> Ayant appris de moy que tres-excellement
> Elle auoit imité Florante, asseurement
> Que pour un peu d'argent elle s'est enhardie
> D'auoir aussi son role en cette Comedie.
>
> (V.4)

In Baro's *Prince fugitif* (1647), Philoxandre avoids explaining his origins
to the King by arguing:

> Ce monde est un theatre où chacun comme moy
> Peut faire en mesme iour & l'esclaue & le Roy.
>
> (IV.3)

Each of these examples, and there are many more, is a deliberate appeal to the intellect of the spectator; he is associated not with a character but with the actor. The specific stage illusion is opposed to reality.
The spectator is made aware of the theatrical nature of the scene he is
watching. The actor becomes himself or, at least, plays the part of the
actor, and, demanding that the spectator acknowledge the illusion as
such, leaves his role aside for a brief moment. Certainly, all the instances given above occur in comedies, and one may argue convincingly

---

3. Cf. p. 67 below: Mareschal, *Le Railleur*, V.6.

that the device is very common in this genre at any time in the theater's history. Bergson has suggested that laughter is possible only if the spectator is intellectually and emotionally indifferent to the victim of his laughter. Thus, the spectator's awareness of the illusory nature of what he is watching prevents any kind of identification with a character, and the comic relationship is made possible. I do not intend to dispute Bergson: the farces and *sotties*, the comedies of Molière, all tend to use the spectator in the same way, and all remind him that he is *watching*. In this context, he may enter a new kind of relationship, where the illusions of the stage become his own: not because his emotions are confused with those of a stage character, but because he stands *with the actor* at the first level of illusion. With comedy it is necessary that he laugh; the methods of suspending his belief need not be too subtle. With other genres, demanding a serious frame of mind, more care is needed, since an abrupt dissolution of the illusion may produce laughter regardless of the tone of the action. There are, however, other means of achieving this fluctuating distance between spectator and character; and these means are the essence of the so-called baroque theater.

If Hardy maintains a certain tension in his theater by means of an atmosphere which restrains a latent conflict involving theme, language, set and action, then the dissipation of that atmosphere implies the disappearance of that particular tension and the release of the conflict. To some extent this consequence is apparent in Tristan's *Mariane*, but there the conflict is already limited in that the spectator may identify with the characters, and the elements composing the conflict are less sharply defined. Roughly in between Hardy's theater and the new illusionistic theater—of which *La Mariane* is an early example—lies this baroque theater in which Hardy's atmosphere plays no part, characters are still purely figments of the language, and the four abovementioned elements of dramatic conflict are treated as separate entities. They dance around one another, they meet, combine and separate again with no reference to the exigencies of plot or character. The dialectical juxtaposition of these elements keeps the spectator aware of the theater and, resuming in aesthetic terms the artist's philosophical problems, takes him into a somewhat primitive form of "total" theater.

The word "primitive" applies because this theater, at least at the Marais and the Hôtel de Bourgogne, still depended largely on the text

to establish the dialectic, in the absence of technical devices designed
for the same end. But although these stage devices first appeared in
the simplest of surroundings, they could hardly be considered crude,
as Lawrenson indicates:

> Long before Torelli was summoned to France the baroque theater
> existed potentially in the streets of its cities. In this particular
> canalization of the dramatic art, the mystery stage, via the Royal
> Entry, becomes the baroque stage, with perspective scenes, ma-
> chinery, ascents, appearances, seen through a columned archway,
> a century before these adorn the court theatre and *without ref-
> erence to the development of the dramatic text.*[4]

Lawrenson, in fact, suggests (and on this point he and Kernodle concur)
that the architectural development of the stage does not simply parallel the textual development of the play, but often precedes it—with
the important exception of the Hôtel de Bourgogne after 1640. This
thesis, of course, reinforces the view that each stage element carries
its own distinctive significance.

The banality of the plots, the predilection for nymphs and shepherds
(whether in pastoral, tragi-comedy or, indeed, comedy), the emphasis
on love and the problems it creates, point at once not simply to the
salons' taste for *L'Astrée* but to the complex theme inherent in the
aesthetic of this new theater. It may be true, as Gill comments, that
the particular originality of *Les Ramonneurs* lies in "cette subordination de l'intrigue à l'intention de faire rire,"[5] although this theory
seems to slight most of the earlier popular comic theater. But whether laughter or something else was the desired end, the playwrights of
this period certainly did subordinate plot to the dialectic of dramatic
elements: "Et jamais on n'a veu qu'au récit d'un poëme, on ait pré-
occupé les spectateurs par la cognoissance du sujet."[6]

If language is approached here as the central link between these
elements, it is partly because a study of these plays must center on
the texts. The language does in fact constitute a springboard for the

---

4. Lawrenson, *The French Stage*, p 46.
5. Gill, Introduction to *Ramonneurs*, p. xxv.
6. Balthasar Baro in his preface to *Clorise*, quoted by Jules Marsan, *La
Pastorale dramatique en France à la fin du xvie et au commencement du
xviie siècle* (Paris, 1905), p. 345, n. 1.

other elements, but not seldom a change in the set may reflect a shift
or progression in theme, while the language is focused elsewhere. In
Monléon's *Amphytrite* (1630), Leandre changes into a rock as he
laments (IV.2), and the lament becomes a counterpoint to the changing form; in *Les Galanteries du Duc d'Ossone* (1634),[7] the shifting
walls and curtains play against the shifting and uncertain relationships
of the characters. The set may also support the language: in the
pastorai, the thick forests seem to echo the complicated tangles found
in the speeches and plots of the lovers.

It may be that such scenes as the binding of Alexis to the tree in
Gombauld's *Amaranthe* (V.2ff) are deliberately planned to reflect a
theme: in that case, the intangible obstacles dividing the lovers from
one another. The continual change of scene in de Brosse's *Innocens
coupables* (1643) is another case in point. At times the language
seems to bear no relation to the set, as a character tries to convince
the spectator of a reality entirely apart from his apparent situation
(in madness, for example); or the language itself may create that situation, as at the end of Mairet's *Sylvie* (V.2) when the growing tension
of the spell eventually bursts into the storm which Florestan drives
away.

In certain cases the set neither opposes the text nor echoes it, but
adds a further dimension to the idea evolving through the drama. In
the text of d'Aubignac's *Pucelle d'Orleans* (1641), where the angel
warns Joan of her future, there is a marginal notation reading "Icy
paroistra en perspectiue une femme dans vn feu allumé, & vne foule
de peuple à l'étour d'elle" (I.1). In La Calprenède's *Mort de Mithridate* (1635), as Pompée welcomes Pharnacc to fight with him against
his father, Mithridate, a curtain opens and "Mithridate paroist auec
Hypsicratee & ses deux filles." This semi-cinematographic effect occurs some dozen lines before the first scene closes, and makes a deliberate appeal to the spectator as a spectator; such an effect can be
achieved only when the spectator retains his identity apart from the
characters. Kernodle has shown that this device of the inner stage is
of very ancient origin, and that it has been frequently used in the theater of northern Europe since the Middle Ages.[8]

7. In *Le Théâtre français au xvie et au xviie siècle*, éd. Edouard Fournier,
2 vols. (Paris, n.d.), II, 217-79.
8. Kernodle, *Art to Theatre*, pp. 108, 123, 128 and *passim*.

On these occasions the individual spectator is not left to sense the
play between the various elements for himself: on the contrary, the
author is often at pains to indicate it. *Sylvie* provides a particularly
fine example. As Florestan climbs the steps toward the magic mirror
which he must break in order to set Sylvie and Thelame free from the
spell and thus win the hand of Meliphile, he exclaims:

> L'espouuantable objet, l'horrible vision!
> Courage, tout cecy n'est rien qu'illusion.

(V.2.2071-72)

Here the author shows how this theater plays to the full with the confusion of reality and illusion; for the thunder and lightning, the flashes
and shadows were actually produced, and thus *real* both for the spectator and Florestan.[9] What the prince refers to as illusion is seen and
heard by the spectator. This is an inversion of the usual situation
where the character believes in something which the spectator can re-
ject. The prince's remark counteracts the realism of the technical effects. His acceptance of the magical atmosphere can only be equated
with the spectator's awareness of the theatrical atmosphere. Though
the full horror of the prince's discourse could not be reproduced
through physical effects, the spectator sees enough so that the character's words only emphasize the scene's theatricality:

> Mais pourquoy s'amuser à ces objets trompeurs
> Qui ne peuuent donner que de legeres peurs?

(V.2.2083-84)

As the scene progresses, the action remains obviously unreal. After
Thelame has been brought out of the enchantment he continues to
think he is dead, and tries to convince Sylvie accordingly. Even after
the spell has been broken, Thelame's illusion is not fully destroyed;
only the combined efforts of an oracle, Sylvie and the King finally
suffice to dispel his madness. Here, the discrepancy between language
and visual appearance leads to a whole series of differing illusions:

---

9. The following props are required: "Il faut une nuict au cinquiesme acte,
un tonnerre, des eclairs, des socisons [espèce de fusée dont on se servait pour
les feux d'artifice (editor's note, p. 76)], des dards, des houlettes et un miroir
enchanté" *(Le Mémoire de Mahelot,* éd. Lancaster, pp. 90-91).

first the King observes the illusion of Thelame and Sylvie (he and Florestan are as much an audience as the spectators); then Florestan battles an "illusion" which is not an illusion: its effects are real for him, as for the spectator, even though they parallel the illusion of Thelame and Sylvie which the spectator perceived as fictional a moment before. Finally, Thelame maintains his illusion after the original illusion is broken, while Florestan and the King look on and Sylvie seems to fluctuate. Similarly, the spectator is fluctuating all along between several different illusions, identifying with none and altering his attitude toward the stage as it passes from illusion to illusion.

Less dramatic, usually, are those occasions when the set appears to provoke the language, as with lyrical passages on the beauty of the countryside (for example, *Sylvie*, I.2.111-16 or Auvray, *La Madonte*, I.3).[10] These passages, to a reader, seem inspired by literary convention; but for the spectator they are stimulated by the visual stage effects.

10. I quote part of the passage from *La Madonte*, since the play is not easily consulted:

> L'Echo que l'on entend dans ces deux fortes tours
> N'a pas dit ce matin vn mot de ses amours,
> Toutes les fleurs encore ont la teste baissee
> Le soucy seulement entretient la pensee,
> S'étonnant toutes deux de ce que mon Soleil
> Semble perdre auiourd'huy le soin de son reueil,
> I'entens fort peu de bruit, le Zephir a son aise
> Baise toutes les fleurs pour eteindre sa braise,
> Il semble entretenir les eaux de leur fraicheur
> Les Oeillets de leur feu, les lys de leur blancheur,
> Et leur rebellion qui le rend plus superbe
> Le contraint quelquefois à les coucher sur l'herbe;
> Ces ruisseaux de cristal, & ces veines d'argent
> Ne coulent qu'à regret, et d'vn pas negligent.

(Jean Auvray, *La Madonte, tragi-comedie, dédiée à la Reine* (Paris, 1632), I.3).

It is hardly necessary to remark on the erotic nature of this admiration; what is of significance is that the stage setting becomes a kind of springboard for the thoughts of Damon, although one supposes the set as envisaged by the lover to be somewhat imaginary. (Though not entirely: Mahelot calls for "un beau jardin" and "des rossignols" [*Mémoire*, p. 70]). The actor transposes the visual into a realm of the imaginary existing only in the mind and in the language which reflects it.

This intertwining of dramatic elements is of course extremely complex, and one hesitates to discuss them separately for fear of obscuring the problem. Such a discussion, however, may be focused if one first determines the central preoccupation of all these dramatists, then examines this preoccupation more closely through two *explications de texte.*

Madness, love and illusion

> Lovers and madmen have such seething brains,
> Such shaping fantasies, that apprehend
> More than cool reason ever comprehends.
> The lunatic, the lover and the poet
> Are of imagination all compact.
> *(A Midsummer Night's Dream,* V.1)

The representation of madness on the stage, as noted by Van Roosbroeck[11] among others, is by no means limited to the period under consideration here. However, it does reach a peak between 1625 and 1635, as his examples show, and stresses almost exclusively the close connection between madness and love.[12] Since love forms the knot of the intrigue in most plays of this period, this connection is of considerable significance even when there is no obvious madness in the play, for it suggests that the ostensible theme is tightly linked with the major problem of reality, illusion and the reliability of human perception. This madness has three main characteristics: it leads to a desire for death, it reveals the depth of the victim's attachment to the beloved, it is pleasing to the afflicted: "Agreables transports! importune raison!" shouts Pyrocle in Mareschal's *Cour bergere* (1638);[13] and Scudéry's Ligdamon explains "Je me plais dans l'excés de ma melancolie," to which Sylvie replies, "Ne flattez point

---

11. See Gustave L. Van Roosbroeck, "A Commonplace in Corneille's *Mélite:* the Madness of Eraste," *Modern Philology,* XVII, 3 (July 1919), 29-37.

12. Ibid., p. 30.

13. I.1; a little later (I.3) he adds: "J'adore la prison, & la main qui me tue."

son nom, appellez là folie."[14] These traits are evident in the stage description of madness, but they do not by any means define its nature. Foucault has noted four distinct types of unreason in the theater of the period, and supplied definitions for each:[15] "la folie par identification romanesque," illustrated by *Les Folies de Cardenio*, where a character takes himself for a literary type or behaves according to some essentially literary ideal, after the fashion of Don Quixote; "la folie de vaine présomption," as in *Les Visionnaires* or *Le Pédant joué*, where a character believes himself capable of anything (this category must include the matamore, who believes himself all-powerful, first in war, and second in love); "la folie de juste châtiment," as in *Mélite*, with Eraste's confession of guilt in his madness; and finally "la passion désespérée," illustrated by Rotrou's *Hypocondriaque*, or by the mad lover, Liridas, in de la Croix's *Climène*. What is common to all these variations is their creativity: whatever its cause, whatever form it takes, madness creates a completely new world, a world in itself perfectly logical and admirably well-ordered.[16] Indeed, as Monléon's

14. Georges de Scudéry, *Ligdamon et Lidias, ou la ressemblance, tragicomédie* (Paris, 1631). It may be well to comment here on the important words *hypocondriaque* and *mélancolie*, since their meaning in the seventeenth century was not what it is today. According to Pierre Richelet in the "nouvelle édition" of his *Dictionnaire françois* (Amsterdam, 1706), the word "hipocondriaque" meant "bizarre, foux, capricieux" (p. 418). Of "mélancolie," Charles Marty-Laveaux says: "Le mot n'a aujourd'hui rien de sinistre; il exprime d'ordinaire une douce et aimable tristesse, dans laquelle on se complaît; il n'en était pas de même au dix-septième siècle. Cette expression désignait alors le chagrin le plus invétéré, le plus profond, et *mélancolique* était un synonyme fort rapproché d'*atrabilaire*" (Pierre Corneille, *Oeuvres*, éd. Ch. Marty-Laveaux, 12 vols. [Paris, 1862-68], XII, p. 78]. Indeed, Richelet gives for *atrabilaire* only the word "melancolique" (p. 87), which he defines as: "Espece de délire sans fievre, accompagné de crainte & de chagrin sans raison aparente à cause que le chagrin & le jugement sont blessez par l'abondance d'une bile noire & brulée. Tristesse" (p. 500). Since the pastoral hero's complaint of *mélancolie* is a perennial one, one should note that it means considerably more than mere sadness.

15. Michel Foucault, *Folie et déraison: histoire de la folie à l'âge classique* (Paris, 1961), pp. 44-46.

16. Foucault *(Folie,* pp. 253-303) quotes Paul Zacchias, *Quaestiones medicolegales* . . . , 2 vols. (Avignon, 1660-61), and Ysbrand van Diemerbroek, *Disputationes praticae, de morbis capitis,* in *Opera anatomica et medica* (Utrecht, 1685), who both make this observation from a medical standpoint at about this time.

Amphytrite suggests, the premise upon which the madman bases his world may be no different from that employed by the supposedly sane person—an idea that enables the author to confuse his audience as to where true reality lies, if anywhere.

Now the possible significance of madness in the theater becomes more clear: as the characters accept or refute this world, as this world contradicts or adapts itself to the visual world of the stage or even changes it, so the spectator's affective response will fluctuate. Illusion replaces illusion, and, in this theater, will shift again to return the spectator, not to the first illusion whose fragility has become apparent, but to reality. Foucault has remarked on the essential lightheartedness of stage madness during this period. The tragic madness of an Ophelia or a Lear, of a Saül [17] or a Tiribaze,[18] can no longer have any place here, for these victims are *real* and each dies as a result of his folly: their madness does not compel the spectator to question reality, because it is simply another facet of a single reality. It may be, as Foucault suggests, that to the Renaissance mind the madman is in a privileged position between life and death; but this position lies on a single line of reality encompassing both these extremes, while the madmen in the French plays mentioned above seem to be placed parallel to "reality." Thus, the spectator to these plays may not readily determine where madness ends and reality begins—an effect Foucault considers of critical importance.

> Sa fonction dramatique ne subsiste que dans la mesure où il s'agit d'un faux drame: forme chimérique où il n'est question que de fautes supposées, de meurtres illusoires, de disparitions promises aux retrouvailles.
>
> Et pourtant cette absence du sérieux ne l'empêche pas d'être essentielle—plus essentielle encore qu'elle n'était, car si elle met un comble à l'illusion, c'est à partir d'elle que l'illusion se défait.[19]

It is not simply a question of Eraste talking in his madness and revealing all his plotting to those affected by it, nor of the madness feigned by the lovers Alfrede and Luciane in Beys' *L'Ospital des fous*, to cheat those who would separate them or to communicate without

17. In Jean de la Taille's *Saül le Furieux* (1572).
18. In Jean de Schélandre's *Tyr et Sidon, ou les funestes amours de Belcar et Meliane. Tragédie* (1608).
19. Foucault, *Folie*, pp. 48–49.

arousing suspicion. These destructions of illusion do not annihilate
the essential illusion of the theater: it may be somewhat shaken, but
it continues to bewitch. This is the case also with *L'Hypocondriaque,*
with *La Bague de l'oubly,* where effects of the ring's spell may be
viewed as a form of madness, and indeed with the majority of plays
of this period: the spectator's distance fluctuates, but is not destroyed.
In a few plays, however, the spectator is returned to a reality in which
the stage is on a level with the auditorium, and the theater is specifically revealed as an illusion: the two *Comédies des comédiens* of Gougenot
and Scudéry, Corneille's *Illusion comique,* and to a degree *L'Ospital
des fous* (for different reasons than those suggested above). In these
works, the actors are presented as themselves: they appear simultaneously as the spectator's equal and as an illusion. Monléon's *Amphytrite* is a special case, destroying—or using—illusion in a way common
to many others, but to so uncommon a degree that its effect resembles
that in the other plays just mentioned. In a sense, the spectator is
made to regard the characters in these last plays much as, in the others,
the sane characters are obliged to regard the madmen.

Thus madness becomes just another way of further confusing the illusion. It may be funny or pitiful, but primarily it serves as a foil to
the supposed reality of the other characters, which it puts in doubt because the madman on the stage is their equal: to the spectator he is
neither more nor less illusory than the rest. It is they who remove
themselves from him, as the spectator cannot, for the madman is on
the stage with them. Moreover, it is not rare for them to accept his
madness for one reason or another. Cliton, mistaken for Charon by
the mad Eraste, gives up trying to persuade him otherwise and carries
him off as though he were indeed the boatman of the underworld
(*Mélite,* IV.6). Certainly, this is farce, but behind the laughter lies
Cliton's acceptance, for whatever reasons and however briefly, of the
second illusion.

In Mairet's *Illustre corsaire* (1637), Lepante, prince of Sicily, and
Tenare, one of his officers, feign madness in order to gain access to
the former's love, Ismenie, whom the prince has not seen for ten
years and who is now betrothed to the evil Lypas. This madness
becomes confusing, for Tenare plays at loving one of Ismenie's
maids-of-honor, Célie, who seems to return his love: but the spectator never knows whether the love of Tenare is real or not, whether
Célie accepts his "illusion," or he hers. Nor does the spectator know

just when the "play within the play" rejoins the outer illusion, for here, too, the second illusion has been accepted.

And the situation becomes still more complicated. Love (as I have noted) is itself a form of madness; Mairet, to stress this idea, paints a lively picture of Lepante playing a highly romantic love-lorn prince (which he actually is as Lepante) under the madman's name of Nicas, the shepherd/prince consecrated by countless plays and novels. Then Nicas, in turn, is deliberately presented as playing a role (II.5), for which he needs props and a special king's costume. There is a dual commentary: on his supposed reality as the prince, Lepante, mocked by the mad illusion of himself as Nicas, and on the stage character of the shepherd/prince in general. The original stage illusion has been replaced by a game of multiple illusions, and it would seem that this game is more important than the story.

In Rotrou's *Hypocondriaque,* Cloridan goes mad upon hearing of the "death" of his beloved Perside (III.2) and is cured after seeing two men rise from their graves to the strains of some music supplied for the occasion: one of them shoots at Cloridan in resentment at being brought back to life (V.6). The falseness of Cloridan's illusion becomes manifest when others are involved in it: again, however briefly, illusion is shown as such. Another example occurs in Mareschal's *Le Railleur* (1635):[20] La Dupré, replying to a remark made by Clarimand concerning "un vain Capitain," wonders:

> Est-ce un de ceux qu'on doit jouer à ces jours gras?
> Rodomont, Scanderberg, Fracasse, où Taillebras?
>
> (II.2.163)

It happens that Taillebras has not only already been on stage, but is to reappear in the very next scene. La Dupré speaks of him (and, by analogy, of the equally pretentious and vain poet, De Lyzante, who is always vying with Taillebras in braggadocio) as though he were a stage character, although he appears in the play apparently on the same level of illusion as herself. Thus there is a confusion of levels: for a moment La Dupré steps figuratively into the auditorium. Yet she in turn is held up to ridicule as a grotesque puppet by Clarimand, the *railleur,* and his loved one, Clytie, as are the other characters in the play. Indeed, Clarimand presents himself as a disinterested spectator:

20. In Edouard Fournier, éd., *Théâtre français,* II, 146-208.

Tu sçais que mon humeur est de rire en tous lieux
Que je voy du faux or aux idoles des Dieux.

(II.2.163)

And he puts himself at the level of the spectator in the auditorium by making mocking asides (e.g., throughout I.2). If he finally submits to the very madness which he has mocked in the others, if he is finally "trapped" into a marriage he was actually not unwilling to make, it is because the illusion plays a trick on him: he is obliged to marry by that most conventional of stage devices, the false letter (in fact a marriage contract that he signs unawares).

The spectator, of course, knows about the contract well before Clarimand; and, with the play's closing lines, Mareschal makes sure that the spectator is no dupe of the theater:

Son mariage icy, quoiqu'il fasse et qu'il die,
Viendra comme la farce après la comédie.

(V.6.206)

Beyond the fantastic madness of Taillebras and De Lyzante, beyond the less obvious folly of La Dupré, Beaurocher and the rest (note the similarity of these names to real-life names of certain actors), Mareschal is concerned with the illusory nature of Clarimand himself. These characters move from one level of illusion to another, and in the process cast doubt on each level successively, so that finally the spectator has nothing to grasp. Since costumes were contemporary in style, a character who deliberately stepped aside from the others in order to mock them would take on the aspect of a spectator: particularly at a time when spectators were seated on the stage. Thus, through Clarimand, the audience can watch a *spectator* being slowly absorbed into the illusion.

It is not difficult to see that the stage representation of madness must inevitably lead one to question the nature of reality, an issue made all the more vivid by the stage setting. Leaving aside the several varieties of madman—the fantastic matamore, the equally preposterous poet, the mad lover and so on—the most significant aspect of this portrayal of diverse follies is that it serves to mirror the human condition.

Ce monde du début du XVIIe siècle est étrangement hospitalier à la folie. Elle est là, au coeur des choses et des hommes, signe ironique qui brouille les repères du vrai et du chimérique, gardant à peine le souvenir des grandes menaces tragiques—vie plus trouble qu'inquiétude, agitation dérisoire dans la société, mobilité de la raison.[21]

This loss of the grandeur and gravity that had once accompanied madness transformed it from an ever-present reminder of the supernatural and the extraordinary into a warmer and merrier phenomenon, blurring the very "realities" generally accepted as the norm. Madness has not lost its importance as a symbol, it has simply changed its significance. As Foucault tracks its course, madness at this moment is halfway between its Renaissance position as some form of reality beyond "normal" reality, and its later seventeenth-century position as an isolated segment of reality, walled off for fear it would contaminate "normal" perception: "Le classicisme éprouve une pudeur devant l'inhumain que la Renaissance jamais n'avait ressentie."[22]

The Renaissance spirit seems to subsist in the dramatic literature of the period with which I am concerned. One may suppose that just as the attitude of the other characters toward the madman is one of pity and a desire to help, mixed with gentle mockery—and, very occasionally, a mild fear[23]—so too is the spectator's attitude one of pity and laughter, rather than fright. These characters arouse a certain excitement, they confuse, they pull the spectator into the illusion only to present him with another. They are incapable of arousing that terror with which the spectator will later regard a Cléopatre (in Corneille's *Rodogune*), a Phèdre or a Néron, and which will also spur a later morality to call for the exclusion or punishment of the offender. With the possible exception of Eraste in *Mélite,* these madmen of an earlier generation do not represent a threat to society. Far from it: they constitute a necessary element in a single but very blurred reality.

From a theatrical point of view, they are a means of provoking the spectator to an awareness of this lack of clarity. This provocation, clearly, far exceeds the mere representation of madness: it permeates plot and character. For among all the forms of madness shown on the stage, the most common is the passion of love.

21. Foucault, *Folie,* p. 53.
22. Ibid., p. 179.
23. For example, Cardenio's attack on the *licentié* in Pichou's *Les Folies de Cardenio* (Edouard Fournier, éd., *Théâtre français,* II, 3-67), IV.2. But he and the barber quickly recover and go after Cardenio to see if they can help.

To the seventeenth-century mind, indeed, the madness of a lover was not simply metaphorical. Love itself was considered madness, supposedly caused, like hypochondria, by hot humours rising to the brain; and producing symptoms resembling those of melancholia.[24] Thus the very core of these plays—the intrigues of characters who exist only for love, their amorous language—is already the precarious reality of a madness. And this madness remains linked to death in the midst of life, questioning not only our perceptions and our reliance upon them, but the very nature of life itself. Love disturbs the mind, it inspires the lover to change his nature, to lose himself in the loved one and thus to deny his own reality. It may confuse his reason so much that his perceptions move, as it were, to another level. Finally, it leads him toward death. If his love is accepted, the two souls become one and his essential being is altered; if it is refused he has lost his soul without possibility of recovering it, and will die:

> Si tost que ie le vy, ic perdy ma franchise;
> Mon sang fut tout esmeu, mon ame en fut esprise;
> Ie me perdis moy-mesme, & voulant l'acquérir,
> Ie fus ingenieuse a me faire mourir.
>   (Gombauld, *L'Amaranthe* [1630], I.5)

So love itself appears as the symbol of the problem the playwright faces, for while it leads to death, while it modifies and intensifies the perceptions, at the same time it leads to life. The lovers are surrounded by the warmth of the sun, by the chattering of birds, the rushing of streams; appreciation of the growing trees and flowers around him is a standard part of the lover's repertory in the pastoral. At the same time, this life is not a "normal" one: the true lover is only able to enjoy it to the full if his beloved has accepted his love as a part of her own being. To achieve this fusion, he presents her with his soul (and vice versa). In Du Ryer's *Argenis (Derniere iournée* [1630]), the heroine says to Poliarque as he is about to leave, "Helas! ie suis sans

---

24. See Foucault, *Folie*, pp. 318-59. He cites as authority for this linking of love and melancholy two works in particular. First, Jean Liébaut, *Trois livres sur les maladies des femmes* (Paris, 1649), which was first published in French, I find, in 1589, translated from Liébaut's Latin, in turn an adaption of Giovanni Marinelli's work of 1563: the idea has deep and wide roots. The second work is interesting in this connection for its title alone: Jacques Ferrand, *De la maladie d'amour ou mélancolie érotique* (Paris, 1623).

vous la moitié de moy-mesme"; but he tells her not to be afraid, he
will return from France in three months with a fleet. He cannot stay
without Argenis:

> Que feroient mes subiets d'un monarque sans ame,
> Et qui la laisse icy pour gage de sa flame.
>
> (III.6)

And Arimand, in Mairet's *Chryséide et Arimand*, describes his state
on being separated from his love:

> Ie ne suis desormais qu'vn pauure corps sans ame
> Ie ne suis desormais que l'ombre d'vn viuant,
> Qu'vn fantosme qui parle et qu'vn tombeau mouuant.
>
> (I.2.206-08)

Argenie's ambiguous death-wish in Scudéry's *Prince deguisé* (1634-
35), when she bewails the fate that will oblige her to marry the killer
of Clearque, whom she loved, seems also to stem from this fusion.
When Philise tells her that whoever tries to kill Clearque is more likely
to die himself, Argenie can only reaffirm the intensity of her love:

> Et puis que de l'Himen tout espoir m'est osté,
> Que je puisse mourir, et viure en liberté.
>
> (I.2)

It is this fusion, this "death," that the lover welcomes. In Théophile's *Pyrame et Thisbé,* the heroine soliloquizes

> Mon ame, qu'ay-je dit? c'est fort mal discourir,
> Car l'ame nous fait vivre et tu me fais mourir.
> Il est vray que la mort que ton ame me livre
> Est aussi seulement ce que j'appelle vivre.
>
> (I.1)[25]

---

25. Cf. also Thélame's lament for Sylvie in Mairet's *Sylvie:*

> Car n'ayant eu tous deux qu'une ame iusqu'icy,
> L'vn mort, l'autre deuroit cesser de viure aussi.
>
> (V.2.1963-64)

And Artenice to Alidor in Racan's *Les Bergeries* (published 1625) after she regains consciousness by the river:

Whatever the sexual implications, this loss of the self is scarcely different from that doubt which is a central question in, for example, the work of Rotrou. Though love is not necessarily the immediate cause of this doubt, it is always a contributing factor. In *L'Hypocondriaque*, Cloridan comes from his madness doubting his reality:

> Vos soins injurieux m'ont réduit à ce point
> D'ignorer si je vis ou si je ne vis point.
>
> (V.6.90)

The King of *La Bague de l'oubly* sinks ever-deeper into madness as a result of the magic spell contained in the ring:

> Au pitoyable état où mes jours sont réduits
> Je n'ose m'assurer si moi-même je suis.
>
> (IV.2)

Amphitryon, faced with the somewhat unusual problem of an exact double, loses touch with his own reality: "Je ne me connais plus; moi-même je m'ignore" (*Les Sosies*, II.3). Indeed, both in this play and in *Hercule mourant*, the author makes no secret of his preoccupation with the problem of identity and the questioning of accepted reality.[26]

However, in most plays of the period it is the lover who provokes this doubt. In Baro's *Parthénie* (1641), Alexandre feels himself beginning to go out of his mind as he tries to fight his love for his beautiful captive, and his friend Ephestion remarks:

> Hélas! gardez-vous bien d'avancer vostre mort:
> Je mourrois avec vous; nos amoureuses flames
> Font dans un mesme corps respirer nos deux ames.
>
> (III.4)

In Mairet's *Athenaïs* (1638), Theodose says to Paulin of Athenaïs:

> En ce cruel instant qu'elle s'est éloignée:
> Alors auec douleur, i'ay senty que mon coeur
> S'est détaché de moy pour suiure son vainqueur.
>
> (I.5)

26. For the first, see Judd David Hubert, *Molière and the Comedy of Intellect* (Berkeley & Los Angeles, 1962), pp. 162-88, and for the second, Jacqueline Van Baelen, *Rotrou. Le héros tragique et la révolte* (Paris, 1965), pp. 33-37. Note Hercule's exclamation after he has put on the poisoned robe: "Moi-mesme je m'ignore en ce triste accident" (IV.1).

> Mais pour notre malheur les Destins ont permis
> Qu'un trait d'oeil plus puissant qu'un monde d'ennemis,
> Fasse par un succes qu'ils ne pouuoient pretēdre
> Qu'Alexandre aujourd'hui cesse d'estre Alexandre.
>
> (IV.3)

Alexandre is ready to admit his problem:

> Il est vray, les regards dont je suis enchanté
> M'ont osté la raison comme la liberté,
> Et leur pouuoir injuste autant qu'il est extreme,
> Fait qu'en cet accident ie ne suis plus moy-mesme.

The identity cannot withstand the force of love—it seems to absorb the two personalities in a fusion of souls. It leads to moral and spiritual blindness, to a lack of judgment, to derangement. Values become displaced, because they are regulated by a single passion, because they depend only on this passion and are formed by it. It is a kind of madness, and it leads the lover to interpret everything in a different way.

The lover of this theater already occupies a different reality from that of the spectator, for he exists in the literary world of the pastoral. His appearance on stage brings him nearer to the spectator, of course, than he could ever be to a reader, for his unreality is thus invested with a certain solidity. It is sufficient, at least, to pull the spectator into the *"jeu des illusions."*

Two examples: Monléon's *Amphytrite* and Scudéry's *Ligdamon et Lidias*

At this point it is, I believe, necessary to show how a complete play of the kind presently being examined would affect the spectator. This process may involve a certain amount of tedious repetition, but it is essential if one is to arrive at a clear idea of the whole theatrical event. I have mentioned in the general introduction my reasons for choosing two relatively unknown plays.

Monléon's mythological fantasy[27] is ushered in by the goddess of the title as she languishes after the sleeping Sun, who is foiling her desires

27. de Monléon, *L'Amphytrite. Dediée à Monseigneur le marquis Deffiat* (Paris, 1630).

by dreaming only of a certain Clytie. Amphytrite complains of the god's indifference and cites the strength of her own love:

> Pourquoy l'ay-je troublé, son repos est le mien,
> Ie n'ay point de plaisir qui ne vienne du sien,
> Et ceste passion est tellement extreme
> Que je vis dedans luy plus que dedans moy-mesme.
>
> (I.1)

The customary effect of love is immediately evident; Amphytrite's personality is lost, confused with that of her lover. Since this question is of primary importance, I note here that this blurring of identity through love has implications similar to those created by the representation of doubles (upon which *Ligdamon et Lidias* is centered, as also *Les Sosies* and *Les Menèchmes*) and by the extensive use of disguises (as in Rotrou's *Filandre* and *La Pelerine amoureuse,* Du Ryer's *Argénis et Poliarque, Les Vendanges de Suresne,* Mairet's *Sylvie* and *L'Illustre corsaire,* and a host of others). In Monléon's play, the confusion remains for the present at the level of conventional poetic metaphor: and Amphytrite makes the most of her opportunity to lengthen that metaphor. This is important, for language is always a major element of the confusion to which this madness leads. In this play, when the language gets out of hand it upsets the "dialectical balance," as it were, and causes the whole elaborate fabric of appearance—an appearance created by language in the first place—to collapse.

The Sun finally wakes up and prepares to leave on his daily round, as Amphytrite complains that his assiduity does not reflect any eagerness to work, but rather his desire to be with a certain beauty:

> L'Amour le plus puissant s'affoiblit par l'absence,
> Et pour l'entretenir tu luy dois ta presence,
> Affin que l'vnion de vos diuins accors
> Passe de l'vn en l'autre, & n'informe qu'vn corps.
>
> (I.2)

The eyes of the beloved reveal the essence of the lover. The Sun's essence is his light and heat, and Monléon makes much of the double entendres possible here, linking the "fires" of the Sun with those of love. The Sun's response to Amphytrite when she protests that her

presence is as valuable as Clytie's, or, rather, when she asks whether
he believes Clytie to be worth more than her, is a kind of play on
words:

> Non, mais dans ces beaux yeux, pour que ie meurs d'amour,
> Je treuue tous les feux dont i'allume le iour.

(I.2)

Later, the Sun has cause to regret this comment. After Clytie has
disappointed him, he begs the sea goddess to love him, asking if she
does not see the love in his eyes. Amphytrite then retorts: "Clitie
est dans tes yeux, on y voit ses appas" (I.4). But for the moment,
she is the suppliant, begging the Sun to take his fires from her:

> Ah! si tu veus bien tost le mettre tout en flame,
> Prens seulement les feux qui consomment mon ame.

(I.2)

It is a game, a kind of salon preciosity, played out by the gods seated
in the Blue room: the flame of love, the dart of the eyes, the flame
of daylight, linked by the metaphor of a life-giving sun. And this life,
like the flame that generates it, has no permanence: her love, says
Amphytrite, would empower the Sun to consume the world—while
the Sun reflects that since she is a water goddess, her love would
more probably extinguish him: "On verroit cét essay causer trop de
malheurs" (I.2). Above and beyond the Sun's grief and Clytie's, the
consequence of Amphytrite's love is death, for the earth or the Sun.
There is a confusion here, typical of the language of these plays, between the world of metaphor and the literal world. In the mind of
the speaker, the metaphor describing love becomes a concrete attri-
bute of love itself, and the spectator is presented visually with the
result of this confusion at the end of the play.

In the meantime, Amphytrite goes off on another tack, suggesting
that when the Sun's rays are inspired by her love, her waters will
protect Clytie from their fearful heat (a suggestion of suicide by
drowning, which will recur):

> Tu te pourras servir de l'onde de mes pleurs,
> Affin de guarantir de mes feux ta Princesse,
> Et puis tu m'aduoüeras qu'il faut estre Déesse
> Pour ne consommer pas à la flame des Dieux.
> Et que seule ie puis souspirer pour tes yeux.

(I.2)

Here Amphytrite seems to imply that equality in love is a first necessity. At this, the Sun returns to his earlier protestations that if the couple in love become a single being, external equality is of no consequence. The being created by love exists at a level whose connections with the social order are exactly nil. If the two beings are fused into this unique being, there can be no question of the kind of relationship Amphytrite describes, which presupposes a certain distance between them. The sun is adamant:

> Tout cede à mon amour comme vne autre elle mesme,
> Ie hais ce qu'elle hait, pour almei ce qu'elle aime,
> Ie fuy ce qu'elle fuit, & l'amoureux tourment
> En toute heure, en tout temps, nous touche également,
> En cét astre des coeurs partageant ma puissance,
> A tout (ainsy que moy) peut faire resistance.

(I.2)

Amphytrite, however, disagrees, and reiterates her own ideas:

> Ainsi tout son pouuoir n'est autre que le tien,
> Mais moy ie ne scaurois me seruir que du mien,
> C'est en quoy mon amour d'autant plus la surpasse,
> Que s'il luy faut souffrir tu te mets en sa place.

And the Sun again refutes her, insisting that the power of each individual has nothing to do with the force of the couple in love: "De deux tourments vnis l'excez en est plus fort." Amphytrite is obliged to adopt a position contrary to her own opinions on the fusion of lovers' souls. She knows this fusion makes the social rank of either irrelevant, but her rank is her only trump, albeit a useless one. The "égarement amoureux" is based on an opposition of reason and emotion, with the first inevitably the weaker. Once the emotional premise has been accepted, reason must surrender: Amphytrite accepts the notion of fusion, and can only dispute the couple involved, something at present beyond her power to alter.

Here the discussion is patterned after the salon convention, and the spectator of the play is constrained to follow a dialogue that makes no attempt to involve him. He may admire its intricacy and follow its logic, but his emotions remain quite unmoved as far as the characters are concerned.

However, the total work is designed as a play, not a salon discussion, and the spectator's attention is soon attracted elsewhere. As

the two immortals leave the stage, Leandre enters to comment on the
sun's beauty and to suggest that it must be the result of some love (a
comment which invites the assent of the audience, hence a certain
degree of intellectual involvement). All the world, comments Leandre,
seems to be in love:

> Aussi vid-on jamais sur le sein de Cybelle
> Vn feu plus admirable, vne clarté plus belle
> Que celle que lon void ranimer tous les corps
> Que le somme auoit mis, comme au nombre des morts,
> Sur le bord émaillé de ces claires fontaines,
> Quand vous chassez la nuict, Iris chasse ses peines,
> Et les Nymphes autour de leurs sacrez ruisseaux,
> Pour gouster ces douceurs abandonnent leur [sic]eaux;
> Zephire les courtise, & Flore plus contente,
> De mille objects charmans rauit leur veuë errante,
> Et pour les obliger d'vn plus noble dessain,
> Auecque son haleine il découure leur sein.

(I.3)

This passage, indeed all of Scene 3, demands the accompaniment of
visual effects. Here the scenery is more than a complementary element; it is a direct source of the conversation, which would be mean-
ingless without it.[28] With love, says Leandre, all awakes, beauty
comes alive and hints of death are dispelled (a rash supposition, as
becomes evident). The atmosphere is that of *L'Astrée,* the *Bucolics,*
a hundred pastorals. Even the trees and boughs, "soubs qui l'esprit
soupire / D'vn amant transformé," seem to laugh, as though antici-
pating a general amnesty and metamorphosis into their original
shapes.

   After Sylvie enters, the conversation becomes increasingly precious,
with images as fragile as the water reflection they describe. This language transforms itself on a whim, and is subject to the abrupt intru-
sion of reality or another fantasy, as is the whole idyll. While it
seems to be taking on one shape, its whole character will change as
Amphytrite tries to impose her desires upon it:

---

28. See above, p. 61, n. 10: *La Madonte, Sylvie,* and so on.

SYLUIE: Berger, quel beau dessein, ou quelle inquiétude
Accompagne vos pas dans ceste solitude.
LEANDRE: Le mesme qui peut estre a promis à vos yeux,
De leur faire treuuer vn miracle en ces lieux.
SYLUIE: Il s'en est acquitté, puis que je vous rencontre.
LEANDRE: Seroit-ce en ce cristal, où vostre object nous monstre
Tout ce que la nature, & tout ce que les Dieux
Ont pu faire de beau, de parfaict, ou de mieux.
SYLUIE: Ouy, s'y representant vostre Image en son onde,
Il montroit dans son sein tout l'abregé du monde.
LEANDRE: Mais plutost, s'y formant, vostre rare tableau.
Il faisoit sous vos trais paroistre Amour plus beau.

The entirely visual nature of these figures, as in the discussion between Amphytrite and the Sun, reflects perhaps its dependence on
a visual stage setting surrounding the protagonists, from which they,
like the spectator, take their cue. Indeed, many of these plays seem
to be constructed toward the end of displaying a particular kind of
scenery rather than relating a convincing story. This play of Monléon's is especially inclined toward the visual, but as such it is far
from exceptional.

Having abruptly switched from the immortal pair to the mortals,
the playwright now returns just as abruptly to the gods. The Sun
returns, preparing to plunge into the sea; his love has changed its
course, and he now loves Amphytrite whom he previously scorned:
"Ie vay chercher ma vie, au milieu de ma mort" (I.4). He is proud
of having changed his target:

Douce captiuité, changement glorieux,
Qui me tirez de terre & m'esleuez aux Cieux.
Aux Cieux, que c'est mal dit, vne erreur sans seconde
Me fait prendre le Ciel pour le sejour de l'onde,
Puisque dedans les Cieux ie ne fais que courier,
Et que l'eau m'arrestant me fait viure & mourir,
Viure pour adorer les appas de ma belle,
Et mourir dedans moy pour mieux reuiure en elle;
Donnant à mes desirs ce doux contentement,
Que ie vis pour aymer, & ie meurs en aymant.

(I.4)

Language once more becomes a plaything. As with Sylvie and Leandre, the poetry here builds its own worlds, and at the same time creates its own emotions. The Sun's love exists not in reality, but in this language of fantasy, whose object might in fact be anyone. It is in the figures of language rather than the heart that love is to be found. Thus, pursuing the metaphor of a love which bears him off to the heavens through his uplifted emotions and the divinity of their object, the Sun pauses suddenly (with humorous effect) as he realizes that his new love, Amphytrite, obliges him to descend toward the sea, where in the normal course of his circuit he must in any case spend the night.

The original paradox of a simultaneous life and death, the end of the day marking the birth of his life in love, is now revised to accommodate the ideas expressed at the beginning of the play. The souls of the lovers will unite, life will become a perpetual adoration of the beloved, death will be equated with the sinking of the self into the other—to find a new life. The language seems circular, but in fact it winds along all kinds of paths, leaps about, and creates its own obstacles at the whim of the person using it. It never reaches or discloses any certain reality; the listener only perceives the reality that a given character chooses to entertain at a certain moment. The only thing that is permanent here is the language itself. This situation often produces absurd images; the Sun, theorizing that Jupiter wished to make of Amphytrite another world, finds her superior to the original because she has more than one sun:

> Mais qui peut auiourd'huy, me tenant en seruage,
> En auoir vn au sein, & deux dans le visage.

> (I.4)

Such a simile is absurd, however, only if one links it to some known reality; with this reality left behind and ignored, the image becomes all-important, and the spectator must view the play in this context. When Amphytrite enters again, she extends the Sun's metaphor, and the ambiguity deepens. She has overcome her love for the Sun, frustrated by his constant rejections, and is no longer tormented:

> Cet astre qui les fit naistre dedans mon ame,
> Les a jusqu'au cercueil conduit avec sa flame.

> (I.4)

Thus, neither the god of love nor the sun "ont plus d'empire" over
her heart: "Ces Dieux dedans mon coeur ont treuué leur tombeau."
She, of course, understands the word "tombeau" here in a different
sense from the Sun: for him, it implied the opportunity for rebirth
in love; for her, it means precisely the opposite. To a listener, the
ambiguity of the metaphor would be quite striking.

Clearly, the spectator must keep continually on the alert in order
to catch all these little subtleties of the precious author. The playwright evidently has no intention of pushing the spectator into the
stage movement to identify with the emotions of characters: they
have no identifiable emotions, the language is far too intricate for
that. Rather, the spectator must consciously assess the spirit of the
language, and his interest in the play must lie largely in its intricacies.
This is not to suggest, of course, that the play would lose nothing if
it were read rather than performed: the fact is that these plays were
performed. Moreover, the set often serves to illuminate the language
for the spectator.

No specific reference to the staging of this particular play is available, aside from the directions in the printed text; but it is clear that
some contemporaries at least were aware of the kind of theatrical
relationship such a play seeks. D'Aubignac complains bitterly about
the stretch of imagination *Pyrame et Thisbé* demands of the spectator. When the two lovers converse, they do so through a crack in a
wall which stretches from the back of the stage toward the front:

> Car outre que les deux espaces qui estoient deçà et delà ce faux-
> mur, representoient les deux chambres de Thisbé et de Pyrame, et
> qu'il estoit contre toute apparence de raison, qu'en ce même lieu
> le Roy vint parler à ses Confidens, et moins encore qu'une Lyonne
> y vint faire peur à Thisbé, je demanderois volontiers, par quel
> moyen supposé dans la verité de l'action, cette muraille devenoit
> visible et invisible? par quel enchantement elle empéchoit ces
> deux Amans de se voir et n'empéchoit pas les autres? [29]

The spectator is forced to use his imagination regarding both scenery
and language. The text and the set together guarantee that the spec-

29. L'abbé D'Aubignac, *La Pratique du théâtre,* éd. Pierre Martino (Paris,
1927), p. 104.

tator will always be fully aware that he is facing a stage, that he is watching an "illusion" (since there is no real illusion, this term is something of a misnomer). Yet in spite of all this, the spectator is quite likely to identify with a character, from time to time at least.

D'Aubignac also remarks on the likelihood of identification with Pyrame at the moment of his death despite the unreality of the long speech which precedes it; he is annoyed precisely because such an effect is rare in these plays.[30] Yet is it not this very effect that enables one to characterize this theater? This "fluctuation" of the spectator's mind, which one may call "theatrical distancing," blurs the frontier between the real and the illusory: thus corresponding to the principal theme of the theater of the period, as revealed through the superficial themes of love and madness and the ambiguous use of language. The plays of the theater, the *impromptus* of Scudéry and Gougenot, accomplish the same end through different means.

Already, Mairet's *Sophonisbe* (1634) reflects the beginning of a completely new theater which the public will not fully accept until considerably later, a theater no less experimental than Gordon Craig's, Antoine's or Beckett's in our own time. The very fact that it was so long before the earlier plays gave way to this "neo-classical" theater seems evidence that the public sensed how different it was. For example, the same Scudéry who in 1637 fought so vigorously against *Le Cid* for its supposed infractions of theatrical rules, *bienséances* and language, is able to defend his ideal of the tragi-comic equally vigorously in the 1641 preface to *Andromire*. His defense, similar to that in the preface to *Ligdamon et Lidias* ten years earlier, is based on several premises: "dans chaque Scene, [elle] monstre quelquechose de nouueau;" the play's effect is achieved "par cent moyens surprenans;" and it contains a "grand nombre de figures." It is possible that he is simply trying to justify the type of play he finds easiest to write, but his argument is not a trivial one: "C'est vne chose que le sentiment public a determinée, et que nostre plaisir particulier, nous a fait connoistre a tous par experience." Thus both D'Aubignac in 1657 (although *La Pratique* was already under way in 1640) and Scudéry in 1641 give evidence that a theater which denied illusion, a theater which made no effort to convince the spectator of the reality of its characters, not only existed but was popular.

i.e. by disapproving

30. Ibid., pp. 333-34; and see below, pp. 144-45.

The chief concern of this theater is to emphasize appearance as a guide to actual reality: characters virtually equate the two. They recognize one another by appearance alone, and are moved only by appearance: how many of these lovers fall in love first and foremost with a picture?[31] Like the spectator in the auditorium, they are moved first by the sight:

> Mais, o Dieux! je la vois, & ces rares beautez
> Suspendent mes esprits, qu'elles ont enchantez,
>
> (I.4)

exclaims the Sun as he sees Amphytrite again. The goddess, however, succeeds in escaping from him. As she approaches Leandre in the wood, she feels herself being consumed. She can see no one, but she feels her soul being destroyed by love as she hears a voice. Fearing it may be the Sun in pursuit, she complains, but is powerless; even if it is he, as she thinks, she is constrained to love him.

> Je le pense, & ses yeux plains d'amoureuse flame
> Me bruslent dans le coeur, & consomment mon ame,
> Leurs raiz malgré la nuict du plus sombre sejour
> Font éclatter par tout le charme de leur jour,
> Mes yeux en sont frappez, & ma veuë insensée
> En donne le portrais à ceux de ma pensee.
>
> (I.5)

It turns out, however, that she is wrong: the shepherd, Leandre, is the cause of these flames. He in turn falls in love with her, and, forgetful of Sylvie, pines after Amphytrite who leaves with the promise of a meeting soon. Here Leandre is shown to be no better than a Hylas, that Protean lover, epitome of inconstancy. The Sun changes, Leandre changes, Ligdamon and Lidias are confused, Cardenio goes mad, heroes deceive, disguise, mislead; and these characters are matched by the glittering language: the spectator is drawn into this vortex of confusion and blurred perception. To intensify the chaos, Monléon brings on the Sun disguised as a shepherd.

This ambiguity has no limit, for if reality follows language, it is clear that the appearance which allows us to grasp a reality is subject to the

---

31. See, for example, *Sylvie; Argénis et Poliarque; La Cour bergère.*

same changes as the language which translates it. Amphytrite says of
Leandre, "Ie ne suis plus à moy, son oeil est mon vainqueur" (II.2).
Love, it would seem, can be based only on beauty; and beauty is
visible. The eye can deceive, however. The Sun is disappointed in
Clytie; Leandre, at one moment apparently living, can become a rock
the next. When Neptune comes to woo Amphytrite, having been
made to fall in love with her by Love himself (who also fell in love
with her upon seeing her asleep), the sea god remarks on her beauty.
Replies Amphytrite:

> Souuentesfois nos yeux promettent des rigueurs,
> Lors qu'vn calme & la paix logent dedans nos coeurs;
> Et telle a sur son front les traits d'vne Cythere,
> Qui porte dans son sein l'horreur d'vne Megere,
> Tellement qu'on ne peut auec iuste raison
> Croire aux appas flatteurs de ceste trahison.
> Le charme nous deçoit & sous vn beau visage,
> Couure le plus souuent vn perfide courage.

(II.3)

Appearance, then, is likely to mislead both as to its own surface and
what lies beneath: an idea repeated visually in this scene, when
Leandre becomes a rock. In the second example, Ligdamon and
Amerine are believed dead, when they are actually under the influence
of a cunning potion.

As the play goes on, Neptune begs Thétis and Oceanus for their
daughter's hand, but, given no satisfaction, is angered and begins to
stir up storms. In the meantime, Leandre has been bewailing his lot,
and the lack of understanding among humans:

> Quiconque peint l'Amour sans des confusions,
> Peut bien paindre la nuict sans des illusions,
> La rage sans transport, sans tumulte la guerre.

(III.2)

He sleeps, and during his sleep "Vne Nymphe montre la moitié du
corps qui sort de l'écorce d'vn laurier" (stage direction, III.2). She
tells him he will conquer Amphytrite, but his love will be quenched
in the sea. He awakes in anger and begins at once to speak in *stances.*
Two important distancing devices are functioning here. The audience
is enabled to visualize a completely unreal literary convention, as the

nymph is seen emerging from her tree; and the subsequent use of *stances*, attacked specifically for lack of realism by the classical critics, can only increase the scene's theatricality.

Meanwhile the gods are meeting to decide what to do about the storms being stirred up by Neptune, which threaten to engulf the entire earth. They hold an "assemblée des Dieux" (stage direction, III.5), presumably on the upper stage; located, according to Mme. Deierkauf-Holsboer, above the main stage.[32] Once again there is no attempt at realism (ignoring the fact that the action concerns "gods" in the first place), and the artificial nature of the performance is brought home to the spectator.

The gods decide to resolve the problem by driving Leandre mad, leading him to attempt suicide, at which point they will transform him into "quelque arbre, ou . . . quelque rocher" (III.5). Their plan is fulfilled in front of Sylvie, who has searched out Leandre in the hope that if she tells him of her love, he will return it. Seeing the shepherd approach, apparently grief-stricken, she decides to hide in order to overhear him. The spectator is now treated to a very long

32. S. Wilma Deierkauf-Holsboer, *Le Théâtre du Marais*, 2 vols. (Paris, 1954 and 1958). Speaking of the rebuilding of the Marais in 1644, the author points out that the new theater had this second stage (I, 109-10, and plate X, p. 113), and observes that her discoveries indicate its dimensions: "Il est vrai que plusieurs documents se rapportant au théâtre en France avaient déjà signalé 'un théâtre et un petit théâtre' mais ils n'avaient jamais été dessinés parce que les données relatives à leur disposition et à leurs mesures étaient trop incomplètes" (I, 114). In her later work, *L'Histoire de la mise en scène dans le théâtre français à Paris de 1600 à 1673* (Paris, 1960), she adds: "Mahelot s'est servi plusieurs fois de la seconde scène, lorsqu'il fallait imiter le ciel, la lune, les étoiles ou faire mouvoir les planètes. C'est sur ce deuxième plateau qu'il installait les machines nécessaires pour produire ces effets" (p. 53). (For a more precise study, which corrects her calculations, see Donald H. Roy, "La Scène de l'Hôtel de Bourgogne," *Revue d'Histoire du Théâtre* [1962], 227-35). If it is true that the workings of these *machines* were quite visible, then the illusion is still more obvious, for there can be no doubt that the upper stage was not simply used to hold devices: the machines were representational. Mahelot's description of the set for Durval's *Travaux d'Ulysse* (1630) provides an example: "Au milieu du théâtre il faut un enfer caché et les mesmes tourmens d'enfer. Au dessus de l'enfer, le ciel d'Appolon, et au dessus d'Appolon, le ciel de Jupiter" (*Mémoire*, p. 83).

discourse by Leandre, interspersed with Sylvie's comments aside to the audience. She adopts the position of a spectator, and thus involves the audience closely with the first level of illusion (her own), in juxtaposition with another, stronger illusion: that of madness.

Leandre is determined to overcome this unreasonable love he has for a goddess, but as he realizes it is impossible for him to do so he gradually slips into madness:

> . . . une morne tristesse,
> L'attaque [his mind] en sa douleur, le menasse, le presse,
> L'horreur auec l'object de ses images faux,
> Luy liure incessamment des funestes assauts,
> Mes yeux sont éblouys, mon ouye est perduë,
> Mes sentimens estaints, ma raison suspenduë,
> Et je ne reçois plus que les illusions,
> Qu'vn sang plain de vapeurs forme en des visions,
> Mon jugement troublé ne conçoit que chimeres,
> Que fantosmes hideux, que larmes [sic] que Megeres,
> L'air ne souffle pour moy que des contagions,
> L'enfer a deschainé toutes ses legions,
> Vn esprit plain de feux, de flames & de souffre,
> M'accompagne par tout, le ciel veut que je souffre,
> Les Dieux l'ont arresté, l'imagination
> Me fait voir leurs tourments, & ma punition
> Vn gouffre empuanty de poix & de bithume,
> Où la peste nourrit le charbon qui l'alume,
> Parmy l'infection d'vn funeste élement,
> Où la mort sans mourir meurt éternellement,
> Où le mal desespere, où la fureur enrage.
>
> (IV.2)

The madman has followed an admirable logic up to the point where he decides the only solution is death; his train of thought evolves steadily from a first assumption based on some image in his mind. This logic, as Foucault points out (see above, p. 63 and n. 16), corresponds to the pattern of melancholia: Leandre begins with the possibility and the fact of his loving a goddess, and continues "the gods are far above the level of humans and I am therefore guilty of the most arrant hubris in loving Amphytrite. On the other hand, if I refuse her love, which she has already offered to me, I am again guilty of withstanding the will of the gods: a hubris of no less magnitude than the first. I have, therefore, but one escape: to die."

Sylvie, unlike the spectator, accepts Leandre's first premise; for she is part of this world of fantasy. But although the spectator continues to associate gods and goddesses with unreality, he is drawn briefly into the fantasy when Sylvie directs her confidences to the audience. Here the stage devices cease, momentarily, to function, and when they begin to operate again the sense of distance returns. As Leandre goes to throw himself into the sea, in the midst of his madness and lament, he changes into a stone. The language, the madness in which the spectator is momentarily involved takes, as it were, a separate direction from what occurs on stage, until finally Leandre becomes aware that he cannot move his feet. Now the spectator moves away from Sylvie again as she goes over to the rock, thinking first that he has indeed fallen over the cliff, and finally concluding that he has been changed into a rock:

> Quelque demon l'a-il [sic] soustrait à la nature,
> Ou pour trahir mes sens d'vn trait malicieux,
> Supposé ce fantosme à l'object de mes yeux:
> Est ce toy que i'ay veu Leandre, ou bien l'image
> D'un spectre qui paroîst dessous ton beau visage,
> Reuiens, qui que tu sois, fusses-tu le trépas,
> Tu me plairas tousiours auecque ses appas,
> Esprit d'illusion.

(IV.2)

At this point, both Sylvie and the spectator are still inclined to consider the whole scene an illusion. But the rock shifts slightly and "L'esprit de Leandre de dedans le rocher parle à Syluie," telling her to engrave his fate upon the rock. This she does. As Leandre becomes a rock, then, Sylvie forces the spectator to deal with his concept of illusion (which is different from hers). The spectator now perceives Leandre's madness as illusion, and detaches himself from Sylvie, to whom this metamorphosis is perfectly acceptable if not altogether normal. Here the spectator has fluctuated between an acceptance of madness, an illusion of the stage (though in this case the character is not feigning madness), and his awareness of it as an illusion.

With Leandre's metamorphosis, Monléon employs a familiar technique for reminding the spectator that he is watching an illusion: the creation

of a spectacular event. Scudéry in *Le Prince deguisé*, Corneille in his
Médée, Rotrou in *Hercule mourant,* Durval in *Les Travaux d'Ulysse*
and Mairet in the last act of *Sylvie,* among others, also find this technique useful; it is not, however, the only way to emphasize a scene's
falseness. The same effect may be achieved by disturbing the logic of
the language, or, as Monléon does in this play, by simply extending
the logic of madness to dispel the illusion altogether.

Amphytrite, discovering Leandre's fate, decides she will marry
Neptune for the sake of the shepherd, since from the base of the rock
a stream runs to the sea:

> Puis que ton beau coulant au sortir de sa source,
> Dans son sein & ses eaux va terminer sa course.

(IV.3)

Her logic, of course, is that by marrying Neptune she will be marrying
a small part of Leandre! The humorous tone introduced here is
strengthened, as the following scene sees a total devaluation of the
role of the gods. Oceanus and Thétis are aghast to learn that Amphytrite loved beneath her station, while Mercury assures them that "Des
regards ont esté leurs plus grandes faueurs" (IV.4), a remark which
sends Thétis into praise of her good upbringing:

> Ie l'ay tousiours cognuë assez discrette & sage,
> Pour ne permettre rien à son desauantage.

The incongruity of this exchange in the mythological fantasy world
created by Monléon is quite comical, and has the same effect as the
spectacular scenes: it pushes the spectator away. This device occurs
so regularly in the plays of this period that one cannot ascribe it to
mere ineptitude on the part of the playwrights; it is particularly popular with Rotrou and Corneille (see below, Chapter 3).

Amphytrite agrees to become "emperiere & maistresse en ce lieu,"
and she and Neptune go off to the rock where Sylvie is lamenting the
fate of her Leandre. Neptune releases the shepherd, and there ends
the story of the two mortals. It is by no means the end of the play,
however; Monléon has saved the most spectacular moment for the
end.

As Neptune and Amphytrite rejoice in their happiness, the sky
opens and all the gods appear. Neptune and his new empress "se
retirent pour aller receuoir les Dieux dans la grotte où se doiuent

faire les Nopces" (stage direction, V.2). At the same time "Les
Sirenes & les Tritons font vn concert," and the spectator is entertained with what was probably a kind of ballet. The Sun now reap-
pears to make the most of this opportunity for vengeance: he decides
to burn up the world. Thus the language of love, the logic of madness
of which this love is one form, creates its image. The fires, previously
a simple metaphor, are made concrete. A moment before, the playwright has employed a lesser form of the same device: the two gods
are married, and Neptune praises the good fortune which has enabled
him to possess "ceste diuinité." Here the semi-ironic language of
preciosity has been transformed into its own fantasy; the address to
the beloved, the "goddess," is real instead of simple hyperbole (V.4).
This is a mere prelude to the major effect, however; cries are heard
and the characters notice that everything seems to be on fire. Thétis
cries out,

> Que d'horribles objects espouuantent les yeux,
> On ne voit plus qu'esclairs voller dessous les cieux,
> La terre ouure son sein, & soulageant son ame
> Semble vomir dans l'air mille forests de flame,
> L'onde mesme consomme.
>
> (V.4)

Here the play is reduced to purely artificial spectacle, some of which
must have been staged[33]—an attempt to embody the fantasy of the
language, through which the whole illusion is betrayed. And this revelation emerges in a kind of epilogue which has little to do with the

33. The feasibility of all this staging is indicated by Mahelot *(Mémoire)* and
Nicola Sabbattini, *Pratica di fabricar Scene* (Ravenna, 1638). The latter gives
countless ways of achieving the various effects these plays demanded. Although
his work was published in 1638 (it is available in a modern French edition,
Pratique pour fabriquer scènes et machines de théâtre, trad. Maria et Renée
Canavaggia et Louis Jouvet [Neuchâtel, 1942]), and presumably had no direct
effect in France until the arrival of Torelli in 1645, we may assume that most
of the machines described were those in general use; witness the staging of the
ballets de cour in France years before. The principle Torelli later established
was that, through careful use of space, the set might become an entity separate
from, if connected to, the text and the movement of the actors within that set
(see Bjurström, *Giacomo Torelli,* p. 103).

main action centering on Amphytrite and Leandre, although in a
sense it does conclude the action which began the play. It is almost
as though the author wanted to underline the play's artificiality before the audience left their places; Neptune questions the reality of
these "estranges visions . . . Sont-ce des veritez, ou des illusions?"
(V.4).

The final scene of the play brings the sirens and tritons out again,
as they lament the horror by which they are surrounded. Everything
is confused, cries are heard from suffering humans. "Esprits languis-
sants," "leurs souspirs & leurs plaintes," "la rage du feu," "ces feux"—
the language used to describe the dreadful agonies of humanity is the
precious language of love. It is as though the language abruptly becomes visible to the spectator. The irony is now physically present,
the spectacle the language seemed to create in the mind has become
theatrical spectacle. The spectator is now completely distanced from
the fantasy, for the whole thing is clearly revealed as a stage device.
The final irony is that the sun's rage is quenched by a threat, borne
by Mercury, that Jupiter will send Iris to put out the sun! The spectator is thus brought full circle from the sun's original desire to drown
himself in the waters of Amphytrite and die in her love to his eagerness to escape a more literal quenching in the waters of Iris.

Less spectacular, but abounding with many of the same devices, is
Scudéry's *Ligdamon et Lidias,* published in 1631, one year after
L'Amphytrite. Scudéry's play, like that of Monléon, opens with the
sighs of an unsuccessful lover: here the spectator is presented with
the sight of Ligdamon lamenting over his love for Sylvie (I.1). The
effect of this beginning, which is fairly standard in this theater, is
not comparable to that of Hardy's long prologues, since here the
discourse is kept at a personal level instead of becoming generalized
in the form of a commentary on the human condition or as a prayer.
Scudéry's plays often begin with such introspective soliloquies, particularly *Le Trompeur puny, Le Vassal généreux,* which opens with
stances, and *La Comédie des comédiens.* If these introductions do
not create an atmosphere of the kind sought by Hardy, they never-
theless establish a certain tone for the play: the poet is always very
much in evidence.

If this is true of Tristan's *La Mariane,* for example, it is still more
important in Scudéry's play, where Ligdamon's complaint concerning Silvie's indifference becomes an exercise in preciosity:

> C'est moy chetif, c'est moy qui tente l'impossible
> En voulant émouuoir vn rocher insensible;
> Ha! ie l'appelle mal; un rocher se fendroit,
> Si c'estoit vne roche elle me repondroit
> Lors que ie l'entretiens du tourment que i'endure,
> Mais elle est de matiere et plus sourde et plus dure:
> Tout horsmis cet aspic prend part à mes malheurs,
> L'air pour l'amour de moy le matin fond en pleurs,
> L'onde mesme en murmure, et le vent en soupire.
>
> (I.1)

Having compared Silvie with all kinds of hardness, Ligdamon finally decides to kill himself. But how? He cannot jump, since he has already fallen as far as he can; he cannot drown himself, since he has survived in the midst of so many tears; besides, even the sea could not extinguish the fires that burn within him. He cannot burn himself, since those fires inside him have been unable to do the job; he cannot hang himself, since he is already bound as tight as he can be; nor can he die, like Cleopatra, from the bite of a serpent, if the snakes in his heart have insufficient poison.[34] He is by now fully convinced of the madness of love:

> ... l'esprit plein d'vn poison
> Qui m'entrant par les yeux en chasse la raison.
>
> (I.1)

He cannot stab himself, since even the arrows of Love have left him alive to languish. He concludes his lament with a conceit based on the commonplace confusion of love, life and death (a confusion coincidentally reflected in the quasi-homonymy of *l'amour* and *la mort*):

> Si bien que dans ce mal mon auenture est telle,
> Que pour mourir toujours ma mort est immortelle.
>
> (I.1)

Death seems to take on a life of its own.

---

34. This speech will be paraphrased in the later play of de Brosse, *Les Songes des hommes esveillez* (1644), I.2.

How wrong is Lancaster to suggest, "Nothing can be more absurd
than Ligdamon's monologue in which he is seeking a means of committing suicide" (*History*, I, pp. 474-75). It is this very language that
contains the interest of the play; more, it is the language that creates
the play. Ligdamon's toying with the idea of suicide leads him into
the confusion of life and death. Language here is much more than a
mere expression of perception (as in Tristan, the later Corneille and
Racine, for example), it is a *means* of perception. The characters of
this theater explore with language in the same way that another might
with his eyes or his hands. They explore at random, and they reach
no conclusions (the plot resolution is immaterial) since the possibilities of language are infinite. Thus Ligdamon may speak without
exaggeration of his "peine infinie": this sorrow is the creation of
language, and exists only within that language. Indeed, it is not the
passage of time and the glory he is going off to win that will convince
Silvie of his worth, but the persuasion of Alcidor, who tells him:

> . . . ie n'espargneray ny paroles ny soins
> Pour rendre à tes desirs ployable ta Siluie.
>
> (I.1)

By the same token, it is Alcidor's persuasion that convinces Ligdamon
of Silvie's love for him, despite the evidence of his other senses:

> Ce discours enchanteur me vient ressusciter.
> Ha! bons Dieux, qu'aisément on se laisse flatter,
>
> (I.1)

admits Ligdamon to his friend.[35]

The notion of giving up one's reason to love, a commonplace in this
theater, is linked to the confusion of souls, the relinquishing of one's
particular and separate personality to mingle it with that of the beloved. Ligdamon's emotion, when he sees Silvie coming towards him,
is explicitly defined:

---

35. And later, Clidamant promises to *persuade* Sylvie to love Ligdamon:

> . . . ma parole engagée
> Promet absoluement de la rendre changée.
>
> (II.3)

> O Ciel! fort à propos ie rencontre ma Dame,
> Mais pourray-ie parler puisque ie n'ay point d'ame?
> Oüy, l'objet qui la prit la préte en ce moment
> Pour chanter sa louange & dire mon tourment.
>
> (I.1)

The idea is always near the surface; it reoccurs in the same scene as
Ligdamon and Alcidor bid one another farewell. The latter tells
Ligdamon to be happy, he protests that he cannot; replies Alcidor,
"L'absence bannira peut estre ce soucy," to which Ligdamon ob-
jects, "Oüy, si ie m'esloignois, mais ie demeure icy." He remains, as
it were, in spirit, while his body goes off; but he takes the metaphor
in all seriousness. This "spirit" is his very essence, not simply a
memory—or a memory whose effacing can occur only in death, which
amounts to the same thing: "Il faut dedans mon sang noyer ce sou-
uenir."

In this playing on language, the tone is naturally subject to considerable fluctuation; and Ligdamon's mournful laments give way
abruptly to the humorous mood pervading his amusing scene with
Silvie, which follows immediately. As he sighs, she praises the beauty
of nature, and he picks up each of her lines as a cue to link her
praises with his love:

> SILVIE: Que le bruit des ruisseaux a d'agreables charmes
> LIGDAMON: Pouuez vous voir de l'eau sans penser à mes larmes?
> SILVIE: Ie cherche dans ces prez la fraicheur des Zephirs.
> LIGDAMON: Vous deuez ce plaisir au vent de mes soupirs . . .
> SILVIE: Ce petit papillon ne m'abandonne pas.
> LIGDAMON: Mon coeur de la façon accompagne vos pas.
>
> (I.1)

This discussion continues for some time.

The stichomythia is itself, of course, a totally unrealistic device,
through which the poet is quite visible. To the precious members of
his audience, some of this repartee might appear seriously sophisticated,
lightly amusing and subtle enough to avoid being gross. This play, however, includes more risqué jokes, again at the whim of the speaker,
which have no direct bearing on the situation in question—or, at least,
do not derive from that situation. Ligdamon speaks to Silvie of the
love she has aroused in him:

LIGDAMON: Donc vous mesconnoissez ce que vous faites naistre.
SILVIE: Chaste, ie n'ay point eu d'enfant iusqu'à ce iour.

(I.1)

The praise of nature, from which this little game evolved, now takes
the spectator in quite a different direction. His attention is brought
directly to the scenery which surrounds the characters, and the emphasis here is even stronger than it was in *L'Amphytrite, Sylvie* and the
rest. Scudéry's Silvie continues to admire her surroundings:

Icy l'on ne voit point sous la fraischeur de l'herbe
Ny de serpent rusé, ny de crapaut superbe,
Ou s'il s'en offre à l'oeil, on remarque à l'instant
Que c'est celuy que l'onde a fait en serpentant;
Cette onde est si tranquille, et si claire, & si pure,
Que mes yeux la prendroient povr vne onde en peinture.

(I.2)

As if it were not enough for the actress to dwell at such length on the
scenery (here 44 lines, in addition to Ligdamon's earlier remarks), she
destroys any aura of illusion by describing it as the painting it is.
There is a kind of contradiction here; the spectator is made aware of
the scene's artificiality by her denial of it—"Elle n'emprunte rien de
l'homme ny de l'art"—while in a seeming attempt toward realism the
playwright matches her language to what is probably a scene change:

Dans ces bois innocens on ne connoist encore
Aucun objet sanglant que le teint de l'Aurore,
Nulle dispute aussi ne suruient en ces lieux
Que celle des oyseaux à qui chantera mieux.[36]

(I.2)

Thus the spectator's interest in the set fluctuates to parallel the irony
of the language, and his mental distance from the stage creation (as a

---

36. It is true that Mahelot *(Mémoire,* pp. 69-70) mentions neither dawn nor
birds, but this does not mean too much, since he often omits, quite unsystemati-
cally (see Lancaster's Introduction, p. 33), such effects from his instructions,
although need for them in a play may be obvious. Elsewhere he uses "rossignols"
as props, and calls for dawns; in any case, the necessary lighting would be readily
available in the theater (see Sabbattini, *Pratique,* pp. 168-69).

whole) is kept ambiguous. After Silvie's lines in praise of the sylvan
beauty, distinguished by an unhurried and even rhythm, the playwright proceeds to startle the spectator with a biting exchange between Silvie and Alcidor. He enters and immediately asks what she
is doing "parmy la solitude." She answers him in straight fashion:

> Ie pratique vn conseil de tout temps enseigné,
> Qu'il vaut mieux estre seul que mal accompagné.

Alcidor, not wishing to be outdone, responds with considerable
sarcasm, "Certes ce compliment a mon ame rauie."

Here language is tempered into an instrument of cruelty, and the
listener's relationship to the characters alters sharply as a result.
From afar he has been watching these light-footed creatures of
fantasy flit through woods created by poetry, when suddenly the
mood is broken and he finds himself face to face with two more
familiar people. The tone continues to fluctuate; Alcidor, allowed
to say four words, launches into a description of Ligdamon's despair,
and suddenly the audience is involved with pure comedy, even farce:

ALCIDOR:	I'ay connu Ligdamon, qui la face trempée
	Tournoit deuers son coeur le bout de son espée
	Vous nommoit en pleurant, & lors les yeux bandez.
SILVIE:	Il ne s'est point fait mal.
ALCIDOR:	Patience, attendez,
	Les yeux, dy-ie, bandez tout droit deuers la pointe
	Aussitost à son coeur elle alloit estre iointe.
SILVIE:	Mais vous pour le sauuer y courustes soudain.
ALCIDOR:	Et malgré ses efforts ie luy retins la main.
SILVIE:	Si bien donc qu'à tout mal soustraite est sa personne.

(I.2)

Thus the scene between Alcidor and Ligdamon is placed in a ridiculous
light, at least to the spectator, although in fact the former is relating
the events as they occurred. At the time, the scene was created out
of the language of the lament through which Ligdamon both expressed
and perceived his plight; similarly, the spectator acquired the notion
that Silvie was only pretending not to love Ligdamon; and now Silvie's
language casts doubt on the reality of his suicide. Unlike the language
of classical plays, which may discuss, but never create, a situation, and

through which the characters may come to perceive a choice, these
speeches are not a means of clarifying the material (or spiritual) world.
As has been suggested, the characters play with words and use them
to invent situations: all kinds of possibilities are presented, but no
choice is made, or can be made (since that too is in the language)
among them.

As Silvie now suggests, it is possible that Ligdamon's behavior is
simply a play performed for their benefit:

> Alcidor, Alcidor, veux-tu que ie te die,
> Cet acte peut passer pour vne Comedie,
> Il se fust bien gardé d'entrer dans ce projet
> Si ses yeux n'eussent eu les tiens pour leur objet.

(I.2)

Here Silvie seems to be either placing herself next to the spectators
in the auditorium, as these characters so often do, or creating a third
level of "reality" as intermediary between Ligdamon and the audience.
The spectator must react as he would to a play within a play, and
adopt a "dual" distance in his appreciation of what is going on before
him.

The language is invariably ironic, whatever other devices the author
may employ to confuse the spectator. Alcidor continues to plead
Ligdamon's case:

> Mais dis pourquoy ton oeil son vnique vainqueur
> Ne veut-il accepter le present de son coeur?

(I.2)

He is immediately rebuffed by Silvie's literal acceptance of his question in a passage of some humor:

> Qu'il garde ce beau don, pour moy ie le renoye,
> Ie ne veux point passer pour vn oyseau de proye
> Qui se repaist de coeurs, & ce n'est mon dessein
> De ressembler vn monstre ayant deux coeurs au sein.[37]

37. Cf. also, at a more serious point in the play, Amerine's comment as she
tries to persuade Ligdamon of her love:

> Sçache que i'ay gardé ton portrait dans le coeur,
> Ouure moy l'estomach, tu verras ta peinture
> Qu'Amour pour mon malheur sçauant en portraiture
> Y graua tellement qu'il te fait apparoir
> Aussi bien là dedans comme dans vn miroir.

(V.2)

The whole idea of the fusion of souls, rather than the particular situation, is ridiculed here. On the other hand, in view of Silvie's future love for Ligdamon, this passage contains a different type of irony. And the ridicule continues, as the literal and metaphorical intentions of the words continue to be deliberately confused:

ALCIDOR: A tort de tant d'attraits nature t'a pourueüe,
                 Puisque vray Basilic on meurt en t'ayant veüe.
SILVIE: S'il meurt en me voyant qu'il esloigne ces lieux,
                 Ou s'il n'en veut partir, qu'il se creue les yeux.

Alcidor proceeds to a revolting description of how Silvie's body, horribly decayed in old age, will inspire regret for her treatment of Ligdamon, who is dying for her:

SILVIE: Le Medecin ne peut vn defunt secourir.
ALCIDOR: Bien que ja trespassé, belle & cruelle Dame,
           Vn baiser seulement luy redonneroit l'ame.
SILVIE: Bon soir, pour cet effet i'ay l'esprit trop peu fort,
          Me preseruent les Cieux des baisers d'vn tel mort.

With this the scene is removed to Rothomage, and the spectator encounters the rival team of Amerine and Lidias, whose mutual love is presently being disturbed by Aronthe. This is the first of the changes "de face" which Scudéry discusses in his preface to this play, and which, D'Aubignac and Mairet complain, destroy the illusion by making the spectator adjust to a sudden and extreme shift in locale. Such moves increase in importance, since the two main characters journey from one place to the next, as does Silvie at the end, and an army which is laying siege to Rothomage (although the audience does not see the troops, the officers play a part). It happens that the scene is again a "lieu solitaire," the site of a duel over Amerine between Lidias and Aronthe, won by the former.

Unfortunately, Lidias did not consider beforehand that, win or lose, he would have to leave Amerine if he wished to avoid laying "sa teste au sanglant eschaffaut." He does not go alone, however:

> Adieu belle Amerine, aujourd'huy plein de flame
> Ie t'emporte en mon coeur, & reste dans ton ame.

(I.3)

Amerine now appears on stage, and, seeing Lidias bewailing his misfortunes, is curious. He explains:

> Vous verrez vn amant qu'on ne peut secourir,
> Si vous tournez les yeux qui le faisoient mourir.

After suitable lamenting, he forbids her to flee with him, so she bids
him farewell as he goes off into the forest:

> Amour y soit ton guide, adieu, reçoy mon ame
> Qui passe dans ta bouche en ce baiser de flame.

Despite the difference, then, between the situations of Lidias and
Amerine, Silvie and Ligdamon, the images of their language work
alike: the language creates not only the situation, but also variations through which it runs like a central musical theme, thus acting
as a kind of counterpoint to itself.

The scene is now removed to another place, where Aegide is trying to convince Ligdamon to grieve less: "Estes-vous resolu de
deuenir fontaine?" (II.1). And lest one be tempted to laugh at this,
it is important to recall that where language is the creator, such a
metamorphosis is quite possible, as with Leandre's fate in *L'Amphytrite* and Durval's *Travaux d'Ulysse* where the hero's companions
return to human form after being changed into pigs (II.2); lovers
elsewhere occupy trees or rocks or fountains. Such a prospect does
not in the least deter Ligdamon from his grieving over an infinity
of vicissitudes. Aegide continues to argue about "ce mal qui la
raison offense:"

> Le supreme laurier des belles actions
> S'acquiert à surmonter ses propres passions.

Easier said, of course, than done.

These are not the Cornelian heroes of a decade later: here is no
victory of reason, nor even, if it comes to that, a struggle. The
hero of these plays does not attempt to quit his melancholy—only
the achievement of his love will satisfy, and to leave his "folie"
would be to abandon his beloved. Besides, he cannot struggle, for
the world about him reflects his love. If, as Tristan's plays demonstrate, man is the microcosm, then the relationship operates no
less in reverse. He is, declares Ligdamon with a melancholy glee,
to be compared with a wounded deer fleeing across some plain,
thinking thus to flee also from his pain:

> Tel suis-ie absent de l'oeil mon vnique vainqueur,
> Ie fuis, mais en fuyant i'en ay le trait au coeur,
> I'ay tousiours dans l'esprit ce visage adorable,
> Comme l'ombre d'vn corps se void inseparable,
> Toutes sortes d'objets sont autant de portraits
> Où ie voy son humeur ainsi que ses attraits;
> Ces monts à qui la gresle est tousiours inconnue,
> A cause que leur chef est plus haut que la nue,
> Me vont representant l'excés de son orgueil,
> Les rocs sa dureté qui me met au cercueil,
>
> (II.1)

and so on, for 38 more lines. Yet what is interesting about this passage is not only the way the lover confuses himself with the world around him, or simply that he gets carried away by the words, but rather (thinking of the play in performance) the way this attitude of the lamenting lover becomes that of the creative poet, deliberately showing off for the listener:

> Mais de peindre son coeur, c'est vn acte impossible
> La nature n'a rien de si fort insensible,
> C'est là que le pinceau me demeure perclus.
> Or passons aux beautez que nous ne voyons plus,
> La rose en son esclat me presente sa bouche,
> La neige peint sa gorge, où personne ne touche.

Ligdamon produces a blason to his "Dame" in the style of a multitude of sixteenth-century poets consciously adhering to Petrarchan imagery. This praise mingles always with his laments, until finally he returns to the confusion of love and death:

> Pour quitter cet objet que l'amour me fait suiure
> Il faut premierement que ie cesse de viure.

Not that this would settle matters, however, for he would still follow his lady in "le pays de morts." Thus he is doomed to live and love, with "Vn enfer portatif" everlastingly in his soul.

At the end of this scene another humorous twist of language is introduced, enhancing the effect of distance. Ligdamon tries to convince his servant that since his soul is in prison in his body it is his duty to set it at liberty with his dagger. Aegide remarks on the "rare elo-

quence" with which this "paradox en Sophiste" is presented, and
continues to protest:

> Mais stupide et grossier iusques au dernier point,
> Ce discours est si haut que ie ne l'entends point.

Here he creates the same kind of effect Silvie produced with her re-
buff of Alcidor: Ligdamon's perception of *his* reality is thrown into
doubt, and the spectator must laugh and again view the action from
outside.

Now the two come upon the tracks of an army, and Ligdamon
decides to follow to the camp and enlist, hopefully to meet a glorious
death "au lit d'honneur." As it happens, however, they first meet
one Nicandre, brother of Aronthe, who, taking Ligdamon for Lidias
(here the reader first learns that these two are doubles, but the spectator would know of course from the first moment he saw Lidias),
challenges him and forces him to fight. He is wounded in the arm,
and Ligdamon has Aegide take him to a nearby village, seeing him off
with the angry words "Vous estes moins blessé dans le bras qu'au
cerueau" (II.2). And indeed, the confusion of identity throughout
the remainder of the play are not far from the delusions of a madness. Whether the spectator was also caught up in that particular
confusion would depend on how closely the two actors resembled
one another, something one has no way of knowing. At this point,
however, the spectator again comes face to face with two new characters.

These actors are not in the least afraid of creating their own roles.
Ligdamon has made himself into the suffering lover, Sylvie presents
herself as the hard-hearted and distant lady (always with the reserva-
tion that the role each adopts may not reflect any truth), and now
Merovée presents himself as the magnanimous

> . . . Prince exempt d'ingratitude
> Qui pour son interest ne veut rien butiner,
> Et ne veut tout auoir qu'afin de tout donner.
>
> (II.3)

Clidamant, Ligdamon's lord and liegeman of Merovée, presents himself as Scudéry was probably wont to do: "Le nom de Roy me
manque, & non le coeur de Roy." The King, not to be outdone,
suggests he make Clidamant a sort of Belisaire, partaker of his throne.

This idea is left hanging, and they are obliged to suspend their exchange of courtesies with the arrival of Ligdamon, who now fits into the new word picture being painted. No longer is he the languishing lover, but instead a romantic warrior, as Merovée describes him:

> . . . ce guerrier dont la démarche grave
> Semble forcer les yeux à iuger qu'il est brave.

Ligdamon, in response to Clidamant's astonishment at seeing someone familiar, is permitted to introduce himself, somewhat ambiguously, since the phrase he uses refers to the lover and the liegeman: "Ligdamon, le premier des seruiteurs parfaicts." Clidamant adds a testimonial intended to give him command of the forward ranks, adding finally, as though to convince the King that his praise is sincere, "Sire, la verité vous parle par ma bouche." Once again, the playwright stresses the great power of language.

The tone and import of this pair of scenes (bridging the gap between the second and third acts) represent a departure from the rest of the play: Ligdamon is placed in the midst of a tale of chivalry. Following the introduction of the new characters (including Ligdamon who has neatly effected his change by the ambiguous presentation of his new personality), the romance is continued by a mutual exchange of praise which finally terminates in a discussion between Merovée and Clidamant on how the power of kings should best be used. This scene, in language as high-flown as ever, has little to do with the two pairs of lovers, but the spectator's interest centers on the discussion anyway. The possibility of a battle is of some relevance to the plot, and the argument as to whether Merovée will be clement or harsh toward the Neustriens is important in this connection. Essentially, however, the focus is on the nature and achievement of kingly power, and the response demanded here is not that called forth by the central story, the love intrigue.

As the third act begins, Merovée lauds Clidamant for having saved his life and thus the kingdom, and the political tone is sustained. Clidamant remarks that all this is purely the creation of language, and therefore no more real than its opposite might be (and in fact, it appears that Ligdamon was largely responsible for the favorable outcome of the battle):

> Vous formez ma vertu de l'air comme vn fantosme,
> Et voulez faire grand ce qui n'est qu'vn atosme.

(III.1)

For a while, then, they strive to outdo one another in praise of their mutual valor. Finally, Merovée explains to "vne troupe d'habitans de Paris" the nature of the deed whose glory they have been so busy creating. Once again, the poet appears in Merovée's creation as he describes Clidamant's arrival to rescue himself and rout the enemy like some avenging angel:

> Citoyens, vistes vous iamais l'oyseau de proye
> Fondre sur les perdrix qu'il descouure à sa voye,
> N'auez-vous iamais veu quelque loup bocager
> Escarter vn troupeau qu'il treuue sans berger,
> Ou l'horrible sanglier dont la forte defence
> Escarte en vn moment la meute qui l'offence;
> Tel parut ce Heros.

The battle, as the King relates it, reaches the proportions of a battle in some *geste:*

> A chaque coup donné sans doute on voyoit bas
> Ou la teste, ou la cuisse, ou la iambe, ou le bras;
> L'abondance du sang respandu par la plaine
> Augmenta d'vn ruisseau les ondes de la Seine,
> Et rougit tellement la riuiere en son flus,
> Qu'à l'abord l'Ocean ne la connoissoit plus.

Not that his own deeds are any less incredible than those of his liegeman:

> Moy qui pour espargner le tribut d'vn denier
> Auois fait vn tresor au pasle nautonnier,
> Qui pour sauuer ma vie au milieu des allarmes
> Me couurois d'vn rempart fait de corps de gens-darmes.

All this has absolutely nothing to do with any normal perception of reality, and the listener is not intended to accept it as such. However, this epic interlude, as valid a creation of language as love, provides an alternative context. The spectator is exposed to a constantly fluctuating tone and a continually changing perspective, via the changing aims of the language no less than the play's scenic elements.

This particular interlude comes abruptly to a close when the King promises Clidamant that, as recompense for his valor, they will try to recover Ligdamon from Rothomage, where his friend fears he has been carried as a prisoner. The sense of suddenness derives from a change in both tone and place. The new setting is the wood of the first scene, and the new tone is not unlike that which opened the play. The poet continues to keep himself in sight.

The action returns to Silvie, who has finally fallen in love with Ligdamon (or has simply decided to confess her love) and is begging for his return, in *stances:*

> Reuiens pour te venger & pour me secourir,
> Tu le peux me faisant mourir.

(III.2)

Again she points to the ambiguity of love and death, the typical theme of these scenes. This time, however, she allows herself to sacrifice emotion for irony, inserting a critical comment on the *stances* the playwright has supplied for her:

> Que ces vers sont charmans, i'y treuue vne peinture
> Du malheureux succés de ma triste auanture,
> Celuy qui les dicta plus sçauant que rimeur.

This kind of fluctuation, seemingly designed to immensely extend (if only momentarily) the spectator's "psychical distance," must necessarily be brief if the spectator is to regain his former position with regard to Silvie. So, since it is only by constant fluctuation that the spectator is kept aware of the illusion, the actress is thrust aside to allow the role to reappear:

> Mais où va ce propos? quel excés de folie
> Me faire ainsi flatter dans ma melancholie?

It is at this moment, when the spectator has just been obliged to remark upon the flickering stage illusion before him, that Scudéry chooses to lead him deep into a new confusion. Silvie's melancholy madness is made visible, in a sense, by the arrival of Lidias, pining for his love. She, naturally, takes him for his double, Ligdamon, and seeks to comfort him accordingly. Being an honorable youth, Lidias refuses her advances, disclaiming any acquaintance with her. His name, he tells her, is Lidias, not Ligdamon, and he is a Neustrian. Silvie refuses to accept his story, claiming it is a pretense, and the confusion of the ensuing dialogue is reminiscent of madness:

> SILVIE: O Dieux! soyez tesmoins de cette trahison
> LIDIAS: Demandez leur plutost la veuë ou la raison.
> . . . .
> SILVIE: Ie ne sçais que respondre à son extrauagance.

Lidias now asks to be directed to Marsilly,[38] and Silvie, ironically, accepts the new personality she thinks Ligdamon is creating for himself:

> Neustrien de Forests, ie m'en vay vous l'apprendre
> Pourueu qu'en méme temps ce bel oeil mon vainqueur
> M'apprenne le chemin qui meine à vostre coeur.

The spectator, obliged to make a swift readjustment in the face of one set representing several places, is removed once more to Rothomage. Amerine, in a long lament (68 lines), protests the imprisonment of her "Lidias"; but, as always, even the expression of the most wretched grief is permeated with an irony which practically negates its force and repulses the spectator once again. Amerine goes on to complain to the gods of their severity:

> Mais où va ce propos? ces Dieux imaginaires
> Dont le vulgaire parle en ses mots ordinaires,
> Ce sont des Dieux de bois, ou de bronze, ou d'airain,
> Qui n'ont que le seul nom d'vn pouuoir souuerain:
> Ou si cette creance a rien de veritable,
> Ce sont des Dieux gourmands qui sont tousiours à table,
> Le nectar fait aller leur cerueau de trauers,
> De la mesme façon qu'ils guident l'uniuers.
>
> (III.3)

Lidias' mother now comes on stage to persuade Amerine to save her "son" by marrying him, as the law of the city provides. Amerine, despite her blushes, agrees, and the scene closes with a neat little piece of irony, since the spectator is well aware of the vanity of Amerine's hope:

> O ciel! ne permettez cet acte executé,
> Que ie puisse esprouuer mesme infidelité.

38. If there is a reference here to Auvray's *Dorinde* (published, like *Ligdamon et Lidias,* in 1631, and also known as *La Prise de Marsilly* [see Mahelot, *Mémoire,* pp. 81–82, and the identification made by Lancaster, p. 81, n. 3]), this request would further detract from the illusion (the whole play, of course, recalls *L'Astrée*).

Knowing that Ligdamon must refuse, and that Amerine will react as though to an infidelity, the spectator's role becomes that of an omniscient observer, and remains so. Not that he is completely distanced from the stage throughout; rather, he will now be able to anticipate the reactions of the characters, and within this framework Scudéry is free to maintain the same kind of fluctuation as before.

In the following scene, Ligdamon laments his imprisonment—now a matter of fact instead of metaphor (III.4).[39] At the same time, afire with the light of his memory of Silvie, he attains a kind of exaltation: not the tragic madness of a Hardy hero crushed by his universe, but a kind of pleasant melancholia which enables him to affect a new role:

> Car si la mort venoit me prendre à cet instant
> Ie finirois en cygne & mourrois en chantant.

Aegide has another name for this attitude, and refuses to allow Ligdamon to turn himself into a lyrical martyr:

> Mais forcer la nature & creuser son tombeau,
> C'est estre maniaque & foible de cerueau.

By degrees, the spectator is now prepared for the resolution of the confusion. First Amerine has a dream which takes on the same force of "reality" as all the other creations of this language. She has dreamed of her own death at the hands of someone "Que vostre oeil abusé prit pour vn autre absent" (IV.1), as she is informed by the soul of Lidias.

Another sudden change of place returns the spectator to Lidias, now expressing in *stances* his bewilderment at the mad way the world is treating him:

> Que le destin iniurieux
> Qui trouble toutes mes delices
> A pour moy d'estranges malices,
> Et qu'il se monstre furieux;

39. For a discussion of the set as an echo of the language in which characters express their emotions, see above, pp. 58 ff.; and below, pp. 122 ff. There are many other instances in this play. Ligdamon asks Aegide to set his soul free (II.1); Sylvie blames herself for her harsh treatment of "vne ame prisonnicre" and comments that if Ligdamon returns he will see her "languir en prison comme [lui] dans les fers" (III.2), and so on.

> Il fait qu'vne fille aueuglée
> D'vne passion desreglée
> Dont son foible esprit est charmé,
> Me poursuit d'vn dessein fantasque,
> I'en suis aimé sans estre aimé,
> Et croy moy mesme auoir vn masque.

(IV.2)

This train of thought leads him inevitably to the notion that he is perhaps something other than he thinks. The conflict here is the same as that which occurs in *Les Sosies,* in *Les Menèchmes,* and so on (see above, pp. 69ff and n. 26): one's own conception of oneself as opposed to the view of others. It appears to Lidias that Silvie is trying to create a new personality for him:

> La Nymphe qui me persecute
> En m'accusant de trahison
> Tasche dans vne erreur extreme
> De m'oster auec la raison
> Le creance d'estre moy mesme.

This uncertainty as to his true personality, it need scarcely be said, echoes that doubt already created in the spectator by the continual fluctuation of distance, which has thrown into question the whole nature of reality and his perception of it.

Despite the danger, Lidias is willing to return to Rothomage with Silvie, to find his own personality and to prove his claim that he and Amerine are in love. So the scene returns to Rothomage, site of Ligdamon's trial, and stays there for the remainder of the play. After a fiery condemnation by the three judges for his supposed murder of Aronthe and support of their enemy Merovée (they have refused indignantly to hear the testimony of Merovée's herald), Ligdamon is sentenced to die fighting lions. Aegide provides a running commentary on the fight, which one may safely assume occurred offstage, although the lions themselves apparently did appear, since Mahelot asks for "un antre d'ou sort [sic] des lions" (*Memoire,* p. 70). These lions were represented, one supposes, by actors dressed in skins:[40] the least convincing element in the entire play.

40. In the *Romant comique,* Ragotin tries to persuade the comedians to perform his story, which they claim is ridiculous and too hard to stage:

The last act dwells on the confusion of love and death, the problem of the self and its relation to the loved one. Ligdamon is the most confused of all, because he has been saved by Amerine, who is to marry him; while he, resolved to die, complains about Silvie:

> Ha! ie discours fort mal, la raison m'est rauie,
> Il est vray que mon coeur conserue ses appas,
> Mais ce coeur dont ie parle, ô Dieux! ie ne l'ay pas,
> La cruelle le garde afin que ie ne meure,
> Car sçachant que c'est là que nostre ame demeure
> Son oeil larron subtil à dessein l'a rauy,
> Afin qu'en mourant il soit tousiours seruy,
> Et semble que le sort le conspire auec elle,
> Car la Parque pour moi n'est point assez mortelle.

> (V.1)

For a moment, it is as though Silvie's possession of his soul is keeping him alive. As in *L'Amphytrite,* however, the language seems to be winning the battle. Ligdamon, obliged to marry Amerine, tries hard to avoid it: he cannot accept the personality being thrust on him any more than she can accept his "real" personality:

> LIGDAMON: Vouliez-vous que mon coeur par vne offence extreme
> Allast confesser d'estre vn autre que soy mesme?
> AMERINE: Veux tu par vn discours traistre, malicieux,
> Abuser ma memoire & démentir mes yeux?

> (V.2)

The use of "vous" and "tu" emphasizes this dual vision. By "offence," Ligdamon means not only the potential damage to Amerine and to his love for Silvie, but also a denial of his own essence. Faced with this duality which he cannot resolve, he must die. Indeed, he and Amerine have already taken the poison he requested. Perhaps here he may be

---

". . . si l'on doit juger des choses par l'effect qu'elles font dans l'esprit, toutes les fois que j'ay veu jouer Pirame et Thisbé, je n'ay pas esté tant touché par la mort de Pirame qu'effrayé du lion" (Paul Scarron, *Le Romant comique,* in *Romanciers du xviie siècle,* éd. Antoine Adam [Paris, 1958], p. 570). The comedians find this absurd, presumably because the lions were not real but actors in suitable skins. This interpretation is strengthened by Ragotin's apparent affirmation that this is how animals were produced on stage: he has just remarked proudly that he has "fait autrefois le chien de Tobie."

compared with Leandre, who, faced on the one hand with his consciousness of himself as essentially human and thus unable to love a
goddess, and on the other with another essence that is loved by a
goddess, also resolves to die.

Finally Ligdamon "dies," with a final plea that Silvie be informed:

> Reua-t'en en Forests, Aegide, vers ma Dame,
> Dis-luy que dans ma cendre encor reuit la flame,
> Et que pour ne fausser ce que i'avois iuré
> Ie suis mort en martyr de son oeil adoré.

Real death is confused with an erotic death, and Ligdamon, like
Amerine, has become more of a metaphor than a physical reality:
he has succumbed to the language. As Aegide says to Sylvie, who has
now arrived and whom he accuses of causing Ligdamon's death, she
need scarcely be upset: "Peux-tu bien craindre vn corps dont tu pos-
sedes l'ame?" She accepts the challenge, and undertakes to recall
Ligdamon from his apparent death. The confusion between the
metaphor and its intent is now complete:

> Vous m'auez cent fois dit que la voix de Silvie
> Pourroit vous rappeller de la mort à la vie,
> Et que malgré le sort qui commande aux humains
> Vostre destin estoit enfermé dans mes mains;
> Sus donc, cher Ligdamon, paroissez veritable.

Silvie's demand is rapidly fulfilled, for it turns out that Ligdamon and
Amerine had only been given an opiate, and the doctor who sold it is
easily able to revive them with the necessary potions. Both Amerine
and Ligdamon, upon awaking, confuse life with death; so although
things are finally clarified at the last minute, the play ends on the
same note of ambiguity which has dominated throughout.

It would seem, then, that by maintaining a constant fluctuation in
the spectator's "psychical distance" and preventing him from adopting a fixed position toward either the characters or the action, both
Ligdamon et Lidias and *L'Amphytrite* concentrate his attention on
the ambiguity of his own perception of reality. In both plays, perception may be communicated only through the medium of language,
which thus often takes on the role of the senses; the set and props,
partly realistic and partly non-realistic, are described in suitably ambiguous terms; the actor is regularly stripped of his role; and so on.

Thus the major (and perhaps only) theme of these plays may be summarized in this remark Amerine makes to Ligdamon:

> Ie ne te connois point? tu veux dire peut-estre
> Que changeant tous les iours on ne te peut connestre.
>
> (V.2)

3. Language as Creator and Destroyer
of Character

> Estans imitateurs de toute la Nature,
> Ils doiuent auoir peints tous les Etres diuers,
> Que la Nature estalle en ce grand Vniuers:
> Et comme la terre est vn vaste eschaffaudage,
> Où chacun dit son roole, & fait son personnage;
> Pour la representer ils ont deu faire choix,
> De ce qui peut seruir les Bergers & les Roys,
> Afin que leur Theatre où tant de peuple abonde,
> Puisse estre l'abbregé du Theatre du monde.
>
> (Beys, *Les Illustres fous* [1653], IV.5)

The examples of *L'Amphytrite* and *Ligdamon et Lidias* show how deliberately precarious is the illusion created by the playwrights of the early seventeenth century. In these plays, madness is more often the framework of the playwright's creation than simply the illustration of a theme. As a result, the spectator himself is made to experience a kind of hallucination, though not in Baty's sense, when he insists that a playwright must achieve "un univers expressif et cohérent et de provoquer dans la salle une hallucination collective."[1] The theatrical universe created here is coherent enough; but it is coherent in its incoherence. That is to say, it deliberately sets out to confuse the spectator and to include him in a hallucination—not simply by absorbing him in the new and possibly unfamiliar world on stage, but by subjecting him to a kind of madness punctuated by abrupt intrusions from the "real" world of normal perception. The spectator must be constantly reminded that the world these plays depict is unreal, but as they progress he also becomes conscious that a reality *beyond* the norm has been established on the stage. He does not merely observe the madman's imbalance or feel an impulse to identify with the madman. Rather, as the play unfolds his doubts on the nature of reality multiply—and he is urged into that very imbalance himself.

1. Gaston Baty, *Rideau baissé* (Paris, 1949), p. 219.

One of the playwright's best techniques for creating this doubt is
to bend his play's action toward a visual realization of his metaphorical language, rather than a logical evolution of the intrigue. When
Monléon's fantasy is suddenly made tangible before the spectator's
eyes, or when Scudéry's pastoral tragi-comedy gives substance to an
apparent metaphor, the impact on the spectator—already confused
by the constantly fluctuating psychical distance—is a devastating one.
Similarly, in the last act of Mairet's *Sylvie*, Florestan must conquer
a series of physical obstacles to ensure the happiness of four lovers:
the emotional problems facing them are thus embodied and actively
overcome. And in the fourth act of Corneille's *Clitandre*, the stage
storm reflects the tumultuous personal relationships of the characters as it furthers the action, leaving the prince stranded without
his horse and so in a position to save his love.

A more subtle but equally common device for confusing the issue
of reality involves the extensive use of language to destroy its own
creations, as when the actor's persona is suddenly bared in *Ligdamon
et Lidias*. Scudéry's use of this device is less methodical, however,
than that of Rotrou and Corneille.[2]

The actor and his language

The very fact that language can, and does, destroy not only its own
credibility but also that of the characters and situations visible through
it, implies—even depends upon—its prior ability to create these things.
The madman in Du Ryer's *Argenis* comments on his appropriation of
Poliarque's name and person:

> Ie l'ay trop bien acquis . . . la mesme renommee
> A force d'en parler s'est presque consomee.
>
> *(Derniere iournee, I,5)*

And Alidor gleefully tells Cleandre in Corneille's *La Place royalle*
(1633-34) of his control over Angelique:

2. Corneille's *Le Menteur* (1642-43) is the most obvious play of approximate-
ly this period where language creates a world deliberately presented as mythical
by the author. Here, however, the spectator accedes to this world *through* a
character, so that the play should properly be considered as belonging to a later
style and as a kind of summing up of the development we will follow in Corneille's own theatre (see Chapter 5).

Cleandre elle est à toy, i'ay flechy son courage
Que ne peut l'artifice, & le fard du langage!

(III.6.905-06)

Since the play's very existence during this period depends in the main
on the creative power of language, I shall concentrate here on its use
for destructive purposes. I shall have more to say of *La Place royalle*
later, for it already suggests the close of an era in its opposition between language and character, in a way Mairet's *Sophonisbe* (1634),
for example, a play generally considered "classical," does not. The
average play of the period does not raise doubts on the truth of its
language in a systematic fashion, as does *La Place royalle;* rather,
most authors prefer to interrupt the action occasionally by comment-
ing in various ways on the language and its creations, to divert the
spectator's attention. Such comments are almost always "destructive," for they devalue the character or his situation so as to cast considerable doubt upon his reality. They seem to fall in two basic cate-
gories (although in the final analysis they become virtually indistin-
guishable). The language itself may simply be devalued by numerous
different means, or a character's existence may be thrown into question by mockery of the terms he uses. One may argue, with some
justice, that whenever the language is brought into doubt, then so is
the character who is using it.

Since there are fewer examples in the second category, I shall begin
with those. In *La Place royalle,* Angelique is forced by Alidor to refuse the love which exists for her (at least, as far as the spectator can
see) only in terms of preciosity: but it is this very language which
has created her as a character. This play will be more closely examined in the chapter on Corneille, but here I shall glance at the
scene in which Philis congratulates herself on having speedily dis-
carded Dorante, and tells Lisis that he can now "Me conter de quels
feux tu te sens l'ame attainte" (II.6.518). This is already a mockery,
since Philis's role throughout has been to laugh at the "perfect" lover,
and to make comments whose essential purpose is to deny the existence of this lover; here the mockery goes further, for Lisis takes her
seriously and proceeds to view himself as the very lover whom the
spectator already knows to be nonexistent:

> Vous estes ma Maistresse, & moy sous vostre empire
> Je dois suiure vos loix, & non y contredire,
> Et pour vous obeir mes sentiments domptez,
> Se reglent seulement dessus vos volontez.   (529-32)

Often this doubt as to a character's true essence is cast by the figure in question. Lysimant, who at the start of Rotrou's *La Diane* (1632-33) is betrothed to Orante, feels quite cold toward his fiancée, anu in a monologue comments on the deceitful nature of his praises of her charms:

> Je les vois, je les loue, et je parle en amant:
> Plus libre que jamais, et plus froid pour Orante
> Que je ne le serois pour une indifférente,
> Je parle toutefois et d'amour et d'attraits
> Comme si ma froideur se rendoit à ses traits.
>
> (II.3)

It almost appears here that the actor himself is talking, an impression reinforced by the absence of other characters: the scene is between the actor and the spectator alone. This kind of doubt is, naturally, less common than that which remains *inside* the play, when the character as such begins to doubt his nature. In the same author's *Les Occasions perdues* (1633), there is considerable confusion toward the end as to which man is with which lady. Clorimand, who happens still to be out on the street, overhears other characters say that he is with both the queen and Isabelle (this last bit of information coming from the lady herself!). Not surprisingly, Clorimand himself is left somewhat confused by this state of affairs:

> Ah! que tout est contraire à mes chastes faveurs!
> Dieux! quand finirez-vous ce dédale d'erreurs?
> Lysis, puis-je etre ici, chez elle, et chez la reine?
> Hélas! quel Jupiter baise mon Alquemène?
>
> (V.9)

Numerous examples of the same phenomenon are discussed above (see pp. 70-71, n. 26, and p. 104).

Here I shall turn to the first category of techniques a playwright may use to undermine the credibility of his language. Usually, this devalua-

tion is accomplished through a ridiculing of language itself; vulgarity
is the most obvious means, but, for reasons of *bienséance* which will be
apparent, becomes the least common. One of the best examples occurs in Auvray's *Innocence descouverte* (1608), where Thomas continually mocks Marsilie's passion in vulgar terms. Nearer to the period
under examination here is Schélandre's *Tyr et Sidon* (1628), in which
the vulgar is reduced to the obscene in the scenes between the old
lecher Zorote, the page dressed as a girl, and Zorote's eunuch *(Premi-
ère journée,* III.5; IV). This tone recurs throughout the play: at the
end, Zorote and Almodice, nurse of the Tyrian princesses, are to be
burned alive together, the first for having caused the death of Léonte,
prince of Tyre, who was having an affair with his wife, and the second
for provoking the suicide of Cassandre, princess of Tyre, through her
efforts as an *entremetteuse.* Pharnabaze condemns them in terms
which inspire a risqué joke by the *archers:*

PHARNABAZE: Et qu'un mesme buscher soit leur lict à tous deux
                        Comme en un mariage egal et digne d'eux.
ARCHERS: Vieillard, si, toy vivant, ta femme estoit trop belle,
                    Ne crains point que là bas un tel sort te martelle:
                    Tu ne deviendras pas cornu par celle-cy.
ZOROTE: Je serois bien mieux veuf que d'espouser ainsi.

(IIe J, V.5)[3]

This kind of an ending mocks the high-flown language occurring
elsewhere in these plays; the traditional laments, and so on. In Rotrou's *Hypocondriaque* (1628), the innocent shepherdess, Cléonice, is
to be carried off by Lisidor and his friend Eristhène. They come
across her sleeping in the meadows, as the former is busy justifying
to his friend his project to place "ce soleil dans mon lict" (II.2). He
kisses her, and she wakes accusing him of a lack of discretion. There
follows a rather indecent discussion based on the not very ambiguous
conceit of "ces deux monts de roche." The lady is not at all abashed
by this turn of the conversation, and keeps up her end undismayed.

Language is here debased by a false confusion between real and apparent meaning. False, because in fact there is no "apparent" mean-

3. Jean de Schélandre, *Tyr et Sidon, tragi-comédie,* in *Ancien Théâtre Français,* éd. Viollet-le-Duc, 10 vols. (Paris, 1856), VIII, 5-225.

ing, although the manner of their conversation seems to imply one. The terms of preciosity are applied to the indecent: the metaphor is so transparent as to lose its *raison d'être*. In this particular instance, it also changes the character of Cléonice, who will no longer appear to the spectator as the innocent she originally pretended to be. Her subsequent attempts to seduce Cloridan confirm this new character.

A similar mockery of language occurs in de Brosse's most interesting play *Les songes des hommes esveillez* (1644) when the nobles, constantly playing pranks, trick the peasant Du Pont, whom they have brought into the castle in a drunken stupor and clothed in fine silks and jewels. Lucidan feigns to be an old friend of the poor victim, and after a little fooling on this theme, introduces his lover, Clorise, as his sister, whom Du Pont, he says, could have to wife if he wishes. Ariston, who is posing as Du Pont's friend and valet, tells him that he had better come up quickly with some compliment. The peasant does so, grotesquely and not altogether decently:

DU PONT: . . . Vostre gorge est de laict, & vos tetons encore,
            Sont plus beaux que le py, de nostre jeune taure.
CLORISE: Ce grand nombre d'attraits, & de perfections,
            Me donnera-t'il part en vos affections?
            Me pourrez vous aymer?
DU PONT: Que dites-vous Madame,
            Vos yeux ont enflamé la paille de mon ame,
            Et si vous n'arrestez leurs violents efforts,
            Ils reduiront en feu la grange de mon corps.

                                                      (III.5)

One must concede that for an uneducated peasant Du Pont does rather well in applying traditional metaphors to his own experience.

A parallel technique for the devaluation of language, not involving vulgarity, is based on the servant/master relationship. I have noted Aegide's use of this device in *Ligdamon et Lidias,* and Sosie employs it in *Les Sosies.* The servant degrades the words of his master, either by applying them in a less elevated context or by mocking them outright. In Rotrou's *Bague de l'Oubly* (1628-29), Fabrice, the jester, makes fun of the king's love for Liliane:

            Quel avantage, ô Dieux! Fabrice a sur des rois,
            Et combien je me ris d'amour et de ses lois!
            Ce prince à cet enfant voit son ame asservie,

Il forme ses desseins, il gouverne sa vie,
Il trouble sa raison, il engage sa foi,
Et peut autant sur lui que Bacchus sur moi.

(I.7)

And in Du Ryer's *Vendanges de Suresne* (1633), Guillaume mocks
Polidor's constant lamenting of the apparent relationship between
Tirsis and Dorimène:

POLIDOR: Je viens de voir piller les plus grands biens du monde.
GUILLAUME: Comment! quelques soldats en secret assemblez
Sont ils venus piller et nos vins et nos bleds?
Ce sont les plus grands biens que nous sçaurions
attendre.
POLIDOR: Je parle des baisers que Tirsis vient de prendre.
GUILLAUME: Vous parlez de baisers, c'est un precieux fruit,
Cela merite bien qu'on fasse tant de bruit.
Je prefere aux baisers des plus belles du monde
Les humides baisers d'une tasse profonde.

(III.5)

In *Les Occasions perdues,* Clorimand apostrophizes the heavens as
he approaches an evening rendezvous, asking that all light disappear,
since his love dare not be seen. His servant, Lysis, finds an appropriate twist to mock his conceit, echoing Isabelle's ironic question to
her mistress the queen earlier in the play, when the latter was bewailing the difficulties of loving a man below her in rank: "Aimez-
vous un rocher, un arbre, une fontaine?" (II.1). Now Lysis asks his
master:

Adorez-vous quelqu'un de ces oiseaux de nuit
Qu'on ne peut jamais voir quand le soleil nous luit?
Un Hibou cause-t-il votre amoureuse peine?
Auriez-vous bien, Monsieur, une âme si peu saine?

(III.2)

Fabrice, again, of *La Bague de l'Oubly,* mocks Alphonse's pining for
love:

Avoir donné son coeur, c'est être en mauvais point:
Moi, j'ai besoin du mien, et ne le donne point.

(I.2)

The mockery in these examples is not far from that already mentioned (see above, pp. 94-95 and n. 37), where the metaphor becomes real. Here the humor, which changes the attitude of the spectator, is a consequence of reducing an analogy to a reality all its own, so that the response is made (in these cases by the servant) in terms quite alien to the original thought. It is as though the author, in searching for a stage verisimilitude not dependent on a purely literary illusion, were constantly reducing his literary world, holding it up to ridicule.

As yet, however, he appears to have no illusion to replace the literary one—or rather, no definite or permanent illusion. He has not yet discovered personality. Thus the destruction of language simply uncovers layers of illusion, which always remain apparent. Metaphors and other tropes, which are essentially literary (and therefore, in this theater, in conflict with a more conscious *setting* of the play, where earlier they might have created a satisfactory illusion), are taken apart as soon as they are created; or rather, as soon as they are repeated, since these are the clichés of preciosity that are being mocked.

It is, of course, quite clear that the "classical" theater by no means scorned the precious cliché. The difference may be that it did not oppose this cliché to another reality, but presented it simply as the mediator between the stage reality and the reality of the spectator: it cannot be torn down, because it is no more than the interpreter of a personality. That is to say, it fulfills the normally accepted functions of language: to convey a single meaning through itself, not a multitude of meanings reflected off its glittering surface. There it is the *signifié* which is important, here it is the *signifiant*. Language in classical tragedy cannot afford to question itself; it cannot disrupt the even tone of the play, or wonder at the type of illusion it is offering. It thereby permits the spectator to do what his predecessor never could: enter into a character and take on his emotions. This earlier spectator is at one moment held aloof from a character, at another urged toward him. The mockery of language is also the mockery of the illusion.

There are other ways of achieving this effect. The pun is one; and, in a sense, it plays a similar trick, as when Amerine makes the rather hideous request that Ligdamon open her up and find his image graven in her bosom. In *Les Folies de Cardenio,* Fernant, who is trying to force Luscinde to marry him in accordance with her father's wishes but against her own, since she loves, and is loved by, Cardenio, manages to get a word of acquiescence from her when they are both before her father. Her grief at having seemed to surrender is such that she falls to the floor in a swoon, to all appearances dead. Indeed, as she falls, she says she has killed herself:

> ... quittant Cardenie il falloit bien mourir,
> Puisque l'on me vouloit separer de mon ame.
>
> (II.4)

Fernant, annoyed at this, says that after such temerity and cruelty

> Je ne te verray plus, ma raison retournée
> Ne sçauroit supporter ta froideur obstinée.

Such hair-raising puns are very common. Not necessarily based on a confusion between image and reality (in this particular case, the pun might be obvious to the spectator only because of Luscinde's apparently dead body lying on the stage), they may depend on the confusion between two different images: such as Théophile's much maligned blushing dagger in *Pyrame et Thisbé*.

Confusion between image and reality does not necessarily lead to humor. In *L'Hypocondriaque*, Lisidor courts Cléonice before attempting to carry her off. She demands sòme proof of his love, and his reply is reminiscent of the approach to love in *L'Amphytrite* and *Ligdamon et Lidias:* "Que je quitte le jour?" (I.2). His question is a rhetorical one; Cléonice is unlikely to accede, knowing that his love would weigh on her forever. His death would consecrate his love by making him a martyr to it. The issue here is that death is the center of love for these lovers: the self is "dead" whether the love is accepted or refused, in that the lover's soul is given over to his beloved. Lisidor's physical death would be only an outward symbol of his intense love: if Cléonice accepts this symbol, she accepts his soul, and would have to accept his love. Again, the metaphor is taken for the reality; but this time, instead of detaching the spectator from the play, it thrusts him deeper into it.

If language can be destroyed by a kind of internal twist, it can also be subjected to direct mockery. This mockery, too, seems to adopt two principal manners: first, the speech of a character may be compared to a literary model; second, it may appear that an actor is using his role to display his eloquence.

When one character suggests that another is imitating the language of a literary stereotype, he effectively demonstrates the illusory nature of their present situation. In Rotrou's *Clorinde* (1635), Lisante turns to the heroine with the words:

> Ou eut prisé jadis l'ardeur qui vous transporte,
> Mais le siècle n'est plus d'aimer de telle sorte.
> Représentez-vous point ces reines de romans
> Qui ne l'ont pas été des coeurs de leurs amans,
> Dont l'amour fut ingrate et la constance vaine,
> Et qu'au théatre même on suffriroit à peine?
>
> (IV.2)

In Corneille's *La Veuve* (1631-32), Geron, mocking the conversation of Florange (a rich and foolish provincial who never appears), says "Il dit ce qu'il a leu" (I.4.274). And in his *Galerie du Palais* (1632-33), Lysandre comments on the kind of lovemaking customary among these characters:

> . . . Le style d'un sonnet
> Est fort extravagant dedans un cabinet;
> Il y faut bien louer la beauté qu'on adore,
> Sans mépriser Vénus, sans médire de Flore,
> Sans que l'éclat des lis, des roses, d'un beau jour,
> Ait rien à démêler avecque notre amour.
> O pauvre comédie, objet de tant de veines,
> Si tu n'es qu'un portrait des actions humaines,
> On te tire souvent sur un original
> A qui, pour dire vrai, tu ressembles fort mal!
>
> (I.7.167-76)

A similar instance occurs in *La Veuve,* where Alcidon, who is actually Philiste's rival, accuses the latter of pretending to help him, Alcidon, obtain his sister's hand, when he actually knew of this sister's betrothal to Florange. Alcidon knows his accusation is untrue, since the sister's nurse (with whom he concocted the story in an effort to force Philiste into a duel) specifically told him Geron had contrived the liaison in secret. The spectator knows as well as Alcidon himself that the story is false. Alcidon makes the illusory nature of this entire incident even more obvious when he likens his actions to those of a stage character:

> Comme alors qu'au Théâtre on nous fait voir Mélite,
> Le discours de Cloris quand Philandre la quitte,
> Ce qu'elle dit de luy, je le dis de ta soeur,
> Et je la veux traiter avec mesme douceur.
>
> (III.3.955-58; see *Mélite,* III.5)

Clarimond, in Mareschal's *Railleur,* responds to the "poet" Lizante's laments over his suffering in the name of love by classifying him as one of a species:

> Les poëtes, les amans, quand l'ardeur les convie,
> Meurent tous, et jamais ils ne perdent la vie.
>
> (III.3)

And in Scudéry's *Le Prince deguisé,* Argenie, who has just seen the new gardener (the disguised prince), says to her friend Philise:

> . . . cét homme est si charmant,
> Qu'on voit en sa personne un berger de Romant.
>
> (II.1)

In a play like de Brosse's *Songes des hommes esveillez,* with its several inner plays invented by Clarimond to help make Lisidor forget his grief over Isabelle (believed drowned in a shipwreck) this kind of confusion occurs all the time. In the last act, Isabelle, who has appeared safe and sound, is put on the stage by Clarimond to act out her story for the benefit of Lisidor, who knows nothing of her survival. The two plays finally intersect when Isabelle brings her story up to the present time, and is joined by an ecstatic Lisidor on the inner stage.

In each of these cases the spectator is specifically intended to observe the characters as such, to recognize that their language is not that of real creatures: or, to be more precise, that "real" characters (the ones who comment on the language) are playing alongside stage characters. Similarly, a playwright may use literary references to detach a character from the stage. In his *Aveugle clairvoyant* (1648-49), de Brosse has an elaborate pun scene (V.5) which concludes in praise of Corneille's *La Suite du Menteur* after a short discussion of the vogue of this play. In an earlier play, *Le Curieux impertinent* (1644), the same author mocks the countless heroes who fall in love with portraits: Lotaire jokes about Anselme's suspicions of his wife, and laughs, "Vous pourriez à ce conte adorer des portraits" (I.1). He is making a direct appeal to the spectator, bringing the audience into his confidence. Lepante, in Mairet's *Illustre corsaire* (1637), does the same thing, of course, when he mocks the notion of the shepherd-prince. The kind of allusion may vary, but the effect remains the same.

Some of these plays utilize well-known or easily recognizable dialogues, almost all use *stances,* and all contain laments and other long monologues. The most famous dialogue may well be that of Philene and Sylvie in Mairet's *Sylvie* (I.3), probably composed by Mairet himself, but published separately from the play and familiar before the play was produced. The same author's *Sylvanire* contains a shorter dialogue (III.7.1296-1327) of the same nature. The use of stychomythia, echo (where the last syllable or two of the last word in a line is repeated as an echo answering the speaker, usually in a contrary sense to the one he would like to hear) and similar techniques was customary. They obviously serve to remind the spectator that he is watching something essentially unreal. Pierre Corneille, in his *Examen* (1660) of *Clitandre,* comments on these popular literary devices of the period: Les monologues sont trop longs, et fréquents en cette pièce [*Clitandre*]; c'était une beauté en ce temps-là, les comédiens les souhaitoient, et croyoient y paroître avec plus d'avantage. (p. 118) The actors may have prized such monologues, but the authors often used them toward comic ends, undermining a noble speech the moment it was over. In *Les Occasions perdues,* following Clorimand's lengthy soliloquy (III.2), Lysis proceeds to a commentary on his "caquets":

> Qu'une étrange manie a troublé sa pensée!
> C'est bien là se flatter d'une amour insensée.
> Combien de longues nuits il passe à s'abuser
> D'une vaine recherche, et qu'il dut mépriser!
> Il l'adore, il la croit de mille attraits pourvue,
> L'élève jusqu'au ciel, et ne l'a jamais vue.
> O la parfaite amour que l'amour des laquais!
> Ils ne s'amusent point à de si longs caquets;
> Jamais les envieux sur leurs desseins ne mordent:
> Deux mots ruinent tout, ou deux mots les accordent;
> Sans autres complimens, tel de telle a joui,
> Qui n'avoit dit encor que le seul mot d'oui.

In Mairet's *Sylvanire,* the heroine comes very close to mocking her
own eloquence: supposedly on the verge of death, she expounds upon
her love for Aglante and her desire to marry him (at great length in
view of her condition), and pauses in the midst of this lament to cry
out "O mort! n'acheve pas que je n'aye achevé" (IV.4.1686). And
the monologue becomes patently superfluous. This phenomenon is
later repeated, when Tirinte delays opening the tomb in order to
rhapsodize:

> O précieux tombeau, qui dedans ta closture
> Gardes comme en depost l'honneur de la Nature,
> Fidelle gardien de la gloire de l'Amour.
>
> (V.2.2112-14)

Not unnaturally, considering that what they are doing is strictly il-
legal, his friend Alciron is rather annoyed by this eloquence:

> Tirinte despeschons avant qu'il soit plus jour,
> J'ay besoin de ta main, et non pas de ta langue,
> Une autre une autre fois tu feras ta harangue.
>
> (2115-17)

Here language is openly described as a hindrance to the action. It is
clearly existing purely for its own sake, and actually becomes an element quite distinct from the action being pursued concurrently on
the stage. It is a showcase for the actor as an actor, and he presumably viewed it as such, if one can accept the full implications of
Corneille's comment (indeed, as late as 1663, in the *Impromptu de
Versailles*, Molière remarks on the delivery of certain actors—notably
Montfleury and his companions of the Hôtel de Bourgogne— who
break the *vraisemblance* of a play).

This mockery of the language inevitably extends to the mockery
of its creations. Thus certain conventional figures are acknowledged
to exist solely for the amusement of the spectators. As Corneille indicates in his *Examen* (1660) of *L'Illusion,* the matamore in that
play is such a figure:

> Il y en a mesme un [character] qui n'a d'estre que dans l'imagina-
> tion, inventé exprés pour faire rire, et dont il ne se trouve point
> d'original parmy les hommes. C'est un Capitan que soustient
> assez son caractere de fanfaron, pour me permettre de croire qu'on
> en trouvera peu dans quelque Langue que ce soit qui s'en acquitent
> mieux. (p. 123)

The fanfaron and others like him are almost always presented by the other characters as frauds. In Gougenot's *Comédie des Comédiens,* where the levels of illusion are particularly confused, Bellerose remarks on the Capitaine (here supposedly an actor like the rest) "tant il y a que cest hipocondriaque croit sur peine de la vie que nous l'estimions tel qu'il se repute estre."[4] I have already noted that in Mareschal's *Le Railleur,* La Dupré remarks on the "vain Capitain" as though he were in a different reality from her own. This "apparent illusion" is not limited to character, but includes any obviously theatrical convention. If an actor takes on a certain language and bearing to define characters such as the captain, the doctor, the valet, if figures such as Gaultier and Gros Guillaume are clearly stage creatures, this criterion may also be applied to the genre itself and the theme.

In Rotrou's *Diane,* the heroine (disguised as Célirée) is trying to obtain from Lysimant the admission that he still loves Diane rather than Orante, and that he is marrying the latter only because his father wants him to marry someone wealthy. She suggests to him that Diane no longer loves him:

> Le changement du sort peut changer ses esprits,
> Et d'une ardente amour faire un lache mépris.
>
> (I.9)

In response, Lysimant can only sigh, "Hélas! quel changement arrive à des bergères?" His apparent meaning—that Diane will never be rich enough to warrant his father's approval—is confused with an ironic comment on the nature of the pastoral, typical of Rotrou, who delights in such remarks. The irony here is intensified in that Diane's material status is destined to change.

I have already suggested that the stage representation of madness is the symbol of a major theme. It is also, however, a recognized opportunity for the author and actor to delight the audience in a context aside from the action. In his *Examen* (1660) to *Mélite,* Corneille reiterates:

> La folie d'Eraste n'est pas de meilleure trempe. Je la condamnois deslors en mon ame; mais comme c'estoit un ornement de Theatre qui ne manquoit jamais de plaire, et se faisoit souvent admirer, j'affectay volontiers ces grands egaremens. (p. 137)

4. Le sieur Gougenot, *La Comédie des comédiens,* in *Ancien Théâtre Français,* IX, 303-426; this quotation is from Act I, Scene 2.

As I have indicated, it is not uncommon for the playwright to ridicule
the language which creates genre, character or theme. Garapon[5] provides many more examples, in demonstrating how humorous language
enables an actor to show his virtuosity. In the process, the illusion is
totally destroyed, for the actor either steps out of his role, or that
role is presented as a deceit. The galimatias of Bruscambille and the
chansons of Gaultier-Garguille are obvious illustrations, as is the
Galimatias of Deroziers.[6] If these extremes are rare in the tragi-comedy of the period in question,[7] the equally unrealistic and conventional
speech of set characters and themes is not; and while this last is less
humorous than the devices examined by Garapon, it serves as well to
prevent "suspension of disbelief."

The actor and his set

Each of the situations mentioned above destroys the illusion because, in effect, it shows the actor at work; the same loss of illusion
follows when the *mise en scène* is designed with no attempt at
vraisemblance.[8] In Corneille's *Galerie du Palais,* a curtain is drawn
aside and the audience sees "le libraire, la lingère, et le mercier chacun
dans sa boutique" (I.4, IV.12 and 13). As Corneille points out in his
later *Examen:*

> J'ai donc pris ce titre de *la Galerie du Palais,* parce que la pro-
> messe de ce spectacle extraordinaire et agréable pour sa naïveté,
> devait exciter vraisemblablement la curiosité des auditeurs; et ç'a
> été pour leur plaire plus d'une fois, que j'ai fait paraître ce même
> spectacle à la fin du quatrième acte, où il est entièrement inutile.[9]

In *La Place royale,* his efforts to present another attractive and
pleasing decor result in a similar conflict between the action and the

5. Robert Garapon, *La Fantaisie verbale et le comique dans le théâtre
français du moyen âge à la fin du xviie siècle* (Paris, 1957).
6. Le sieur Deroziers Beaulieu, *Le Galimatias, tragi-comédie,* in *Ancien Théâtre Français,* IX, 427-503. Three other plays contained in this volume are
equally good examples: *La Comédie des proverbes, La Comédie des chansons*
and *La Comédie des comédies.*
7. Garapon, *Fantaisie verbale,* p. 148.
8. See above, Chapter 2, pp. 57ff., p. 87, and notes 32 and 33.
9. Corneille, *Oeuvres,* éd. Marty-Laveaux, II, 12.

set. Corneille states in the *Examen* that, finding it unlikely that Angelique would grieve in the street over her precipitous agreement to accept a marriage she does not want (III.5), he decided to place her in her boudoir so that the audience could see her in a more natural manner, through the window. Yet the scene itself remains obviously illusory:

> I'ay mieux aimé rompre la liaison des Scenes, & l'vnité de lieu qui se trouue assez exacte en ce Poëme, à cela près, afin de la faire soupirer dans son cabinet auec plus de bienseance pour elle, & plus de seureté pour l'entretien d'Alidor. (p. 114)

The set, in fact, often seems to take over from the text. I have already discussed the manner in which Mairet, in *Les Galanteries du Duc d'Ossone,* makes use of a moving wall to reveal the various bedrooms which the action demands. *L'Illusion comique* relies on a similar technique, and how many of Mahelot's directions call for a curtain to be drawn aside and reveal another part of the scenery? Witness his instructions for *La Bague de l'Oubly:* "A costé du jardin et du palais, il faut un eschaffaut tendu de noir qui soit caché; il s'ouvre au cinquiesme acte, a la premiere scene."[10] In *Ligdamon et Lidias,* even more scenery must be suddenly revealed: "A l'autre costé, il faut une prison, sous la prison un antre d'ou sort [sic] des lions, il faut des chaisnes; et, contre la prison, il faut aussy un temple ou autel; une barricre garnie de ballustres, et le tout caché."[11] Du Ryer's *Arétaphile* needs "un palais caché," Durval's *Travaux d'Ulysse,* "un enfer caché," Rayssiguier's *Calirie* requires "une belle salle" which is kept concealed until the last act, Mairet's *Sylvie* calls for "un autel: qui ne [paraît] qu'au cinquiesme acte." The instructions for Durval's *Agarite* are not unlike those for Mairet's *Ossone:* "Au milieu du theatre, il faut une chambre garnie d'un superbe lict, lequel se ferme et ouvre quand il en est besoing."[12]

Auvray, in his *Dorinde,* works out an interesting rapport between set, action and theme: Sigismon is to be rescued from the tower in which he is a prisoner by climbing down a rope to a boat where his *confident,* Ardilan, is awaiting him; they will then pursue Sigismon's mistress, Dorinde:

10. Mahelot, *Mémoire,* p. 69.
11. Ibid., pp. 69-70.
12. Ibid., p. 80. For an attempted reconstruction of the setting of Durval's *Agarite,* see Lawrenson, Roy and Southern, "L'*Agarite* de Durval."

ARDILAN: Sus, attachez la corde, & sans perdre de temps
             Allons chercher ailleurs des Astres plus constans.
SIGISMON: Ie suis prest, la voicy;* ie vay quoy qu'il auienne
             Mettre au bout d'vne corde & ta vie & la mienne;
             Mes yeux sous cet habit ne me connoissent plus.
ARDILAN: Ne nous amusons point de discours superflus
SIGISMON: Pour sortir aisement la Tour est vn peu droite,
             Cette corde assez rude, & la fenestre étroite
             **Dorinde sans mentir ie serois sans soucy
             Si nos liens estoient aussi forts que ceux-cy.
ARDILAN: Tenez-vous ferme aux noeux, mon bateau se recule;
             Il faut en cét endroit auoir vn bras d'Hercule:
SIGISMON: Dépesche, que mes mains toutes pleines de feux
             Ne brûlent cette corde auecque tous ses noeux.
             Est-il bien?
ARDILAN: Descendez.
SIGISMON: I'ay pensé lacher prise. •
                                                        (IV.4)

  *Il attache la corde à la fenestre de la tour pour en descendre.
  **Descendant & tenant la corde.

Here Auvray employs several of the devices already mentioned. The
metaphor of the bonds of love is made visible in the chord which
burns Sigismon's hands; the tower itself may represent the obstacles
he must overcome before he may finally approach his beloved. Even
the theme of the fusion of souls is brought in. At the same time, the
actor deliberately calls the spectator's close attention to the set, to
the form of the tower and its window, to the water supposedly carrying Ardilan's boat away from the walls despite his efforts to hold
it.

This same mixture of theme, language, set and *jeu de scène* occurs
in an interesting scene in Scudéry's *Prince deguisé*. Clearque, the
prince disguised as a gardener, is cultivating flowers when Argenie
appears. He picks some and presents them to her, linking flowers
and love in the common metaphor. The symbolism in this *jeu* extends the superficial meaning of their polite conversation, as
Clearque suggests that the flowers are

          Trop heureuses pourtant si vous daignez connoistre,
          Qu'elles meurent pour vous, qui les avez faict naistre.

                                                        (II.5)

The flowers are there because he was in the garden to cultivate them in order to be near her, but as he speaks the flowers clearly represent his own life and love. This poetic metaphor is echoed in other *jeux* during the same scene: when Argenie wishes to drink at the fountain, Clearque washes a cup in it and gives it to her, saying "Ce vase n'est pas beau, mais il est bien lavé." As she drinks from it, she exclaims:

> Ha tu luy fais outrage!
> Et je ne veis jamais un si parfaict ouvrage.

For an action depending entirely on movement, one cannot do better than examine the false execution in Mareschal's *Cour bergère,* where the author's stage directions control the action. The evil Cecropie has managed to persuade her son, Amphyale, to "execute" Pamale in order to frighten her sister, Philoclée, into marrying him:

> Pamele paroit, les mains liées, les yeux bandez, la gorge nuë, & vn Bourreau derriere elle, qui tient vn coutelas à la main, & suit deux hommes qui menent cette Princesse au lieu du supplice, qui sera dans vn lieu éleué au fonds du theatre, & qui se découurira, la tapisserie estant leuée. (IV.6-8)

The spectator (and Philoclée) then sees the executioner about to let his arm drop as the "tapisserie" is allowed to fall. Philoclée faints (perhaps the falling curtain echoes her fainting), but regains consciousness in time to see the curtain rise to reveal "le corps de Pamele tout ensanglantée, & la teste dans vn bassin sur vne table." She was jolted from her faint as her real lover, Pyrocle (disguised as an Amazon maiden), fainted on top of her. The scene's climax is no less extraordinary: first Cecropie appears on "vne platte forme du Chateau;" then Amphyale gets up, grabs his sword and runs to the platform "pour s'y tuer deuant elle." Fate is now enjoying itself: "Il se tuë; & Cecropie reculant de peur, tombe de la platte forme en bas, sur le theatre." All this activity forms a kind of backdrop to the lamenting of Amphyale, the curses of Cecropie, and the fears of Philoclée and Pyrocle. It also puts an end to the sub-plot with the deaths of Cecropie and her son.

One could analyze all these techniques in great detail, but the end result would be a rather dull list, not indicative of the spectator's

reaction to an entire play.[13] It is worthy of note, however, that the
relationship between set and language, reflected in the examples given
above, is not the only source of audience doubt (or support) of the
illusion. In some plays the author emphasizes the irony of the opposition between reality and fantasy; here the best examples are Corneille's *Mélite* and *Place royalle,* where the irony seems restricted almost entirely to the language. These plays, which illustrate in part a
development peculiar to Corneille, will be examined in the chapter
on that author.

In none of the plays discussed thus far is the spectator intended to
believe in the lighthearted games that are being performed. He is not
expected to identify with these nymphs and shepherds; they are a
literary and theatrical game. Rather, the author is working toward
that dialectical juxtaposition of dramatic elements described in Chapter 2. Scudéry seems to recognize this when he suggests in his *Au
lecteur* that the success of *Le prince deguisé*, "cette Peinture parlante,"
was perhaps not solely a matter of its poetry, the effects present in
the text:

> Le superbe appareil de la Scene, la face du Theatre, qui change cinq
> ou six fois entierement, à la representation de ce Poëme, la mag-
> nificence des habits, l'excellence des Comediens, de qui l'action
> farde les paroles, & la voix qui n'est qu'vn son qui meurt en nais-
> sant.

The variable nature of love, that most popular of superficial themes,
the continual playing of the characters with one another, the everlast-
ing deceptions (which may be deliberate, as with Alcidon and the nurse
in *La Veuve* or Fernant in *Les Folies de Cardenio,* or simply emotional,
as with Philiste and Clarice in *La Veuve)*; the physical disguises; the
ease with which the lovers transfer their love; the use of irony in the
language, the set and the actor's manner: it is these factors which reflect the true theme of these plays. In many, the tone seems to alter
sharply with the denouement, but this effect is negated if the spectator

---

13. For agreement concerning this juxtaposition of scenes in terms other than
those of the "subject" in the theater of Rotrou, see the recent detailed and complete commentary of Morel, *Jean Rotrou,* pp. 180–87, where the author terms
this an "esthétique du discontinu," and justifies it in terms similar to mine. See,
in the same volume, pp. 227–49.

understands what lies behind the action.   At the end of *La Diane,* the peasant Sylvian, excluded from the happiness of the others because the heroine's hand is denied him, bitterly remarks:

> Puisque tout est contraire à ta persévérance,
> Va dans un broc de vin noyer ton espérance,
> Malheureux Sylvian, et venge sur les plats
> La perte que tu fais de ses rares appas.

(V.10)

Any humor in Sylvian's comment is nullified by the sullen anger of his tone.   A similar bitterness marks the conclusion of Corneille's *La Suivante,* when Amarante laments for reasons like Sylvian's.   At the end of *Mélite,* the defeated nurse swears she will get her revenge, as does the "vanquished" Erphore in Mairet's *Illustre corsaire.*

This kind of "open" ending is by no means rare, indeed the multiple marriages that so often conclude these plays are a distinctly theatrical means of avoiding the problem: questions raised in the course of the drama, regarding the uncertainty of the human condition, the unreliability of human perception, and so on, are left quite unanswered.   The tragi-comedies and comedies of this period do not attempt to answer a moral problem; indeed, they are rarely concerned with what Gaiffe terms "la peinture des mœurs et . . . l'analyse psychologique."[14]   Their focus is a more general one.

The theater on the theater

The emphasis these authors place on the problem of reality and illusion leads naturally and quite rapidly to plays whose subject is the theater itself.   It is clear that their reliance on theatricality to achieve a certain rapport with the spectator, their refusal to conceal the essence of the theatrical moment, brings them to examine that very theatricality.   As a result of this examination—perhaps under the influence of a changing philosophical outlook, an evolving social temper, or simply the increasingly powerful critics, perhaps in the course of experimenting—what is presently known as the "classical" theater came to the fore.

The first two such self-conscious plays I shall glance at are the two by Gougenot and Scudéry both called *La Comédie des comédiens;*

14. Fernand Gaiffe, *Le Rire et la scène française* (Paris, 1931), p. 89.

the first has been dated 1631 or 1632, the second 1633, but they
probably appeared closer together.[15] Despite their similarity in form
and title, there is in fact an important difference between them. Both,
of course, center on the reality and non-reality of the actors as such;
but in the case of Gougenot's play, the actors are presented as playing
themselves, while in Scudéry's they are supposedly pretending to play
at being actors. In both plays, the first two acts are presented as a
kind of prologue; Scudéry's, however, also includes a true prologue
in which Mondory presents himself as the director of the troupe, before his first play begins. That, in turn, leads in Act III to a second
play, introduced by a second prologue—or rather, an "anti-prologue,"
consisting of a dispute between the prologue and the argument, whose
conclusion is that both serve no purpose. The play ends with a further
comment by Mondory/Blandimare to the spectators, which returns
them finally to the second play, where it rejoins the primary play.

    Gougenot's play might seem simple by comparison, but in fact is
equally complex. Bellerose walks onto the stage with an apology to
the audience because, he says, two of his best actors have had an argument and come to blows, with the result that they cannot perform
the play they had intended, and will have to produce something else.
His apology is presented as a prologue, but it is a false prologue, for
as Bellerose "feint de vouloir rentrer," having asked for the audience's
silence, Gaultier and Boniface appear on the stage still arguing and
both with their arms in slings. Bellerose comes back to try and stop
them. Thus, throughout the first two acts the actors are supposedly
playing themselves. The action is fairly straightforward from this
point, although it gradually shifts emphasis to the question of the
troupe's organization and the problems of arranging the contracts
of Guillaume and Turlupin, who wish to be partners in the company
and not actors "à gages."

    These first two acts seem to constitute an apology for the theater.
They are filled with comments on the theater's purpose, the problems
actors must face and the way they are treated. Bellerose tells the two
disputants that they are losing time when they should be looking to
the terms of the company's contract and drawing up a list of all the

15. See Henry Carrington Lancaster, *A History of French Dramatic Litera-*
ture in the Seventeenth Century, 9 vols. (Baltimore, 1929-42), II, p. 472, n. 4;
and my Appendix 1, pp. 186-87.

costumes and props necessary for the performances, since the theater
is "une figure racourcie du monde." In the next scene, he extends
this definition:

> ... le theatre estant un abregé du monde, on y doit representer
> en abregé toutes les actions du monde; et c'est avec beaucoup de
> peine, d'autant que douze acteurs, pour le plus, dont la scène est
> composée, doivent en cinq actes et en deux heures representer ce
> qui dans l'univers aura peut-estre succedé en vingt années à mille
> personnes; et, de plus, c'est que dans le theatre universal nul n'est
> attaché qu'à sa propre condition; mais, au comique, chacque ac-
> teur doit representer la qualité, la condition, la profession ou l'art
> que les subjets requièrent, et c'est ce qui fait le theatre bien dif-
> ferent de l'opinion du vulgaire, et qui monstre l'estourdissement
> de ceux qui croyent, par le rapport d'un miroir et par l'applaudis-
> sement d'un vent populaire, que quelque beauté du corps que la
> nature leur a donnée ou quelque affeterie de langage qu'ils ont
> glanné au champ des Muses les rendent capables d'attirer sur eux
> les yeux et les oreilles d'une assistance composée bien souvent des
> plus beaux esprits d'une province. (I.2)

Earlier, Turlupin comments on the various "ruses, inventions, sub-
tilitez, equivoques, feintes et persuasions" involved in the practice of
love on the stage; he had carefully listed them, and he complains that
Madame Boniface destroycd his list out of spite. Bellerose warns,
after Turlepin's departure, that they must be careful not to upset him,
as one of "des plus gentils garcons qui se puissent rencontrer pour le
theatre." This kind of reference reminds the spectator that he is before actors speaking of themselves, and of their art. Yet one must
remember that, for the audience of the time, the real personalities of
these actors are confused with their stage personalities. Mme. Valliot
is not really Gaultier's wife, and there is no evidence to show that the
unidentified *farceur* Boniface is the same person as Nicolas Lion,
known as Beaupré, husband of the actress who here plays Mme. Boniface; but to the audience, accustomed to see these actors and actresses
always in the same roles, they may appear as such. Many spectators
no doubt believed (correctly in some cases) that traits like Boniface's
avarice, Gaultier's jealousy, the bragging of the Capitaine and Guillaume's legendary drunkenness belonged to the actors offstage as well

as on.[16] As though to further this impression, actors in farces often made distinct and recognizable references to events either in their own lives or in those of the spectators,[17] a pattern followed in this *Comédie des comédiens*. The actor played certain set roles: the lover (Beauchasteau) was the hero, surrounded by a number of other established characters. This practice survives into classical drama: the brave, handsome lover, who can always be played by the same actor, is backed up by an old man (no longer ridiculous as when played by Gaultier), an opponent of some kind, a lady to love, and so on. The spectator knows the nature of a character as soon as he recognizes the actor, and if given the chance to confuse actor and role, as in the *Comédie des comédiens*, he will be very likely to do so. Indeed, the actors themselves do so: Mme. Gaultier comments on her "husband's" jealousy, and remarks to Mme. Boniface that anything might happen if she had to kiss someone else on stage in the course of her performance: "Et que sçay-je encor si la rage du docteur ne passera point jusqu'à l'extremité de luy faire representer au naturel les folies du docteur Gaultier?" (II.2). This confusion must have intensified the spectator's sense of fluctuating psychical distance.

With the end of this two-act "prologue" the company supposedly goes off to rehearse a tragi-comedy, and from then on the theatrical situation is guided by the usual devices of this genre, already described. As I have suggested, Scudéry's play appears slightly more complex at the beginning than Gougenot's. Mondory enters and delivers a true prologue:

16. For the connections of these characters with the italian improvisers, whose stage and real personalities are quite intertwined, see Gustave Attinger, *L'Esprit de la Commedia dell'Arte dans le théâtre français* (Paris, 1950), pp. 100-09; and I. A. Schwartz, *The Commedia dell'Arte and its Influence on French Comedy in the Seventeenth Century* (New York, [1931]), pp. 50 and 59.

17. See Edouard Fournier, éd., *Chansons de Gaultier Garguille* (Paris, 1858), pp. xii-xv; and Tallemant des Réaux, *Les Historiettes*, éd. Georges Mongrédien. 8 vols. (Paris, n.d.), III, 232-33, and VII, 127. For biographies of the actors themselves, see the two volumes by Mongrédien, *Dictionnaire biographique des comédiens au xviie siècle* (Paris, 1961), and *Les Grands Comédiens du xviie siècle* (Paris, 1927).

Ie ne scay (Messieurs) quelle extrauagance est auiourd'huy celle
de mes Compagnons, mais elle est bien si grande, que ie suis forcé
de croire, que quelque charme leur dérobe la raison, & le pire que
i'y voy, c'est, qu'ils taschent de me la faire perdre, & à vous autres
aussi. Ils veulent me persuader que ie ne suis point sur vn Theatre;
ils disent que c'est icy la ville de Lion, que voila vne Hostellerie; &
que voicy vn jeu de paume, où des Comediens qui ne sont point
nous, & lesquels nous sommes pourtant, representent vne Pastoralle,
ces insensez ont tous pris des noms de guerre, & pensent vous estre
inconnus.

He goes on to mock his troupe's idea that he should call himself Monsieur Blandimare ("bien que ie m'apelle veritablement Mondory"),
and that they should pretend they are going to be there for twenty-
four hours—the spectators would have to send out for food and beds.
In fact, he says, they are quite mad, and he would be going for help if
it were not already too late in the day. He concludes that the spectators should make no noise so as to avoid upsetting them, "parce qu'es-
tans melancholiques, ils sont amateurs du silence."

With this introduction, the spectator expects the troupe to offer
some kind of performance. But when it does appear, Belle Ombre is
complaining of the bitterness of life as an actor. He briefly protests
their lack of success in the provincial town and his desire to be back
in Paris, but this soon gives way to discussions among the actors of
the troupe on their profession, while the actresses complain of the
importunities to which they are subjected. Throughout all this they
are supposedly in the inn to which Mondory referred in the prologue,
and at this point the director himself appears, playing M. Blandimare,
ostensibly in search of his nephew. It is, of course, clear to the spectator that Blandimare and Mondory are a single person: hence, the
entire performance that follows takes on the air of a rehearsal to
which the public has been admitted. Belle Ombre turns out to be the
long-lost nephew, and the remainder of the first play (the second act)
becomes an attempt to show M. Blandimare the value of the acting
profession (which includes some praise of Scudéry himself).

This second act becomes even more of an exercise when the troupe
decides to prove itself with the recitation of an "Eglogue Pastoral."
Blandimare is so impressed that he asks to join the company, and
suggests that the next day they perform a "*Tragi-comedie Pastorale,*

intitulee, *L'Amour caché par l'amour*," which Blandimare happens
to have in manuscript form. He likes it so much, as "tout ce qui vient
de cet Autheur," that he has learned it by heart. It is this play that
fills the next three acts, beginning (as noted) with an argument between *Le Prologue* and *L'Argument*, which ends when the first recognizes himself to be "inutile" and the second allows he is "superflu."
Subsequently the spectator is placed before a completely new scene:
"Le Theatre change de face & paroist Bocager." The pastoral continues until Blandimare closes the triple play with a final comment to
the audience.

While Scudéry's play is somewhat more complicated than Gougenot's,
more accomplished still is Corneille's *Illusion comique* (1635).[18] Until
Rotrou's *Saint-Genest* (1645),[19] Corneille's play is without doubt the
most interesting example of this self-conscious theater. It has accordingly met with considerable critical attention, but I wish here to consider it as a milestone toward the final metamorphosis of the French
theater described at the outset of this study.

The discussion by Professor Nelson, while helpful, is not entirely
suited to my purpose. Alcandre, he suggests, is "both playwright and
metteur en scène," adding that Corneille "has dramatized his dramaturgy" so that his subject "is not the theatricality of life but the theatricality of the theater."[20] As I have been trying to show here, the
theater to these playwrights is never just the theater; even if it is important to them to make a comment on the theater, their primary purpose is the creation of "un abregé du monde."

Like the magician, Polistène, in Racan's *Bergeries*, Alcandre is depicting what purports to be life. The difference is that where Polistène in
fact reveals a lie (Ydalie and Alcidor are not really lovers), Alcandre,

18. For this dating see Pierre Corneille, *L'Illusion comique, comédie*, éd.
Robert Garapon (Paris, 1957), pp. xv-xvi.
    19. See Judd David Hubert, "Le réel et l'illusoire dans le théâtre de Corneille
et dans celui de Rotrou," *Revue des Sciences Humaines* (1959), pp. 333-50;
Morel, *Jean Rotrou, passim;* Robert J. Nelson, *Play within a Play. The Dramatist's Conception of his Art: Shakespeare to Anouilh*, Yale Romanic Studies,
Second Series V (New Haven, 1958), pp. 36-46; Francesco Orlando, *Rotrou
dalla tragicommedia alla tragedia* (Turin, 1963), pp. 237-94; Van Baelen,
Rotrou, pp. 145-64.
    20. Nelson, *Play within a Play*, pp. 52 and 56. The discussion of *L'Illusion
comique* covers pp. 47-61.

in *L 'Illusion comique*, is showing the truth—or rather, is evoking a
past truth. It is not until Act V that truth and illusion are actually
mingled, most effectively, for neither Pridamant (Alcandre's stage
audience) nor the spectator can clearly distinguish between them. In
Les Bergeries, the lie is surrounded by theatrical effect, and in any
case the spectator knows beforehand that Polistène is tricking
Arthenice. By contrast, an audience must feel chastened after viewing Corneille's play: the first inner play (the truth) is presented
deliberately as a play; and the second (the lie) duplicates the tone of
the first, so that if one accepts the truth of the first he will also accept that of the second.

Thus, at least before the final revelation, the spectator perceives
only two levels of action. One is the conjurations of Alcandre; the
other, the life and play of Clindor and his companions. From Alcandre's point of view, also, there are only two levels: his conjuration (which, although it actually has two parts, a truth and a lie, is
formulated as a unit), and Pridamant's reactions to it. The spectator's
reaction cannot be fused with Pridamant's, for he is always in a corner
of the stage with Alcandre, cut off from the audience. Alcandre, and
through him Corneille, may see Pridamant as a substitute for the actual spectator; but the spectator himself cannot. From inside the play
Pridamant may seem to be outside it, but to those outside the play he
must always be within it. Although Nelson identifies three levels and
sees them collapse into one during the play's action, meeting in the
"anxiety" which causes the father to identify with his adulterous and
murdered son of the final act (which act is for the father but a con-
tinuation of the second level), this collapse cannot occur for the spectator. Pridamant and Alcandre are always there to remind him that
he is watching a play within a play. For him there are always two
levels of action, until (as mentioned) the final revelation of the third
level, when Clindor is disclosed after the stage play, counting up the
company's takings. The spectator's chastisement lies in his confusion
of the second and third levels, a confusion for which Alcandre is not
alone responsible: elements which can only exist in the theater are
constantly intruding into the second level, supposedly a representation of real life.

From the play's outset, Alcandre himself is presented not only as
the playwright and *metteur en scène* but as an actor. Dorante remarks to Pridamant on how carefully he controls every movement
and gesture:

> Son corps malgré son aage a les forces robustes,
> Le mouvement facile et les desmarches justes:
> Des ressorts inconnus agitent le vieillard,
> Et font de tous ses pas des miracles de l'art.
>
> (I.1.85-88)

At first, then, the magician is presented as what, to the spectator, he is—an actor; and the first level is established as an illusion.

Alcandre then assures Pridamant of his son's safety, honor and happiness, not to mention "sa fortune esclatante." Going on to mock the elaborate rituals of charlatan wizards, he knocks with his wand: "Il donne un coup de baguette & on tire un rideau derriere lequel sont en parade les plus beaux habits des Comediens" (stage direction, I.2). The purpose here, of course, is not simply to display the actors' costumes, but also to utilize the "traditional system of warning that a play is about to begin."[21] The spectator is thus involved with the second level of action, which concludes with the final "death" of Rosine and Clidamant, and the "abduction" of Ysabelle; here the curtain falls, according to the 1644 edition, and presumably the same direction applied in 1635.[22] When it opens again, it reveals the falsehood of this last part of Clindor's "life"—which represented his reality of the moment.

Alcandre, then, introduces the spectator to a play. He is first actor, then *metteur en scène,* and indeed playwright, since he selects what Pridamant is to see; but this choice, he reminds us, is made from life:

> Sous une illusion vous pourriez voir sa vie,
> Et tous ses accidens devant vous exprimez
> Par des spectres pareils à des corps animés:
> Il ne leur manquera ny geste ny parole.
>
> (I.2.150-53)

These "spectres parlans" will show Pridamant his son's life "en spectacle," and he must not be disturbed by what he sees, but remember that his son is now living in honor. He sunk fairly low before beginning his upward climb, however, even to the point of writing for a living: "Des chansons pour Gautier, des pointes pour Guillaume" (1. 181).

---

21. Ibid. p. 50.
22. See Garapon, *Illusion,* p. 116, note.

These names were surely intended to recall the immortal *farceurs* of the Hôtel de Bourgogne[23]—Corneille is maintaining the idea of spectacle at both primary and secondary levels. Furthermore, Alcandre reassures Pridamant (and the spectators) that eventually his son's present occupation will be unveiled in all its glory:

> Lors que de ses amours vous aurez veu l'histoire,
> Je vous le veux monstrer plein d'esclat et de gloire,
> Et la mesme action qu'il pratique aujourd'huy.
>
> (I.3.201-03)

This reassurance may come to mind at the end, when the spectator finds he has been completely fooled by the two illusions; confusing them with one another, that is, not with the first level of Pridamant and Alcandre.

At this point, the secondary level is established with the appearance of Clindor and his master, Matamore:

> . . . Voyez desja paroistre
> Sous deux fantosmes vains, vostre fils et son Maistre.
>
> (II.1.217-18)

Here too comes the catch to which I have referred, for the matamore, as Corneille himself remarked in his later *Examen*, is essentially a stage character, a character created to make an audience laugh, one for whom there is "point d'original parmy les hommes." Thus the reality that Alcandre is creating is still mixed with a stage pretense, a pretense submitted to the spectator as a real part of Clindor's life. The matamore is a kind of madman who creates himself and his own "reality" as he goes along:

> Et selon qu'il me plaist, je remplis tour à tour
> Les hommes de terreur, et les femmes d'amour.
>
> (II.2)

He lives out his fantasy completely. Clindor and Ysabelle both agree with his creation, and he takes them with utter seriousness. He has also a page, whose purpose is to bring him messages from various dignitaries. The spectator is fooled into believing that the theatrical matamore is a real madman. Even Clindor's irony may not suffice to make the spectator realize that his madness is contrived. The fantasy

23. Ibid., p. 16, n. 4.

of the tragedy played out in the last act intrudes on the reality of Alcandre's evocation.

And the matamore is not the only obviously theatrical element in
the play. What of Ysabelle and Clindor themselves? The lament of
Clindor in prison is the kind of standard piece any actor made part of
his repertory. Corneille commented (*Examen, Mélite*) that madness
was a favored condition because it offered the actor an opportunity
to show his virtuosity; D'Aubignac has applied the same complaint to
stances and other lengthy set speeches. The spectators have long
been familiar with the stage lament, as in *Les Bergeries; Pyrame et
Thisbé*; Auvray's *Dorinde,* where the hero, Sigismon, laments at
length as he languishes in prison; Scudéry's *Ligdamon et Lidias;*
Schélandre's *Tyr et Sidon* (1628), where Belcar bewails his imprisonment with even more gusto; and so on. In the *Examen* to *Clitandre,*
Corneille says that the title role of that play existed only "pour
déclamer en prison," and (as I have noted) he inserted monologues
only to satisfy the actors' desire to show their ability. Actresses, of
course, had their chance as well—Ysabelle's lament in *L'Illusion
comique* is the counterpart of Clindor's, and the other plays mentioned above contain similar examples.

The point here is not the indebtedness of Corneille to his predecessors, which is obvious and inevitable.[24] What should be noted is that
these patently theatrical devices, created to enable the actor to display his talents, are linked not with the final tragedy, but with the
apparent truth being presented by Alcandre. The spectators are intended to accept the reality of his evocation of Clindor's past life, despite these evidences of its unreal nature, and they endow the final
act—Nelson's third level—with that reality. It is not, clearly, so easily
distinguishable from illusion as one would have liked to think; the
two levels of Alcandre's conjuration remain one to the audience until he decides to separate them. It is indeed a play in which "Une
série de miroirs y recule au delà du réel une humanité romanesque et
baroque qui finit par s'effacer sous le fard et le masque tragique."[25]

The spectator does not really, as Garapon suggests,[26] come face to
face with "la plus stricte réalité," because that would entail his viewing

24. Ibid., pp. xxi-xlii, for a very complete examination of sources.
25. Octave Nadal, *Le Sentiment de l'amour dans l'oeuvre de Pierre Corneille*
(Paris, 1948), p. 118.
26. Garapon, *Illusion*, p. lvi.

Alcandre and Pridamant as actors, whereas in fact only those presented as actors all along actually play out their roles to the end. In the process, however, one does catch a glimpse of his own present reality—the reality Garapon has in mind. The question posed concerns, really, Nadal's mirrors: where do they stop? Indeed, where do they start? One is not a spectator only in an auditorium, but outside as well—how can one distinguish between the two kinds of observation?

What divides these plays from those discussed in the preceding chapter is that, while dealing with the problem of illusion and reality, they remain plays on the theater. The problem which in earlier plays was thrown into the audience is now pushed back into the play by a convenient frame. The spectator is now distanced from that problem; for, if he identifies with anyone, it can only be the characters on the first level, and (through Pridamant) perhaps with Clindor. However, this "second identification" cannot be continuous, for its theatrical nature holds it apart from the first level of the magician and father. In the plays of Scudéry and Gougenot the frame itself tends to waver and become confused on occasion with the picture it contains, where in Corneille's the frame consists of the continual visible presence of two characters watching the second action.

The spectator's "psychical distance," under these circumstances, no longer fluctuates, but remains constant. The playwright's former doubt as to the nature of reality and his own awareness of it is disappearing. He will now go on to create convincing characters whose problems—essentially moral and social—may become the spectator's own.

4. Spectacle and the Language of Illusion

The doctrine of verisimilitude and the problem of aesthetic distance

> La représentation n'est pas une sorte d'épisode qui s'ajoute à l'oeuvre; la représentation tient à l'essence meme du théâtre; l'oeuvre dramatique est faite pour être représentée: cette intention la définit.[1]

This essence of which Henri Gouhier speaks is the relatively simple notion that the theater has two attributes found in no other art simultaneously: it is both "présence et présent." It has the effect of a reality in action, because the actor is as real as the spectators; he is in fact present in their midst, and participates in an action which occurs before their eyes. Hence illusion is built into the theater, and the men of the theater need seek only the precise nature of the illusion they want to foster.

Since, of all the arts, the theater comes nearest to breaking down the barriers between illusion and reality, it is scarcely surprising that critics of all ages have paid it considerable attention, with the result that our heritage of writings on the theater is now inordinately large. Oddly enough, however, only very recently does one find any attempt to discover a complete aesthetic of the theater; perhaps, in France at least, Diderot was the first to do so.

Certainly, and evidently, most writings on the theater will contain some insight into the precise way it affects the spectator, but until the eighteenth century these were little more than slight interruptions in treatises on the rules of writing works of art. During the seventeenth century in France these insights were beginning to occupy such tracts more, while the craft of play-building took a proportionately smaller part (although the tracts themselves grew longer). Hence Bray, in his *Formation de la doctrine classique en*

1. Gouhier, *Essence*, p. 15.

France, was able to contrast the sixteenth century "arts poétiques" with the seventeenth century "théories poétiques." Summarizing his chapters on the origins and foundations of classical doctrine, Bray wrote: "L'instruction morale assignée comme but à la poésie, la foi dans l'art et dans la règle, le culte de la raison, les dogmes de l'imitation de la nature et de l'imitation des Anciens, voilà le credo de l'esthétique classique, les fondements de toute la doctrine."[2] These bases in no way amount to an aesthetic. They precede the work of art, describing how and why the work should be created, but they do not attempt to explain the possibly more complex problems which a complete aesthetic must pose on what happens to a work after its presentation to the public—or, even better, *during* its presentation to the public. These problems must be examined not only in terms of moral functions but also in the more delicate area of a psychological or aesthetic exchange between the work and the spectator. The question of how great a part such an exchange plays in the creation of the work of art affects not only its definition, but its very nature.[3]

If this chapter seems to emphasize critics of the second half of the seventeenth century, it is because I wish to arrive at a fair conception of the ideal being sought. Since the "theories" are for the most part descriptions rather than prophecies, the obvious source of this critical ideal is in the praise of a theater supposed to represent the perfection an earlier theater missed. The fame of Ogier's preface to Schélandre's *Tyr et Sidon* (1628) stemmed from its acute commentary on a theater then quite standard. During this early period one piece of truly subtle commentary takes the opposite position: Gombauld's extraordinary preface (1631) to *L'Amaranthe,* which, it should be noted, echoes to some extent Chapelain's *Lettre à Godeau sur les vingt-quatre heures* (Nov. 1630),[4] and which will be commented upon at greater length in Chapter 5. Scudéry's *Apologie* (1639) and la Mesnardière's *Poétique* (1640) preface a whole series of later theories which encompass D'Aubignac, Rapin, Boileau and the rest, and come after the emergence of this "new" theater from its earliest manifestations. Indeed, Scudéry's

2. Bray, *Formation,* p. 191.
3. See Jan Doat, *Entrée du public. La psychologie collective et le théâtre* (Paris, 1947), pp. 69-92.
4. See Antoine Adam, *Histoire de la littérature française au xviie siècle* (Paris, 1962-68), I, 442-46; and Bray, *Formation,* p. 75 and *passim.*

own doubts on the critical ideal are made clear by his contradiction of the *Apologie* in his 1641 preface to *Andromire*.

The basic general rule of classical doctrine was that of verisimilitude.[5] But, somewhat surprisingly, the relationship between play and spectator at this level is only slightly touched on and almost never clearly developed in the theoretical writings of the seventeenth century. Public opinion was the authors' guide, and public reaction served as a standard only to the extent that mores were not to be offended by the behavior of those on stage. Broadly speaking, verisimilitude was accepted as the mode in which the basic "credo" had to be cast in order to convince the public.

How little most theoreticians took into account the inclusion of the spectator in a kind of overall theatrical experience is demonstrated by the treatment of verisimilitude from Deimier (*Académie de l'Art poëtique* [1610]) to Chapelain, and through almost all the classical critics and theorists. The notion is reduced from Aristotle's belief that anything that appears possible or that one thinks is possible is good for the stage[6] to a belief essentially governed, as Bray puts it, by the notion of what is within reason. The simply possible gradually becomes scorned, and it is on these grounds (among others) that Scudéry, for example, criticizes *Le Cid*.

The critics often seem to confuse the imagination with the reasoning faculties. Mairet, for example, argues that the credibility of the stage action should not strain the imagination of the spectator. Since imagination does not enable one to jump temporal or spatial barriers (a function of memory) it should not be forced to attempt to do so by the nature of the play. If the spectator is made to create, as it were, his own verisimilitude, he will be too occupied to be moved by the play. The imagination must be helped into the illusion by *vraisemblance*, it should be able to accept the play as "real" from the outset, not impelled first to justify the illusion.[7] The implication of this approach is that the spectator must find the play credible so that he may more easily enter into the action. The changes I have ex-

---

5. Bray, *Formation,* pp. 191-214. For briefer comments, similar to my own, on this subject, see Jean Rousset, *L'Intérieur et l'extérieur. Essais sur la poésie et sur le théâtre au xviie siècle* (Paris, 1968), pp. 170-73.

6. Aristotle, *Poetics* 9.

7. Jean Mairet, préface to *Sylvanire,* éd. Richard Otto (Bamberg, 1890), pp. 16-17.

amined from Hardy's *Mariamne* and *Panthée* to Tristan's *Mariane* and *Panthée* are evidence of this effort.

This belief later becomes explicit in the claim that only when the emotions are deeply involved in the action can the moral teaching of the play truly be passed on to the spectator. Rapin, for whom "l'intention principale de cet Art est . . . de rendre agreable, ce qui est salutaire,"[8] continues to add some interesting thoughts.

> La Tragedie ne devient agreable au spectateur que parce qu'il devient luy-mesme sensible à tout ce qu'on luy represente, qu'il entre dans tous les differens sentimens des acteurs, qu'il s'interesse dans leurs avantures, qu'il craint, et qu'il espere, qu'il s'afflige, et qu'il rejoüit avec eux. Le theatre est froid et languissant, dés qu'il cesse de produire ces mouvemens dans l'ame de ceux qui y assistent . . . la crainte et la pitié sont celles qui font de plus grandes impressions sur le coeur de l'homme . . . En effet, dés que l'ame est ebranlée, par des mouvemens si naturels et si humains, toutes les impressions qu'elle ressent, luy deviennent agreables: Son trouble luy plaist, et ce qu'elle ressent d'emotion, est pour elle une espece de charme, qui la jette dans une douce et profonde resverie, et qui la fait entrer insensiblement dans tous les intérêts qui jouent sur le theatre. C'est alors que le coeur s'abandonne à tous les objets qu'on luy propose, que toutes les images le frappent, qu'il epouse les sentimens de tous ceux qui parlent, et qu'il devient susceptible à toutes les passions qu'on luy monstre: parce qu'il est émü.[9]

Rapin tells how this was the effect on the spectator when "Mondory joüoit la Mariamne de Tristan au Marais," and how "le peuple n'en sortoit jamais que resveur et pensif." It is clear that his ideal is a theater which, while emotionally placing the spectator in the play—not simply in sympathy with the characters but empathically involved in the action—also provokes him to reflect upon what he feels.

This does not mean that the intellect should meet with any appeal during the action of which it can be aware. On the contrary, Balzac, Sarrasin, Chapelin, La Mesnardière and the rest are all strongly opposed to any attempt to present ideas as such on the stage. The

8. Le père René Rapin, *Reflexions sur la poetique d'Aristote, et sur les ouvrages des poetes anciens et modernes* (Paris, 1674), p. 19.
9. Ibid., pp. 173-74.

moral teaching of the theater for them lies in the spectator's reflection
upon his emotions. Ideally, they see the spectator as totally involved
with a character:

> Enfin l'Auditeur honneste homme, et capable des bonnes choses,
> entre dans tous les sentimens de la Personne theatrale qui touche
> ses inclinations. Il s'afflige quand elle pleure; il est gay lorsqu'elle
> est contente; si elle gémit, il soupire; il frémit, si elle se fasche;
> bref il suit tous ses mouvemens, et il ressent que son coeur est
> comme un champ de bataille, où la science du Poëte fait combat-
> tre quand il luy plaist mille Passions tumultueuses, et plus fortes
> que la raison.[10]

This desire to cause the spectator to confuse his emotions with those
of the stage character is usually left implicit, but it can be seen at the
base of the varied suggestions intended to produce greater verisimilitude in the theater. Thus, like Voltaire a century later,[11] D'Aubignac,
La Mesnardière and Corneille all suggested that one ideal would be
for the author to have the actual time of the play coincide with the
supposed time of the action.[12] Corneille and La Mesnardière both
reason themselves toward the *drame bourgeois* on the same grounds
that Beaumarchais was later to use in his preface to *Eugénie:* that
spectators of a lower social status would identify more easily with
characters of their own level than with the more lofty ones of classical tragedy.[13]

10. Hippolyte-Jules de la Mesnardière, *La Poetique* (Paris, 1640), p. 74; see
also D'Aubignac, *Pratique,* pp. 314-15.

11. See Voltaire's *Discours de la tragédie* (preceding *Brutus*) in his *Oeuvres
complètes* (Genève, 1775), II, 266.

12. "Il seroit meme à souhaitter que l'action du Poëme ne demandast pas
plus de temps dans la verité que celuy qui se consume dans la représentation"
(D'Aubignac, *Pratique,* p. 123). See also La Mesnardière, *La Poetique,* p. 48,
and Corneille, *III*^{e} *Discours* and the *Examen* of *La Veuve.* As André Villiers
explains it, "[O]n ne vit vraiment dans le présent avec 'l'autre' que dans la
même durée; ainsi, pour revivre pleinement un épisode du passé, cherche-t-on
autant que possible à recréer l'évocation dans les mêmes conditions de durée"
("Illusion dramatique et dramaturgie classique," *XVII*^{e} *Siècle,* LXXIII [1966],
21).

13. Corneille, preface to *Don Sanche;* La Mesnardière, *La Poetique,* p. N.

These suggestions, like so many others,[14] all have as their aim the intermingling of the spectator's emotions with those on the stage. Recently this relationship between stage and public has been considered by philosophers, psychologists and critics as well as theatrical directors and others. Unfortunately, in most cases they[15] approach the problem with a definite bias in favor of some particular type of theater, which takes many of their essays out of the area of description and into that of dogma, leading simply to distortion. The one significant exception is M. Gouhier, but he is viewing the question from an angle somewhat different from mine, being concerned with the theater in more general terms than this essay claims to be.

Most modern western theater has, until recently, tended toward a reduction of psychical distance—toward making the theater as illusionistic as possible—despite the fact that, historically, this type of theater is the most unusual. Oriental theater is much more ritualistic and stylized, and the entire event seems to have more importance than what is presented on the stage alone. The use of music and dance, of stylized movement and makeup, the wearing of masks and so on are all devices which take the spectator beyond the mere stage presentation by bringing to his attention the ceremonial nature of the event of which he is a part. They make him look for what is behind and beyond the symbolism. In this sense eastern theater is not very different from that of ancient Greece or the mystery plays of the European Middle Ages.

It remains to be seen whether the contemporary ferment in almost all of western theater will achieve its aim of complete participation by the audience in the theatrical event. In all the modern experiments, whatever the precise framework—theater-in-the-round, actors in the

14. See, for example, Villiers on physical perspective: "La science impose une nouvelle manière de voir. Satisfait de la justification des lois de l'apparence par la représentation géométrique de l'espace selon les lois optiques, on exige plus encore: la soumission des données parfois trompeuses des sens aux rectificatifs de la raison" ("Illusion dramatique," p. 9).

15. Works by men of the theater containing remarks on this problem include Antonin Artaud, *Le Théâtre et son double* (Paris, 1964); Jean-Louis Barrault, *Réflexions sur le théâtre* (Paris, 1949); Louis Jouvet, *Réflexions du comédien* (Paris, 1952); Pierre-Aymé Touchard, *Dionysos: Apologie pour le théâtre* (Paris, 1949); and Jean Vilar, *De la Tradition théâtrale* (Paris, 1963 [first published 1955]).

audience, spectators on the stage, a barrage of stylized theater forms mixed with propaganda (as presented by the San Francisco Mime Troupe) and so on—the goal is to transcend the devices of the theater by making them as apparent to the spectator as they are to the actor. In this way, ideally, all participants may achieve some kind of "common communication" unattainable through a traditional performance.

This was, as I have noted, what apparently occurred in Hardy's theater. His style, however, emerged at a time when an audience capable of sharing in the occasion, and willing to participate, was on the verge of disappearance. This same change in audience would help explain the very radical changes that occurred in the *ballet de cour*[16] and the disappearance of the old style of farce. The contemporary western theater has not yet found—or produced—such a participatory audience.

While illusion, the reduction of distance, was the general aim, the theater relied perhaps on the de facto unreality of the theatrical situation itself (its being in a theater, on a stage) to maintain a distance. Still, Fielding's Partridge (who goes into a veritable trance at a performance of Shakespeare) may be more common than Büdel[17] supposes: his rarity is denied by examples ranging from Stendhal's tale of the soldier at Baltimore who actually shot at an actor playing Othello as he was about to kill Desdemona[18] to the child at a pantomime who shouts a warning to Whittington as King Rat approaches him from behind. For my present purpose, there is an even more significant example in D'Aubignac's *Pratique du théatre;* the critic praises Théophile's *Pyrame et Thisbé* for the emotion aroused as Pyrame goes to kill himself bewailing Thisbé whom he believes dead: "[J]'ay veu dans cette occasion une jeune fille qui n'avoit encore jamais esté à la Comédie, dire à sa Mere, Qu'il falloit l'avertir que sa Maistresse n'estoit pas morte; tant il est vray que ce moment portoit

---

16. See Appendix 2.

17. See Oscar Büdel, "Contemporary Theater and Aesthetic Distance," *PMLA,* LXXVI, 3 (1961), 277.

18. Stendhal, *Racine et Shakespeare,* in *Oeuvres complètes,* éd. Georges Eudes, 25 vols. (Paris, 1946-56), XVI, p. 15. See also P. A. Michelis, "Aesthetic Distance and the Charm of Contemporary Art," *Journal of Aesthetics and Art Criticism,* XXVIII, 1 (Sept. 1959), 3.

les Spectateurs dans les interests de ce Personnage!"[19] This seems to be the moment of identification urged by the classical critics—not for its own sake, as in Rapin and La Mesnardière, but because later it will make the spectator meditate. This, too, is the opinion of Giraudoux in the *Impromptu de Paris,* where Jouvet tells the spectator (who goes through all kinds of mental and physical contortions while watching a play in order to understand it), "Ne vous donnez pas ce mal, cher Monsieur. Vous n'avez qu'à attendre, vous le saurez demain!"

·To achieve this empathy the play must maintain an even tone. If any incident or action, speech, or spectacle is presented to the spectator which does not fit the general tone of the play—if, for example, a violently realistic murder is suddenly introduced into a fairy tale, or an overly realistic piece of scenery is added to a stylized set—then the spell is immediately broken. The emotions may remain involved, but the judgment will withdraw as from a sudden absurdity (this being one of the comic principles).

The principal unity advocated by the French classical critics is essentially an unstated one: the unity of tone.[20] For it was the ideal of the classical theorists that psychical distance should be closed, so that the ideas and emotions of the poet might gain complete control over the spectator. Afterwards this spectator might break them down again to their moral and social precepts:

> Comme la pierre d'Aymant communique sa vertu au fer qui l'aproche, et ce fer à l'autre fer qui le touche ensuite; de mesme dans les Poëmes dramatiques, les passions bien representées, ayant premierement atteint le Poëte, passent de luy à l'Actuer qui recite, et de l'acteur au peuple qui l'escoute.[21]

This is how the theater "conduit les hommes vers l'instruction, feignant de ne les mener qu'au divertissement," adds Scudéry. The illusion of truth must be created in this way so that the spectator's knowledge is

19. D'Aubignac, *Pratique,* pp. 333-34. The abbé is actually criticizing the long speech which precedes this death and wishing that Théophile had been capable of sustaining the spectators' identification.

20. See particularly, on this "cohérence," although in a different context, the introduction to Judd Hubert's excellent volume, *Essai d'exégèse racinienne: les secrets témoins* (Paris, 1956).

21. Georges de Scudéry, *L'Apologie du théâtre* (Paris, 1639), pp. 6-7.

finally rendered the more intense. The author has to bring the spectator to the very situation and sentiments that he himself underwent and felt at the moment of creation; he has to make him feel with the stage characters.

It is as though the playwright were forcing the spectator to go through his own process of creation in reverse. This intensity of the spectator's feeling, the search for the total closing of this distance, is summed up by Rapin when he remarks that "une passion imparfaite et avortée peut ébranler l'esprit de l'auditeur: et cela ne suffit pas, il faut l'enlever."[22] Even as the critics strove to remove all obstacles to the reduction of distance, they realized full well that the removal of scenic and spectacular barriers did not suffice: language could become a more subtle barrier, one far more difficult to overcome.

Language and transparency

Given that the aim of the theater as seen by the classical theorists is instruction through pleasure by means both "subtiles" and "delicates,"[23] it is clear that they wanted maxims, aphorisms and all rhetorical turns of language ultimately banished from the theater. Naturally, it was impossible that the theorists should have their way entirely: in a theater whose dramatists were for the most part poets first and foremost, in an age when the more sophisticated segments of society were almost excessively conscious of language, there was bound to be an occasional "récit de Théramène" even in the most serious theater.

Strictures on language, perhaps for this reason, did not come until somewhat later than other classical demands. Although La Mesnardière did devote a chapter to problems of language—in which, with many examples, he made a case for a more austere use of it[24]— in the main, as far as critics of the theater are concerned at least, it was not until the 1670s, with Saint-Evremond and Rapin in particular, that rules were actually prescribed. Saint-Evremond, referring

---

22. Rapin, *Réflexions*, p. 99.

23. Jean-Louis Guez de Balzac, "Responce a deux questions. Ou du caractere et de l'instruction de la comedie," in *Oeuvres diverses du sieur de Balzac* (Paris, 1664), p. 86.

24. La Mesnardière, "Le langage. Quatrieme partie de la tragedie," in *La Poetique*, pp. 325-409.

specifically to the pre-classical theater, complains that the dramatists
pay insufficient attention to demands of the stage and to the need
for realism so that the spectator may identify. For, he says, if a
lament goes on too long (as in the example D'Aubignac cited from
Pyrame et Thisbé, and particularly if it is too stylish, the spectator
can no longer "become" the character or identify with the action.

> Quelquefois l'esprit du spectateur qui poussoit d'abord son
> imagination jusqu'à la personne qu'on represente, revient à soi-
> meme, desabusé qu'il est, et ne connoit plus que le poëte, qui,
> dans une espèce d'élégie, nous veut faire pleurer de la douleur
> qu'il a feinte, ou qu'il s'est formée.[25]

This passage is particularly interesting because it shows a perfect understanding of Bullough's "psychical distance" and reveals quite
clearly that the classical theorists wished to keep it as unobtrusive
as possible and to prevent its fluctuation. Saint-Evremond demands that the artist withdraw completely to allow the spectator
to identify with the character; anything less will strike him as ridiculous:

> Un homme se mécompte de moi, en ces occasions; il tombe dans
> le ridicule, quand il prétend me donner de la pitié. Je trouve
> plus ridicule encore qu'on fasse l'éloquent, à se plaindre de ses
> malheurs. Celui qui prend la peine d'en discourir, m'épargne
> celle de l'en consoler. C'est la nature qui souffre, c'est à elle de
> se plaindre: elle cherche quelquefois à dire ce qu'elle sent, pour
> se soulager; non pas à le dire éloquemment, pour se complaire . . .
>   Je suis aussi peu persuadé de la violence d'une passion qui est
> ingénieuse à s'exprimer par la diversité des pensées. Une âme
> touchée sensiblement ne laisse pas à l'esprit la liberté de penser
> beaucoup, et moins encore de se divertir dans la variété de ses
> conceptions.[26]

The "transparency" of language in the classical theater is actually
as illusory as the world represented on the stage, for that world is
created within and by the language itself. Unlike the theater of the

25. Charles de Saint-Evremond, "Sur le caractère des tragédies" (1672),
in *Oeuvres melées*, éd. Charles Giraud, 3 vols. (Paris, 1865), I, 338.
  26. Ibid., p. 338. See also Rapin, *Réflexions*, p. 181.

previous generation, the spectacular aspect of the theatrical production
was gradually reduced until, with Racine most evidently, the complete
lack of all but the most general scenic indications forced language to
translate what was lacking in physical presence on the stage into a
mental image for the spectator.

In such a theater language is transparent in a sense different from
that used by Starobinski in talking of Rousseau's frustrations, where
ideally language reveals the speaker's feelings.[27] Here language is
forced to use the fact that it is an obstacle (in a sense) to complete
understanding: it no longer tries to act as a bridge to certain actions
or to a sense that lies behind it, but rather produces, at its own level,
a sense, a series of images, of sentiments and ideas, which go to make
up the whole play. Language, in the fullest sense, means what it says.
Yet it must give the spectator the *impression* of effacing itself before
character.

Since there is no action going on outside the language, the mere
amassing of tropes would reduce the play to nothing, presenting the
spectator with no single action. If everything had as many meanings
as the poet cared to give it, the audience could no longer follow the
plot, at least in the sense that they sought to follow it. This multiple
level in the theater is precisely what Boileau is complaining of in *L'Art
poétique,* when, speaking of the old pastoral, he comments:

> On vit tous les bergers, dans leurs plaintes nouvelles,
> Fideles à la pointe, encor plus qu'à leurs belles;
> Chaque mot eut toujours deux visages divers.
>
> (11.350-52)

The "baroque" theater, on the contrary, uses language quite dif-
ferently. With ample movement, color, and spectacle, language becomes a counterpoint to the action. As I have indicated, what is carried over the footlights in terms of language may well be something
other than what is implied by the action and setting. Since there is
spectacle, a set in which action may take place, there is a constant
which the spectator may recognize, and around which language may
weave all kinds of patterns. Here ambiguity may be rampant, whereas in the classical theater clarity must come first.

27. Jean Starobinski, *Jean-Jacques Rousseau: la transparence et l'obstacle*
(Paris, 1957).

While the classical audience receives a single impression, being virtually forced to take up a certain attitude, the pre-classical spectator is divided between the visual and the aural. Receiving two (or more) impressions at once, he is unable to identify in the same way as his successor *with a character*. Under these circumstances, the author may present a spectacle in opposition to the language. There may often be a separation of theme and action not found in the classical theater.

Both the baroque and classical theaters create unreal worlds (as by definition any theater must), which are seen by the spectator as either real or illusory. The difference between them is less a matter of theatrical means of expression than of the attitudes toward the relationship between language and theme. The world created by the theater of the second half of the century is one of themes; it exists only by virtue of the translation into action of themes which in fact exist only through the language which translates them.[28] Language, action and themes cannot be played off against one another simply because the first is the medium for the other two. On the other hand, in the theater of the first half of the century the action does not necessarily coincide with the themes the dramatist is treating, and the movements of language are not necessarily due to the exigencies of either the action or the themes. The set seems often to have been a deliberate obstacle to the spectator's entry into the stage world.

The earlier creation seems to be admirably suited to the *Weltanschauung* of the baroque (or "mannerist?") artists and, in one sense at least, is not so far from the theater of the Middle Ages (I am thinking particularly of the mysteries, although its manner has certain similarities with the lower levels of theater). It regularly attempts to encompass far more than one man's actions, not by analogously raising them to a higher plane as the classical theater does, but by weaving them into a multiplicity of patterns. Its special theme seems to be, in fact, the problem of the nature of reality: hence the madness, the magic events, the disguises, the misunderstandings, the rapidly changing scenes, and so on. Under these conditions, one man's character is a part of the situation and is important only insofar as it helps to reveal that situation.

28. See La Mesnardière, *La Poetique*, pp. 12-13.

The classical theater, on the contrary, uses character as the starting point of the action, making it responsible for any peripeteia, as well as for the final outcome. Naturally, I do not mean to imply that the classical theater does not have illusion as a theme. But its treatment starts at a psychological level and can be raised to the metaphysical only if the spectator happens to think along such lines.

Even in its comedies the classical theater is quite serious: it may mock character, but only very rarely will it laugh at itself. Self-mockery, on the other hand, is the very marrow of the pre-classical stage. It treats the problem of illusion and all its implications as a game, whatever seriousness lies behind it; and these implications are certainly consciously envisioned. This is probably the reason why, during the 1630s, so many plays appeared whose main concern was with the nature of the theater itself.

The difference between the two theaters may be briefly indicated here by comparing Rotrou's *Saint-Genest* with his *Venceslas* and *Cosroès.* The last two start with a character and deal with themes, on the surface at least, eminently material and social. Their plots, far from being separate elements, exist only as a function of the themes: each involves a conflict between power, love, and duty in a clearly understandable situation. *Saint-Genest* starts from a situation and sets out to confuse the spectator just as it confuses the characters themselves. Its theme, if relatively clear, is much broader and tries to reveal more about "man in the universe" than about man in a social situation. *Saint-Genest,* however, has lost the gaiety of the game, which is perhaps why, although it is the masterpiece of the baroque theater, it is unique. Whatever the reason, no other play of so broad a theme with such continuous gravity and without a character with whom to identify came to join it. Perhaps *Athalie* is nearest to it, but the differences are greater than the similarities.

How far the classical theorists had moved from this concept of theater by the end of the century, and how successful they were, is made clear by Bossuet's objections to the stage: not on the grounds of immorality (always a fine excuse for church condemnations), but because the spectator is made to feel spurious emotions, which whether sinful or not by nature are sinful because false. In one of his sermons, speaking of the frame of mind the listener should be in for a sermon, he complains, after Saint Jean Chrysostome, that people often listen to sermons as though to a play:

Comme je rencontrois souvent ce reproche dans ses divines prédi-
cations, j'ai voulu rechercher attentivement quel pouvoit être le
fond de cette pensée, et voici ce qu'il m'a semblé: c'est qu'il y a
des spectacles qui n'ont pour objet que le divertissement de
l'esprit, mais qui n'excitent pas les affections, qui ne remuent pas
les ressorts du coeur. Mais il n'en est pas de la sorte de *ces repré-
sentations animées qu'on donne sur les théatres, dangéreuses en
ce point, qu'elles ne plaisent point si elles n'émeuvent, si elles
n'intéressent le spectateur, si elles ne lui font jouer aussi son
personnage, sans être de l'action et sans monter sur le théâtre.*
C'est en quoi ces spectacles sont à craindre, parce que le coeur
apprend insensiblement à se remuer de bonne foi. Il est donc
ému, il est transporté, il se réjouit, il s'afflige de choses qui au
fond sont indifférentes. Mais une marque certaine que ces mouvemens ne tiennent pas au coeur, c'est qu'ils s'évanouissent en
changeant de lieu. Cette pitié qui causoit des larmes, cette colère
qui enflammoit et les yeux et le visage, n'étoient que *des images
et des simulacres par lesquels le coeur se donne la comédie en
lui-même, qui produisoient toutefois les memes effets que les passions véritables;* tant il est aisé de nous imposer, tant nous aimons
à nous jouer nous-mêmes [italics mine].[29]

Elsewhere he complains that because of the presence of the actor on
the stage, these passions touch us all the more. They become "de
vrais mouvemens, qui mettent en feu tout le parterre et toutes les
loges"; the mind and spirit, he says, are laid open to "d'imperceptibles
insinuations."[30] When he speaks of the sinful nature of these emotions themselves, their falsity supposedly put aside, he returns continually to the same reasoning, here applied to *Le Cid:*

Dites-moi, que veut un Corneille dans son *Cid*, sinon qu'on aime
Chimène, qu'on l'adore avec Rodrigue, qu'on tremble avec lui
lorsqu'il est dans la crainte de la perdre, et qu'avec lui on s'estime
heureux lorsqu'il espère de la posséder? Si l'acteur ne sait pas in-
téresser le spectateur, l'émouvoir, le transporter de la passion qu'il

29. Jacques-Bénigne Bossuet, "Sermon pour le iie dimanche de Carème,"
in *Oeuvres complètes*, éd. P. Lachat, 31 vols. (Paris, 1862-66), IX, 129.
    30. Bossuet, "Maximes et réflexions sur la comédie," *Oeuvres*, XXVII, 25
and 40.

a voulu exprimer, ou tombe-t-il, si ce n'est dans le froid, dans l'ennuyeux, dans l'insupportable, si on peut parler de cette sorte?[31]

Thus, for Bossuet, the problem (from a religious point of view) is not simply that what is presented on stage, or the whole outlook of the acting profession, is sinful: it is that the spectator is made to *feel* emotions and to share actions that are possibly sinful but certainly false. He is complaining of the very thing for which the classical theorists were striving throughout the second two-thirds of the century.

The dangers and values of spectacle

The difference in the concepts of the theatrical relationship between the classical critics of an illusionistic stage and the early authors of a "dialectic" theater is evidence of a difference in general outlook:

> C'est peu de dire qu'une certaine manière de voir, de contempler, d'estimer temps et espace, est impliquée par les règles dramaturgiques et les impositions du jeu et de son instrument. C'est la nature meme de l'échange entre acteur et spectateur qui est en cause, un type de participation.[32]

The type of theater which attempts to place the spectator "dans l'acte même"[33] removes the barrier to his "identifying," enabling him to establish more direct contact with the stage characters. This essentially is the significance of Jouvet's tale about Auguste Renoir, who, as a child, was upset by the use of a real piano as a stage prop; for, says Jouvet, the different types of illusion, in opposition to one another, destroyed the effect of either.[34] The "palais à volonté" became the habitual scenic instruction of the classical theater, because it removed all the barriers which were the chief concern of the classical theorists. To begin with, the spectator was obliged to pursue a character across many countries, to watch him gain several years in the course of a play, to follow him and others through multiple criss-crossing per-

31. Letter from Bossuet to le père Caffaro, *Oeuvres,* XXVII, 4; see also "Maximes et réflexions," p. 23.
32. Villiers, "Illusion dramatique," p. 4.
33. Doat, *Entrée,* p. 59.
34. Jouvet, *Témoignages sur le théâtre* (Paris, 1952), pp. 157-62.

sonal relationships, to accept the most fantastic of situations and events, whether supernatural or terrestrial. When, in addition, he was expected, at the level of language, to comprehend many meanings and infinite slight nuances expressed in the most varied of tones (to a point where a live encounter in terms of the stage action might become an essentially literary exercise contradicting that very action), then that spectator found it impossible to enter the action as the classical spectator could.

It is this very variety which makes it possible for communication of quite a different kind to occur. Unable to communicate empathically with a character, or with an action, the spectator becomes a part of a theatrical situation somewhat in the sense meant by Sartre in the above-mentioned article.[35] For while the fluctuating tone, the spectacle, scenic effects and so on will reduce the characters as often as not to so many puppets, with whom identification is not possible, yet these "barriers" are part and parcel of another type of theater. They can be used to set up different levels of illusion by which the playwright achieves a fluctuating "psychical distance" or "theatrical distancing." The spectator, urged into comprehension at one level and abruptly faced with a situation properly belonging at a different level, is obliged to abandon the assumptions and anticipations at which he has comfortably arrived.

In such a theater the problem of illusion and reality becomes a principal theme (and perhaps the very reason for its existence in the first place) to a degree where the play itself finally becomes its own theme. The spectator's empathy with a character for a moral purpose is of no interest to the playwright, who is concerned with placing him in a situation more metaphysical than social (although it will obviously have social overtones and will often throw doubt on social mores).

This wish to express the human condition on stage, rather than simply a small part of it from which moral instruction may be drawn, is expressed by Ogier in his preface to Schélandre's *Tyr et Sidon* (1628):

> . . . car de dire qui est mal seant [sic] de faire paroistre en une mesme pièce les mesmes personnes, traitant tantost d'affaires

---

35. Sartre, "Forgers of Myths."

serieuses, importantes et tragiques, et incontinent après de choses
communes, vaines et comiques, c'est ignorer la condition de la vie
des hommes, de qui les jours et les heures sont bien souvent entre-
coupés de ris et de larmes, de contentement et d'affliction, selon
qu'ils sont agitez de la bonne ou de la mauvaise fortune.[36]

Such a theater includes the spectator in the way sought by Baty and
Jouvet, among others: "Il s'agit pour lui [le metteur en scène] de ré-
aliser sur la scène le songe d'un univers expressif et cohérent et de
provoquer dans la salle une hallucination collective." So says Baty,
while Jouvet, focusing on the effect of having spectators seated on
the stage (which he dates from the Middle Ages), makes an illuminating comment on the nature of theatrical verisimilitude, and one of
particular significance in the present context:

> Dans cette intimité et cette familiarité du spectateur, la conven-
> tion théatrale m'apparait plus pure et le sens de la cérémonie plus
> impérieux. Le rapprochement du spectateur et des acteurs, cette
> proximité des artifices du spectacle obligent l'esprit à les vérifier
> et à trouver leur signification.
>
> Les règles de ce noble jeu qui est le théatre, me semblent plus
> *strictes sur cette scène* qui tient encore de l'estrade et où la véri-
> table illusion, celle que créent l'auteur et les spectateurs, se moque
> de la fausse illusion de la vraisemblance.[37]

One is almost tempted to say that in such a theater the principal
theme will *always* be the conflict of illusion and reality. Certainly
there will tend to be a preoccupation with subjects on which a
permanent judgment is impossible, either because they deny social
morality, or because they cannot be judged in accordance with that
morality. And the frequently amoral nature of this type of theater
often draws the ire of critics, especially those who firmly advocate
the doctrine of verisimilitude.

During the seventeenth century, critical emphasis gradually shifted
from satisfaction of the eyes and ears toward a plea for upsetting the
emotions. The spectator of a classical play, critics felt, should leave
the playhouse reflecting on the unease of his emotions; his predeces-

36. Jean Ogier, preface to Schélandre's *Tyr et Sidon,* in *Ancien théâtre
français,* VIII, 20.
37. Gaston Baty, *Rideau baissé*, p. 219; Louis Jouvet, *Réflexions,* p. 147.

sor was supposed to leave contemplating a kind of allegorical revelation of the human condition. The comment of the one must be closely bound with social mores, that of the other must be free to show the wider context of those mores. In a sense, the later theater will seek to demonstrate the perils of deviation from a set social code, while the earlier reflects an era when a definite code of morality had yet to be formed, and is the mirror of its uncertainty. The essence of the baroque theater clearly does not lie in the classical type of psychological movements, but rather in its varied spectacle:

> La poesie, et particulierement celle qui est composée pour le théatre, n'est faite que pour le plaisir et le divertissement, et ce plaisir ne peut proceder que de la varieté des evenements qui s'y representent.[38]

In these terms Ogier, once again, praises this variety not simply because it contents the spectator, but because it is a reflection of life.

38. Ogier, in *Ancien théâtre français*, VIII, p. 13. I do not wish to imply that the playwrights were necessarily consciously adopting a particular theatrical style in full awareness of what the times demanded. A successful theater is always to some extent the result of a semi-conscious response by the stage to the audience—and vice versa. The various types of theater of the early seventeenth century cannot be as clearly separated as this sketch would seem to imply, and the greatest of baroque plays is probably Rotrou's *Saint-Genest*, which did not appear until 1645. Similarly, the first classical plays—in tone, at least—appeared in the early 1630s. Nor did the generation of 1630 produce its theater in a void: the early plays of Mairet, the theater of Hardy, the translations of the Italian pastorals, had already aroused in the public certain exigencies, to which the theater of the 1630s was the response.

5. Corneille from *Mélite* to *Horace:*
The Spectator and Character[1]

> Je sçay bien que le theatre
> est une espèce d'illusion,
> mais il faut tromper les
> Spectateurs en telle sorte,
> qu'ils ne s'imaginent pas
> i'estre, encore qu'ils le
> sçachent; il ne faut pas
> tandis qu'on les trompe, que
> leur esprit le connoisse; mais
> seulement quand il y fait réflexion.
> (D'Aubignac, *Pratique du théâtre,*
> III.4.210).

The concern with language which Corneille manifests in his later years as a critic of his own theater does not simply reflect his awareness that his plays are not geared to the critical tastes of 1660 audiences. In the *Au lecteur* before *Mélite* in 1633, he remarks that in publishing the play he is at a disadvantage before the public because of his peculiar style: "simple et familiere." This suggestion of a conflict between his style and the taste of his contemporaries is the clue to a struggle between two forms of language which characterizes his early plays, and whose resolution is of immense importance not only to Corneille's own theater, but to that of the following century.

I have already shown how a literary, metaphorical language is perhaps the principal of those warring elements which compose the early seventeenth-century French theater, by virtue of its ability to create or destroy at the playwright's will (and perhaps, more often, his whim) characters and the situations surrounding them. As the madman in Du Ryer's *Argenis* comments upon his "borrowing" of Poliarque's name and person:

1. The first part of this chapter recently appeared in slightly different form in *Yale French Studies,* XLV (1970), and I thank the editors for permission to reprint it here.

> Ie l'ay trop bien acquis [,] la mesme renommee
> A force d'en parler s'est presque consommee.
>
> (*Derniere iournée*, I.5)

While *La Veuve* (1631) and *La Galerie du Palais* (1632/33) seem strongly concerned with literature as an external, distinctly self-conscious interest of the characters, at least two of the plays which immediately preceded and followed them—*Mélite* (1629) and *La Place royalle* (1633)—make this concern a central preoccupation. So significant does it become, indeed, that each play may be seen as an attempt to destroy a certain style of literary language with, as Corneille himself puts it, something more familiar. The staged destruction of literary themes and characters, by forcing the spectator to view them as the literary devices they are, is (as I have shown in previous chapters) by no means unique to Corneille. In his plays, however, the conflict responsible for this destruction does seem to progress toward a résolution more systematically than in the works of others.

The stage character of the time is supplied with an artificial, conventional language (a mask paralleled by a scenic one, as in *La Place royalle*). The playwright may use this language in two ways: either the character himself is aware of its artificiality, viewing it from an objective distance, like the spectator; or the character is presented as an obviously literary figure, whose language is equally stereotyped. Corneille uses both these characters in one play, and it is this juxtaposition which allows the development I would like to follow here. If the first character is to find a language which will enable him to express himself, he must destroy the one he has been given—and, in the process, destroy the literary character who plays opposite him.

At the outset of *Mélite,* Tirsis responds to Eraste's laments concerning his unrequited love for Mélite with considerable cynicism:

> Ces visages d'esclat sont bons à cajoler,
> C'est-là qu'un jeune oiseau doit s'apprendre à parler,
> J'ayme à remplir de feux ma bouche en leur presence,
> La mode nous oblige à ceste complaisance,
> Tous ces discours de livre alors sont de saison,
> Il faut feindre du mal, demander guerison.
>
> (I.1.59-64)

As Van Roosbroeck has observed,[2] with these lines Eraste and
Philandre become comic figures: their protestations of love are so
literary as to seem false. These characters do not adapt to life; rather,
they mouth endlessly the phrases of *précieux* romance. To the spectator they become simply images impressed on a situation. At this
point Tirsis appears as the destroyer of the fantasy Eraste and
Philandre are trying to create for themselves and for the spectator.
He is a foil for the unreality of their characters. What Van Roosbroeck
does not make clear, however, is that Tirsis, a little later, is himself on
the verge of accepting this fantasy when he speaks with Mélite in
terms approaching preciosity (II.8; V.4), although he seems to back
away from it. He is always on the point of accepting a character whose
ridiculous essence he has just revealed to the spectator; he seems to
fluctuate between illusion and a kind of reality. There can be little
doubt that both Eraste and Philandre are completely unreal, at least
before the former's mad confession; with Tirsis the case is more difficult. His stage character is never quite destroyed, yet neither is it completely assured, and the spectator's view of him fluctuates as a result.

   After being mocked by Tirsis, Eraste goes off to see Mélite, who will
also enjoy herself at his expense. He protests his love for her, and she,
who has just echoed Tirsis's cynicism, mocks his love—but in his own
terms:

ERASTE: Vostre divin aspect suspendant mes douleurs
          Mon visage du vostre emprunte les couleurs.
MÉLITE: Faites mieux, pour finir vos maux et vostre flamme
          Empruntez tout d'un temps les froideurs de mon ame.
                                              (I.2.167-70)

The language seems to be bent inward upon itself, revealing a coher-
ence and self-sufficiency which make a mockery of its intended significance. Mélite pretends to accept the terms of Eraste's fantasy,
only to refute them. The language is detached from the reality it supposedly represents, its own metaphors separate it from its intended
meaning. Even the sub-plot serves this demonstration. Cloris seems
to accept Philandre's game (I.4), but the detachment of language from

   2. Gustave L. Van Roosbroeck, "Preciosity in Corneille's Early Plays,"
Philological Quarterly, VI, 1 (Jan. 1927), 27.

reality is reflected in the easy separation of these two "lovers": the love which their language supposedly expresses is in fact absent.

The terms of preciosity never correspond to their surface meaning, but hover above it, playing with it. At times, the irony becomes more direct, as when Cloris remarks

> A travers tes discours si remplis d'artifice
> Je descouvre le but de ton intention.
>
> (290-91)

Further satire is provided with the banter of Tirsis, who reduces the lovers' precious sentiments to their inherent meaning. He happens to enter as they kiss, and feels obliged to "excuse" the importunacy of his arrival: "Vous feries mieux un tiers, que d'en accepter un" (I.5.340). Their fantasy is abruptly joined with the reality that lies beneath it, and is thus destroyed. The spectator is then enabled to view the lovers from a proper perspective, for while Cloris accepts this mocking destruction with small protest, Philandre attempts to continue the fantasy, hoping for marriage. Thus he merits a parting shot from Tirsis:

> Sa nuit est bien plustost ce que vous attendez,
> Pour vous recompensez du temps que vous perdez.
>
> (I.5.375-76)

By suppressing the sexual connotation of these lines in the 1660 edition, Corneille considerably reduced the opposition between reality and literary fantasy which is of prime importance to the play (originally entitled *Mélite ou les Fausses Lettres*).

Eraste, jealous of Tirsis's apparent success with Mélite, decides that if he cannot have her, then neither can his rival. With this in mind, he writes letters to Philandre which are purportedly from her, relying on him to show them to Tirsis. Philandre does, and Tirsis is left lamenting Mélite's infidelity. But he has doubts as to the truth of these letters, thinking they are perhaps only a literary device: "Caracteres trompeurs vous me contez des fables" (III.3.972). He is a little like a modern cartoon character who, playing with a ball, tosses it out of the picture's frame.

For the present, Tirsis accepts the letters and decides to retreat to "quelque lieu desert," there to die. If this were to happen it would signify the death of the reality he represents; the fantasy of preciosity, the deceit of literature in the letters, would have won. But the letters are defeated by yet another literary device: madness.

This victory for reality is echoed by Cloris when she dismisses Philandre for his infidelity (he proposed to make the most of the avowals in the false letters). To his continued cooing, she replies:

> Laisse là desormais ces petits mots de flame,
> Et par ces faux temoings d'un feu mal allumé
> Ne me reproche plus que je t'ay trop aymé.
>
> (V.3.1748-50)

Tirsis and Mélite also decide to do away with all "faux temoings," as the former says:

> Ne parlons plus d'ennuys, de tourmens, de tristesses,
> Et changeons en baisers ces traits d'oeil langoureux,
> Qui ne font qu'irriter nos desirs amoureux.
> . . . .
> Il faut un aliment plus solide à nos flames
> Par où nous unissions nos bouches et nos ames.
>
> (V.4.1792-1804)

While Eraste, who finally repents his falsehoods, is given to Cloris, it is suggested with a laugh that the main representative of the lie—the Nourrice, who has acted as the go-between throughout—should be linked in marriage with the caricature-like Philandre. Her final diatribe against the young lovers (which they do not hear), if not actually representing Lawrence Harvey's "definitive separation of two incompatible attitudes," nonetheless amounts to a "final reiteration of the basic conflict of the comedy."[3] Because this speech is a re-iteration, and the final word of the play, it leaves the spectator more aware of the precariously temporary nature of the separation than of the triumph of "real" love.

In *La Place royalle* the opposition is stronger and the final separation more permanent. The two uses of language are embodied in the two main characters, Alidor and Angelique, and for the first time Corneille sets up a conflict between them. Alidor is seeking a firm freedom in reality, and his love belongs there with him. Angelique's

---

3. Lawrence E. Harvey, "The Denouement of *Mélite* and the Role of the Nourrice," *Modern Language Notes,* LXXI, 3 (March 1956), 200-03.

love is a kind of prison for both of them: for her because she can feel it only when she expresses it in the terms of preciosity, and for Alidor because she seeks to entrap him in those terms. And his love becomes real to her only if he will express it in those terms. Alidor controls language, she is controlled by it—indeed, she seems to exist only as a function of that language.

To some extent, *La Place royalle* may be viewed as a turning-point: throughout, language represents a deliberately unreal level, opposed to a reality for which Alidor himself now stands. But that unreal level, too, has its embodiment in Angelique, so that the opposition has been transformed into one of character.

Alidor's desire for freedom is his controlling passion. The problem with his love for Angelique, he complains bitterly to his friend Cleandre, is that she returns it:

> Ie veux que l'on soit libre au milieu de ses fers.
> Il ne faut point servir d'obiet qui nous possede,
> Il ne faut point nourrir d'amour qui ne nous cede,
> Je le hay s'il me force, & quand j'ayme je veux
> Que de ma volonté dépendent tous mes voeux.

(I.4.212-16)

Under the circumstances, it is natural that Cleandre should suspect Alidor's motives when the latter wishes him good luck in his proposed marriage to Angelique, but Alidor is perfectly well-intentioned. He is not the flighty Hylas of countless novels and plays. His problem is precisely the seriousness of his and Angelique's love, for this very seriousness conflicts with his desire for liberty. Hylas is free in his loves, Alidor is captive, and for this reason he must escape from love. Furthermore, Angelique's love incarnates the literary bond. He is bound by her love, and that love goes no deeper than the words that describe it.

In his attempts to free himself, Alidor insults Angelique, and as his mockery becomes less and less restrained it leads gradually to a destruction of what she represents on stage. She has been created essentially as the precious lover, so she expects suitable contrition from Alidor for his rudeness, and says so. What he scorns, of course, is not Angelique but her language, the language which has created her and which is her only means of expression:

> Vous estes en colere, & vous dites des pointes!
> Ne présumiés vous point que i'irois à mains iointes
> Les yeux enflez de pleurs, & le coeur de soupirs,
> Vous faire offre à genoux de mille repentirs?
>
> (II.2.401-04)

Angelique contemplates suicide, but decides rather to try and overcome her love. As she eschews love, she must try to eschew the language which was her only means of conceiving it, and in her brief attempt to capture reality she becomes an object of pathos. Ironically,
she can express her struggle to repudiate Alidor—and her preciosity—
only in metaphorical terms:

> Restes impertinents d'une flame insensée,
> Ennemis de mon heur, sortez de ma pensée,
> Ou si vous m'en peignez encore quelques traits,
> Laissez-là ses vertus peignez moy ses forfaits.
>
> (II.3.453-56)

The significance of this fluctuating relationship is apparent with its
climax; Angelique, after agreeing in a fit of pique to marry another
suitor, Doraste, is persuaded by Alidor of his constancy and agrees to
elope with him after a ball. His intention is to deliver her into the
hands of Cleandre. When he rejoins his friend, he boasts of his power
over Angelique, and, concomitantly, over language (as though they
were not identical):

> Cleandre elle est à toy, i'ay flechy son courage,
> Que ne peut l'artifice, & le fard du langage!
>
> (III.6.905-06)

That language which creates its own world is presented to the spectator as a pretense, whose purpose is deceit. Earlier in the play, language was viewed as the medium of Angelique's love and Alidor's
struggle for freedom; now it appears as a complicating, unreal factor,
a tool for Alidor and the source of Angelique's defeat.

It is clear at the end of the play that Alidor's reality has triumphed,
and he exclaims gladly:

> Ie vis doresnavant puis que ie vis à moy,
> Et quelques doux assauts qu'vn autre obiet me liure,
> C'est de moy seulement que ie prendray la loy.
>
> (V.8.1579-81)

Angelique, having depended on the *précieux* attitude throughout, must finally accept the loss of freedom inherent in that attitude. Her confusion of reality and language enabled Alidor to mislead her in the first place. Whether she accepts her prison, as Philis calls the convent to which she retires, in the name of Alidor or in that of God makes little difference as far as her personal liberty is concerned.

Angelique's love is really the equivalent of Eraste's letters: both must be defeated to achieve a reality based on character. When a person takes over the role of the letters, the progression is underway. The axis of *La Place royalle* is the alternation between an interior struggle (Alidor's efforts to attain a personal freedom which always conflict with his real love for Angelique) and the external trappings of the theater—letters, abductions, and so on. This opposition of setting (to which Angelique's expressions of love belong) and the real action which needs no setting determines the play's direction.

Here Corneille establishes what appears to be a purely literary conflict, then reveals it to the spectator as a psychological one:[4] a method he developed further in *Le Cid,* and finally perfected in *Horace.* The former play is still bound to literary conventions (which Corneille never fully discards) in a way that *Horace* is not. Thus Elvire, for instance, remarks to Gormas at the play's outset that Don Sanche and Rodrigue, both of whom love Chimène, are equally worthy of her by virtue of their ancestors and their appearance. Their merit is measured not by what they have done but by what their appearance seems to indicate they can do.

Externals are important, but the character may now be influenced by personal inner feelings as well. Chimène is made immensely happy by Elvire's news that her father seems to favor Rodrigue as she does:

> Il semble toutefois que mon ame troublée
> Refuse cette joie & s'en trouve accablée.

---

4. When I use the term "psychological" here in reference to a conflict between stage characters, it is not intended necessarily to imply a profound interchange of emotions, but simply to indicate something that depends on the creation of *individuals,* as opposed to that kind of interchange between literary types which I have already discussed at some length. It may still be a conflict whose sole intention is to inspire a particular reaction in a spectator.

> Un moment donne au sort des visages divers,
> Et dans ce grand bon-heur je crains un grand revers.
>
> (I.2.47-50)

Chimène's fears stem from her own sense of being too happy; they are interiorized even more than Camille's in *Horace,* which result from the words of an oracle and of the images in a dream (I.2)– two forms of divine communication which impose an idea on her own feelings. This combination of exterior and interior influences is important in understanding the behavior of the Infante, whose role may otherwise seem superfluous; Corneille, in the wisdom of later years, elected to criticize the role because of its supposed irrelevance to the action (see the *Examen* to *Horace*).

When Leonor expresses surprise at the Infante's admission of her love for Rodrigue, Dona Urraque agrees that she should not have chosen "un simple chevalier" but adds that she will do nothing unseemly; Rodrigue merits her love, not her hand. The rank of two lovers in the theater of this period is usually the same, so such a division between external appearance (here, Rodrigue's inferior social position) and internal reality (his superior personal merit) is generally resolved in the course of a play. Here the issue is a side one, since the spectator knows there can be no meeting between the daughter of the king and the son of one of his courtiers (there is no hint, as in some other plays, that the true identity of either may be disguised). Precisely because it is a side issue, it is clear that the division must be permanent (which is also why the role of the Infante was criticized, for she can do nothing but lament). This division parallels that between Alidor and Angelique.

Her repose, complains the Infante, depends on the marriage of Chimène and Rodrigue. Until then,

> Je sens en deux partis mon esprit diuisé;
> Si mon courage est haut, mon coeur est embrasé.
>
> (I.3.113-14)

What in *Mélite* was a struggle between an all-powerful language and the reality it was supposed to signify remains a struggle between "signifiant" and "signifié." But the original (if deceptive) "signifiant"– social appearance as expressed by the language of preciosity–has come to equal the personal merit implied by real love (which, in *La Place royalle,* was continually struggling to pierce the artificial language and, unable to do so, was forced to destroy it). This new equivalent—call it "honor," "glory," "duty"—has become a very personal and powerful impulse, thus creating a psychological conflict.

This tension, no longer linguistic, directly involves characters; but its source remains the two opposing kinds of language: artificial and real. First in *Le Cid,* then in *Horace,* this opposition is reflected internally, as the two contrary demands responsible for the emotional conflicts and decisions of the characters: love on the one hand, glory, duty, honor on the other. Not that the submission to one or another of these demands always implies different attitudes on the part of the characters (although it does in *Horace*); nor do the demands always inspire different emotions; rather, they usually represent, at least in the protagonist's mind, two opposite poles between which he must choose.

Apart from Dona Urraque herself, the most obvious conflict of the play—between Chimène's desire to maintain her honor and Rodrigue's concern for his—involves only one side of the duality. The outcome of Rodrigue's justly famous soliloquy is a foregone conclusion, anticipated by his father. When faced with Rodrigue, shocked at the count's insult, Don Diègue advises:

> Ne replique point; ie cognoy ton amour;
> Mais qui peut vivre infame est indigne du jour.
>
> (I.6.285-86)

Since Chimène cannot love Rodrigue unless he is estimable, worthy of her love, he has no option but to clear the honor of his name. If he does not, as he perceives, he loses both love and honor. Nonetheless, in keeping with the different kinds of tension involved here, the soliloquy is absolutely necessary. If Rodrigue is really to be a character and not a literary type, the spectator must watch him arrive at his decision. In a theater where the creation of character is not a major concern, the decision would require no justification; the spectator would have to accept the hero's unhesitating reaction as he would the movement of a piece of scenery. But in this play, Corneille urges a different kind of understanding. What was formerly the actor's set piece has become an essential part of the action, resulting here in Rodrigue's decision to avenge his father.

The same is true of Don Diègue's soliloquy two scenes earlier: "O rage, ô desespoir! ô viellesse ennemie!" The old man's cry of shame, which in previous (and some contemporary) plays would remain just that, here precedes his resolution to place the task of restoring the family's honor in the hands of his son. In the original version this process is clearly traced, but in 1660 Corneille cut the scene with the entrance of Rodrigue as his father apostrophizes his sword: "Passe, pour me venger en de meilleures mains" (I.5.258). The first play included a specific prediction of Rodrigue's decision:

> Si Rodrigue est mon fils, il faut que l'amour cede
> Et qu'une ardeur plus haute à ses flames succede;
> Mon honneur est le sien, & le mortel affront
> Qui tombe sur mon chef rejaillit sur son front.

> (259-62)

Corneille dropped these lines, presumably because they detract from the magnificent following scene and the climactic effect of Rodrigue's decision. Yet they do lend substance to Don Diègue's monologue.

It is also worth noting that four verses concerning the poverty of mere words beside action (in this case a duel) were deleted in the published versions, perhaps as much because they sounded like a school debate as because they formed an apology for the duel.[5] To escape the accusation of excess dialogue, Corneille made sure that most of the speeches in the play were necessary to the action (an exception would be Rodrigue's long description of the battle [IV.4], which unlike that of Valère in *Horace* is quite superfluous, since the spectators already know the essential details). This notion of the futility of mere language is the root cause of the play's central quarrel; Don Gomès informs Diègue that he is too old to tutor the prince, because rather than teaching by example, he is constrained to describe past actions (I.4.185-200). In the original version, Gomès refers to the "froides leçons" the young prince will receive from the older man.

Le Cid remains ambiguous. While the importance of language as a self-sufficient element, as the creator of character and emotions, is reduced, it still remains to confuse the spectator. It is easy to recognize that the Infante's tensions are based on psychology rather than

5. Pierre Corneille, *Le Cid, tragi-comédie*, éd. Maurice Cauchie (Paris, 1946), pp. 27-28, n. 1.

metaphor; but she continues very much a creature of language, always working back to her original position even while wandering in
linguistic circles. Late in the play (V.2), after a long absence from
the stage, she describes in stanzas her own conflict of love and honor,
only to realize that there is no conflict, since whatever may happen,
she can never have Rodrigue. If she suffers from any "pitoyable sort,"
as she imagines, it is not because she is torn between "gloire" and
"desirs," but rather because she can have no hope, as she concedes in
the last stanza: thus negating the first three. In the following scene
with her *confidante,* Leonor, she repeats this process. She has, in fact,
defined her situation in the first act, and throughout the play she
changes no more than Angelique did in *La Place royalle.* Because she
herself contains both sides of the division I have examined, but cannot reconcile them, she is doomed to remain a static figure, useful
only as a theatrical "minor key" reproduction of Chimène.[6]

In a sense the conflict between Rodrigue and Chimène is equally
static. While both must face the tension within themselves at first,
it is very quickly settled and the play's major struggle arises from the
opposition of two family interests. There is no sustained tension between two opposite demands, difficult, perhaps impossible, to resolve;
for Rodrigue and Chimène are equal (an equality reinforced by the
very similarity of their decisions). What interests the spectator is the
resolution of their external conflict—an external which no longer
pretends to hide some other reality. The metaphorical mask of language has been replaced in the equation by the social mask of honor;
the language which represented an opaque obstacle to understanding
and therefore had to be destroyed has been replaced by a "transparent"
language. Thus the conflicting elements are reduced to social appearance and personal desire, on a single level of action. And the lovers
must suffer as a result of their separate decisions, though each knows
that he has made the only possible choice.

The presence in a play of two characters, one apparently "real" and
the other clearly a literary device, is evidently a barrier to the spectator's identification. In a certain type of theater this barrier is essential;

6. For a fuller discussion of this last aspect, see Jean Boorsch, "Remarques
sur la téchnique dramatique de Corneille," in *Studies by Members of the French
Department of Yale University,* ed. Albert Feuillerat, Yale Romanic Studies
XVIII (New Haven, 1941), 121.

Corneille and his contemporaries, with varying degrees of success, were trying to remove it. In *Horace,* for the most part, Corneille succeeded. The conflict of two languages, essence of the tension in *Mélite* and *La Place royalle,* is almost totally transformed into a different kind of struggle, and the spectator finds himself in a different relationship to the play.

Saint-Evremond once made a comment of considerable interest when comparing Corneille's *Sophonisbe* to that of Mairet. The former, he said, failed because the heroine captured too well the spirit of the period in which she lived, whereas "Mairet, qui avait dépeint la sienne infidèle au vieux Syphax, et amoureux du jeune et victorieux Massinisse, plut quasi-généralement à tout le monde, pour avoir rencontré le goût des dames et le vrai esprit des gens de la cour."[7] This remark explains why Mairet's play may be considered a forerunner of the classical theater: the characters are recognizable enough to excite the spectator's sympathy, and ultimately to permit his identification with them. It is equally significant that Saint-Evremond should have found the absence of this factor responsible for the failure of Corneille's play in 1663.

In his often remarkable preface (1631) to *L'Amaranthe,* Gombauld illuminates this aspect of the search for verisimilitude on the stage, confirming and clarifying for a modern reader the later remarks of Saint-Evremond. He describes the reasoning of authors who have sought to reduce the time of a play's action to twelve hours (there were few such in 1631): "ils n'ont pas tant deliberé de representer une chose passée, que d'agir comme si elle estoit presente; & comme si leurs personnages en estoient les vrays Hercules, les Thrasons, ou les Amynthes: qui en ce cas-là ne peuuent auoir d'autre distinction de temps que celle du iour auquel ils agissent." What is important for this study is that, throughout his preface, Gombauld constantly compares two kinds of theater and two distinct types of spectator reaction to them. He is praising a theater which is to become the "classical" theater, because it presents characters in the spectator's time dimension, not as "une chose passee"—and he distinguishes, also, between "une chose" and "personnages." This *present* character may offer the spectator a share in his emotions: Hercules must be Hercules,

7. Saint-Evremond, *Oeuvres melées,* I, 300.

not an imitation of him. Gombauld criticizes a distance which prevents the spectator from knowing a character as "vray," which isolates
the character from the world of the spectator, which suggests that he
is a mythological, hence artificial, being. These characters represent
a seventeenth-century, rather than Roman or Greek, ideal; hence their
dress must be contemporary and their speech a purified version of the
language of polite society. By the same token, Gombauld explains,
authors who are turning in this direction "ont eu bonne grace de
vouloir que le lieu, le temps, les mouuemens, & toutes les circon-
stances du Theatre parussent autant qu'il est possible vray-semblables
& conformes au sentiment du spectateur." All those things represented by the stage must fit into a single and even time scheme, which
the spectator may then adopt for his own; and nothing must disturb
this evenness.

The dialectic clash of elements I have examined as part of the "theater of doubt" has no place in this theater where character is all-important. As D'Aubignac observes in *La Pratique,* if psychical distance
is to be maintained at a constant level, there can be no sudden revelation of the illusion: "Il ne faut jamais mêler ensemble ce qui con-
cerne la représentation d'un poème avec l'action véritable de l'histoire
représentée." He goes on to blame Plautus for precisely that offense:

> Dans son *Amphitryon* Jupiter est supposé dans la ville de Thèbes
> au temps de la naissance d'Hercule; et quand il paraît sous la forme
> d'Amphitryon, il dit aux spectateurs: 'Je suis Jupiter, et me
> change en Amphitryon quand il me plaît, paraissant ainsi et pour
> l'amour de vous,' dit-il aux spectateurs, 'afin de continuer cette
> comédie, et pour l'amour d'Alcmène, afin qu'elle soit reconnue
> innocente.' Où l'on voit qu'il mêle l'intérêt des spectateurs avec
> celui des acteurs, en fait un assemblage des Romains qui étaient
> présents avec des personnes que l'on suppose agir en Grèce.[8]

Here the spectator is abruptly brought face to face with the unreality
of the stage, complains D'Aubignac, and the characters are no longer
acceptable as personalities in their own right, but are visibly a deceit.
There has been a fluctuation in the spectator's awareness.

The staging of these plays, it was thought, had to be unobtrusive in
order to aid the spectator's identification. However artificial the

---

8. D'Aubignac, *Pratique,* pp. 45 and 48.

unity of place in a play like *Horace*, it has the advantage of offering
no obstacle to the spectator's belief in the illusion offered to him.
The scenic continuity of the auditorium and stage, in terms of decora-
tion and lighting, was assured by employing a single set[9] whose lines
communicated with those of the auditorium,[10] and by leaving all the
lights in the theater on throughout the performance.[11]

Another indication of decreased emphasis on theatricality was the
diminished importance of long rhetorical passages, which according
to Corneille's *Examen* to *Clitandre* were included in the first place
solely to please the actors. In *Clitandre*, the hero himself is not very
significant (except insofar as his is the title role), and his laments are
incidental moments in the dialectical opposition of the elements. In
later plays, these soliloquies impel the action, resolve a character's internal struggle or contribute necessary information. Perhaps the
most famous lament of all, Rodrigue's "Percé jusques au fond du
coeur" (*Le Cid*, I.6), expresses (as I have indicated) the resolution of
an internal struggle upon which the play's action depends. Camille's
lament in *Horace*, after she learns the fate of Curiace at the hands of
her brother (IV.4), results in her decision to seek her own death at
his hands and creates a reason for the final act of the play. This decision seems the inevitable fulfillment of her nature, as well as a development integral to the play's action.

As with the laments, the less dramatic *récits* now become essential
to the text of these plays, because the set involved only one location,
so that the stage would not interfere with the spectator's consciousness. Nonetheless, playwrights tried to keep these extended speeches
as unobtrusive as possible. Corneille is careful to interrupt Valère's
lengthy *récit (Horace*, IV.2.1101-61), concerning the real outcome of
the battle between the brothers, with a cry from Camille and an out-
burst from the elder Horace. In addition (as with Racine's "*récit* de
Théramène" in *Phèdre*) the speech evolves naturally from the plot:
it does not seem out of context to the spectator, who is eager to hear
what the character has to say. Furthermore, the *récits* are generally
allotted to secondary characters: they no longer supply the principal

9. See Mahelot, *Mémoire*, p. 110, where *Horace* calls for a "palais à volonté,"
a translation for the sake of the decorator of Corneille's note "une salle de la
maison d'Horace."

10. For further comments, see Villiers, "Illusion dramatique," pp. 28-29.

11. See Sabbattini, *Scenes et machines*, pp. 62-63.

actor with an opportunity to display his virtuosity (the laments, which now resolve a central struggle, are reserved for him). Finally, the *récits* are addressed not to the spectators, but to the other characters, to supply certain information they require. Rodrigue's tale of his battle feats is far less sophisticated than, for example, Théramène's *récit*. In spite of its metaphorical content, Théramène's speech does not intrude; the information it offers, though unusual, is not foreign to the play's atmosphere. Thus, this final revelation of Neptune's fulfillment of Thésée's curse does not take the spectator by surprise.

Horace (1640) seems to me the first play to deliberately accept the *spirit* of the new movement—and of the critics' strictures. I am more doubtful as to the letter, since the unity of time in *Horace* demands some imaginative effort by the spectator (although less so than *Le Cid*). Also, *Horace* seems to complete a definite progression on the part of its author. Corneille's later criticism of the play for its disunified action strikes me as an unwarranted concession to the taste of critics in 1660. Horace does not fall from a public to a private peril, Corneille's *Examen* to the contrary; rather, his victory seems to make him the state's representative, so that any personal insult by his sister is a betrayal of Rome: the final obstacle that must be overcome. The need for such an obstacle is manifest. Camille's death was a well-known episode of a famous story; and after she has served to establish the nature of certain figures and of various tensions, her position at the play's end cannot be left ambivalent. She is essential if the play's tensions are to be fully exploited.

The spectator must, in this theater, be able to identify with a character as a human being. The natures of those on stage must develop according to an internal logic that is not merely possible, but probable; and the behavior of any given figure must be suited to that logic. If these conditions are not met, then the identification—through which this theater makes the spectator aware of certain problems—will not occur. Camille cannot change in the midst of the play: her death must follow that of Curiace, and to be honorable it must come at the hands of Horace, thus negating his victory over her fiancé. Moreover, because her death parallels that of Curiace, it seems to reconcile her with him.

Though *Horace* does not begin as dramatically as Rotrou's *Laure persecutée* or *Venceslas*, Corneille presents at once a character in anguish, as Sabine seeks help from Julie:

Approuvez ma foiblesse, et souffrez ma douleur;
Elle n'est que trop juste en un si grand malheur.

$(I.1.1-2)^{12}$

She tries to overcome her inner despair at the threat posed to her
family: "Le trouble de mon coeur ne peut rien sur mes larmes" (l. 8).
Julie's reproach to Sabine clarifies the reason for her emotion without
seeming extraneous, so that the spectator is immediately interested
and curious. Once he knows that Sabine is lamenting because she is
an Alban married to a Roman, and that war between Alba and Rome
is imminent, he knows the basic *donnée* of the play, and is eager to
learn how this situation will affect the various characters. Surprises,
if Corneille is to produce any, must be created only for the reactions
they will elicit from the characters; thus the interest he has aroused
in the spectator may readily become identification.

The second scene presents a despairing Camille to the spectator.
Throughout her long lament, as with Sabine's in the previous scene,
he is not evaluating her performance as an actress, but instead ex-
periencing her emotions as a character. The lament is no longer a
superfluous comment on the actor's surroundings and the magnitude
of his misfortunes; rather, it exposes the character's interior struggle
—not as a source of embroidered and convoluted language, but as a
way into his soul. Camille's lament also informs the spectator of a
certain rivalry between Sabine and herself, as she reveals that the
family relations are inextricably combined with the relations of the
two cities. The hint of jealousy in Camille's protests that her fate is
as hard, if not harder, than that of Sabine, increases the spectator's
curiosity concerning the characters' struggles with their consciences.

Corneille has now gained the advantage over the spectator, and re-
laxes the tension briefly (the first of three such reprieves) before introducing a greater anguish. The joyous Curiace enters with news of
a "peace" between Rome and Alba—at least, there is not to be a
general battle. But his happiness is short-lived, as he soon learns of
the impending fight between the Horatii and his family. Throughout

12. The edition used is that of the "Grands Ecrivains," edited by Charles
Marty-Laveaux (III, 243-358). I have used throughout, where they exist, the
variants of the 1641 edition, in keeping with the use of the first editions of
the earlier plays.

the play, however, the personality of Curiace will remain essentially
even; the joy he shows at first is matched by his later reluctance—or,
more precisely, lack of eagerness—for the interfamilial battle:

> Que désormais le ciel, les enfers et la terre
> Unissent leurs fureurs à nous faire la guerre;
> Que les hommes, les Dieux, les démons et le sort
> Préparent contre nous un général effort!
>
> (II.3.423-30)

His horror at the idea that the brothers have to fight is in complete
contrast to the reaction of Horace. Further, his joy at the prospect
of peace and his later distaste for the combat, in conjunction with the
spectator's knowledge of Horace, enable the spectator to foresee his
death at the hands of his brother-in-law. While honor is important to
Curiace, his honor is that of the *honnête homme,* not that sought by
the magnanimous hero, to which glory is a necessary adjunct.

It is this sustaining of character, with the toning down of accessory
dramatic elements which it implies, that distinguishes the classical
theater from its predecessor. Corneille purposely does not introduce
his hero until he is in a position to glory in his honor without seeming a warmonger—Horace is reacting to something beyond his power
to affect, indulging in a little false modesty, and above all revealing
the limits of his sensitivity. In response to Curiace, who is torn between love of family and country as a result of the projected duel,
Horace exclaims "Quoi! vous me pleureriez mourrant pour mon
pays!" (II.1.398). Curiace's inability to accept immediately the full
import of Flavian's announcement that he is to fight Horace ("Qui?"
he asks), his subsequent laments, and Horace's immediate hardening
are inevitable. There is no question of changing chameleon-like from
lover to warrior, from softness to harshness, as the script dictates;
this approach prevailed in *Ligdamon et Lidias,* but has no place in the
new theater. Horace and Curiace react entirely predictably to the
duel: for one, an opportunity to win greater glory, for the other
simply a death sentence. Curiace must fight, for the honor of his
family; but for the love of his family he cannot defeat Horace. Curiace, of course, accepts the call, while reproaching Horace for his
harshness: "Mais votre fermeté tient un peu de barbare" (II.3.456).
To Horace's cruelty ("je ne vous connois plus"), Curiace replies with
what seems unconscious irony, but in fact reflects a consciousness of

himself quite in harmony with what the spectator already knows of
him: "Je vous connois encore, et c'est ce qui me tue" (II.3.503).
This self-awareness is apparent again when Curiace responds to Camille's question as to whether his feelings match those of Horace:

> Hélas! je vois trop bien qu'il faut, quoi que je fasse,
> Mourir, ou de douleur, ou de la main d'Horace.
>
> (II.5.535-36)

Horace, in contrast, cannot conceive of any trepidation regarding
the duel; the average spectator will not identify with him. He is a kind
of juggernaut who rolls over those around him, revealing none of his
own feelings, but rousing all kinds of anguish in others. The spectator
may observe Horace, perhaps in admiration, perhaps in horror, but he
feels with Curiace, with Sabine and with Camille, and he is only too
aware of their helplessness. Yet because he feels for them in this way,
Horace is included in his emotions.

The spectator's view of the elder Horace is tempered by the same
distance. Noble, but resigned to his destiny, he too has the blood of
the Horatii; and if he grasps the full horror of a situation which his
son does not yet comprehend, it seems traceable to experience rather
than his nature. Only after telling Horace and Curiace to go and prepare themselves for their duel does he allow himself any tenderness:

> Ah! n'attendrissez point ici mes sentiments;
> Pour vous encourager ma voix manque de termes;
> Mon coeur ne forme point de pensers assez fermes;
> Moi-même en cet adieu j'ai des larmes aux yeux,
> Faites votre devoir, et laissez faire aux Dieux.
>
> (II.8.706-10)

Both the individual personalities of the characters and their family
traits are set off by the rivalry between Sabine and Camille, matching
that of Curiace and Horace. This rivalry is developed from the start
of the play, when Camille seems to tell Julie that her situation is
more painful than that of Sabine: "Croit-elle ma douleur moins vive
que la sienne?" (I.2.136-145). When Corneille introduces a second
relaxation of the tension, with the news that the armies refuse to
accept the chosen champions in view of their relationship, Sabine is
ready, as was Curiace before her, to rejoice (III.2). Camille, however, is less easily convinced: "Ce délai de nos maux rendra leurs

coups plus rudes" (III.3.835). Later the distinction between the two is made clearer, as Sabine responds to Julie's hopes:

SABINE: Comme vous je l'espère.

CAMILLE: Et je n'ose y songer.

                                 (III.3.869)[13]

This exchange is followed by a somewhat banal, but predictable, dispute as to which of them has the greatest reason for suffering (III.4); typically, Camille has the last word.

At this point the elder Horace appears with the evil news that the brothers are now fighting, and the spectator is plunged again into deep anxiety, following the relief (but not disengagement) afforded by the playwright's pause for the "petty" squabble between the two women. Again the laments are Sabine's, while Camille remains silent —not only, one feels, because she anticipated this development, but also because she welcomes it as an opportunity to show her spirit: as though, like Horace, she would have been upset if the hand-to-hand battle between the brothers had been avoided. Already she seems tensed for a final victory, a victory which will lead her in an opposite direction from that of Horace. For her it is love that must win; as noted, she is convinced of the outcome (III.3), and in her dispute with Sabine she makes the spectator more conscious of her self-awareness: "Pour moi, j'ai tout à craindre, et rien à souhaiter" (III.4.894). Her despair is strikingly similar to that of Curiace. But where his fate is the consequence of a situation over which he has no control, Camille's is the result of a deliberate choice: when she learns the true outcome of the combat, she will force Horace to kill her. The false news of the Alban victory inspires only pity for her brothers (two of whom, as her father points out, are dead, while the third is dishonored); she could never go so far as Sabine, who asks that Horace be forgiven and that they make the most of what happiness they can have. In every situation their constant and logically different attitudes maintain the spectator's curiosity.

---

13. In later editions (after 1660), this difference is further emphasized by a slight change:

       Sabine: J'ose encor l'espérer.

       Camille: Moi, je n'espère rien.

When Valère brings news of the battle's real outcome (IV.2), the
emotions of Camille, the elder Horace, and indeed the spectator are
sharply altered. Here again Corneille keeps out of sight those characters whose immediate reactions could not be in keeping with the
framework of his new theater. If Sabine appeared now, her only re-
course would be a lament in the old style, a monologue leading no-
where and resolving nothing: the contrast with Camille would detract from her moral stature. She lacks the kind of initiative pos-
sessed by the Horatii, and at this point her speeches would not serve
as a valuable foil to Camille's. Camille is now in a position to take a
precise stand; her vital complaint results in her decision to die, to rejoin her lover and throw in the face of Horace all the despair to which
he has been blind.

> Offensez sa victoire, irritez sa colère.
> Et prenez, s'il se peut, plaisir à lui déplaire.
> Il vient: préparons-nous à montrer constamment
> Ce que doit une amante à la mort d'un amant.
>
> (IV.4.1247-50)

She succeeds in her object, as she knew she would. And Sabine admits the wisdom of her choice when she begs Horace to grant her the
same treatment:

> Que Camille est heureuse! elle a pu te déplaire;
> Elle a reçu de toi ce qu'elle a prétendu,
> Et recouvre là-bas tout ce qu'elle a perdu.
>
> (IV.7.1380-82)

It is not until the end, however, that Horace, forced to live with
both his glory and his sister's murder, truly perceives his own mon-
strosity. He claims death as his right, but views it as the stamp of his
honor rather than the punishment Valère had demanded:

> Un seul point entre nous met cette différence,
> Que mon honneur par là cherche son assurance,
> Et qu'à ce même but nous voulons arriver,
> Lui pour flétrir ma gloire, et moi pour la sauver.
>
> (V.2.1551-54)

He is refused. He may live because his glory supersedes his crime
(V.3.1760); he may live to serve the state; but he must henceforth
bear the burden of both that glory and that crime. The play terminates at a point when the playwright risks depicting a changed Horace.

Throughout, then, Corneille concentrates on maintaining distinct characters, whose motivations are clearly communicated—and whose actions, therefore, are clearly determined. These characters are recognizable, they are confirmed in their interior anguish, above all they are predictable; thus the spectator's psychical distance is not constantly changing.

The convincing characters, the lack of elaborate but non-illusionary sets, the removal of speeches that interrupt the action, the careful transitions from one scene to the next, the omission of fictional characters, and so on, constitute the result of the playwright's search for *vraisemblance.* As Villiers remarks, "C'est une nouvelle relation entre l'acteur et le spectateur."[14] With the character, the spectator may be brought to feel, and then to reflect upon, a problem that is essentially a moral or a social one. He is not himself put in a total theatrical situation, provoked by the stage but spreading to the entire auditorium; rather, he identifies with a particular character who is facing a moral dilemma, and arrives at an appreciation of that dilemma through an individual sensibility.

14. Villiers, "Illusion dramatique," p. 34.

Conclusion

In a period when men like Copernicus and Galileo were voicing doubts about the nature and form of the universe (and proving the validity of these doubts), when theologians such as Luther and Calvin, de Bèze and Erasmus were questioning the generally accepted views of man's relationship to that universe, and the religious wars were generating uncertainty regarding the nature of man and his modes of thought, it also became necessary for the artist to re-evaluate his traditional forms of expression.

In drama, the kind of aura that made the mystery plays possible, similar to the pervading ritualistic atmosphere of the Greek theater, began to disappear. The feeling of unanimity which might unite a crowd before these mighty dramas was surrendered to a feeling of uniqueness, of individuality, demanding a very different kind of play. The Pléiade artists were more a symptom than a cure; or perhaps the theater-going public was not prepared for them yet. Turning their back on the wider audience, because the theater there was dissolving, they produced a theater that answered a very particular need in its public: a theater based on rules, successful in its milieu because of its originality and poetry, and because its dependence on language appealed to those spectators who were trying to create a new, expressive language. It was unsuccessful as popular theater because its producers did not see—or, more probably, did not care—what had guaranteed the success of the medieval theater, of the mystery, or what compelled the unity of an audience before a farce.

Hardy, on the other hand, was highly conscious of the needs of his audience; he was also aware that the old forms had lost their meaning, and that the Pléiade dramatists had not replaced them. If he did not intellectualize this awareness, he certainly saw that—for one reason or another—theater audiences no longer felt themselves part of a vast machine, unified by an aura of common superstition which reduced man to a single totality under God and permeated the whole of life. And recognition of this change spurred Hardy to create new forms of communication which could be equally meaningful.

He must have been successful, because he remained Valleran's paid
poet and drew sufficient audiences to keep a travelling theatrical company working, at a time when such companies did not receive great
rewards. Though only a small percentage of Hardy's vast output has
survived, it is safe to assume that these plays, though selected to
please readers of the mid-1620s, are fairly representative of his style.
I have tried to analyze this style, which involved uniting those elements central to the stage production under an overall atmosphere
created essentially by the text, the spoken word. Hardy seems to
draw his audience into this atmosphere, into a "mock-up" of the life
they experience outside.

Rapid change in the theater continued, however. Hardy's creation
could not satisfy for long. Playwrights began to work toward a form
that would echo the new emphasis on the individual, a theater where
the spectator would commune with a character, with no dependence
on ritualistic atmosphere.

The period between 1625 and 1640 was marked by a series of experiments, which did conform to a basic trend. The artist must seek
a new mold: he is placed face to face with the problems of a change
from the belief which allowed man to feel part of a unity to one which,
by allowing man to question, freed him of his ties with God (based on
a traditional burden of unquestionable Patristic doctrine) and at the
same time of his mystic ties with his fellows. No longer could he rely
on the ritual of the mystery or on the simple buffoonery of the farce
or *sottie* (although the more ambitious *moralité* might have provided
greater scope had its form been less archaic).

The spectator was becoming more sophisticated, more curious about
the world around him, and he needed something more satisfying than
the farce and less diffuse than the mystery. His world was suddenly
too complex for the author to show it in a single play, no matter how
extensive. The idea of God was no longer so close to man as to per-
meate every aspect of his life and do away with the need for explanation; and the audience would not be satisfied only with the uncompli-
cated situations and attitudes of the farce with its standard types and
plots. The expression of God did not express man and his world
(which explains that lack of familiarity with God which resulted,
among other things, in the banning of the mysteries): eventually the
theater had to choose to represent things more narrow in scope than
the mystery, less simplified than the farce.

The replacement of one theater with the other naturally involved a period of transition. Perhaps inevitably, the problems which interested the playwright during this time reflected his questioning of both his own metaphysics and the theater itself. The struggle he faced as an artist coincided with his struggle to grasp the nature of reality. Thus in his plays (those discussed in Chapters 2 and 3), the illusory world of the theater is thrown into doubt and with it the external world of the spectator.

The change which took place, then, is not simply a question of chaos in the theater world preceding a reign of order. When Lancaster charges that Pierre Mainfray's *Chasse Royalle* (1628) "is at the same time allegorical, mythological, and realistic, a strange medley, typical of much that was written at the time,"[1] and Lebègue comments on the flourish, the breadth of the "baroque theater,"[2] they avoid, I believe, the main issue; for these very characteristics denote an entirely different style of thought from that of the classical or medieval theater. This intermediate theater may, in fact, be compared with the better-known theater that followed, much as Guez de Balzac compared the Latin to the French language. The former has, he suggests, the force of a *thing,* it carries its own significance apart from its ostensible context, lending to authors' ideas "beaucoup plus qu'elle ne reçoit d'eux." French, on the contrary, does little more than express the thought.[3] So with these styles of theater: the earlier relies on the density of its language—that is, speech, scenery, movement, spectacle, actor, spectator—within which the ostensible subject is only a part of a much broader series of themes; the later keeps distractions (both technical and textual) to a minimum, toward a kind of direct communication between the spectator and the character.

Whatever may be the precise intention, or lack of it, in the work of any given author, behind the general change in the theater lies a shift in man's world view. The development of the drama seems to reflect, in microcosm, the great shift from a dialectical mode of reasoning to

1. Lancaster, *History*, I, 229.

2. Raymond Lebègue, "De la Renaissance au classicisme: le théâtre baroque en France," *Bibliothèque d'Humanisme et Renaissance.* Travaux et documents II (1942), 161-84.

3. F. E. Sutcliffe, *Guez de Balzac et son temps: littérature et politique* (Paris, 1959), p. 250. See Jean-Louis Guez de Balzac, *Les Oeuvres,* 2 vols. (Paris, 1665), II, 612.

an analytical one. During this period, of course, a radical new approach to learning evolved under the auspices of Ramus and Descartes in France, and Bacon in England.

P. Bürger, discussing the strange mixture of truth and illusion in Rotrou's *Saint-Genest* (whereby the spectator attains "truth" *through* illusion) views it as an echo of "das Denkschema einer Zeit" during which reality is broken dialectically into being and appearance.[4] The resulting tension between illusion and reality, he points out, is the characteristic mode of thought of the period; it is also the essence of the theater. The spectator is subjected to this tension as a consequence of the playwright's dialectical juxtaposition of theatrical elements.

This form of theater, which involves the spectator in a constant fluctuation between belief and disbelief, forcing him to accept what he normally could not and to doubt his conception of reality, cannot last for long. It throws an equal doubt on the artistic philosophy behind it. It is a speculative theater, by virtue not only of its apparent subjects (the positing of certain relationships followed by their elucidation) but also of its whole method: for in projecting a kind of debate on the notion of reality, on man in the universe, it is doomed to eternal questioning, or at best to eternal repetition of the conclusion at which Montaigne arrived some fifty years earlier.

The "new" theater will replace this uncertainty with the examination of specific situations, involving well-defined characters, and may therefore reach a conclusion: in the form of a moral and social commentary. The spectator is cut off from the tension of a situation, as this tension is "framed" by the viewpoint of a single sensibility: the very precise definition of this action, creating the tension, also affords a degree of relief to the spectator.

The magician and his one-man audience, who, in *L'Illusion comique*, offer the spectator a means of sensing that anxiety, also represent a means of escaping it. By identifying with a character, the spectator feels his anxiety, but, as it were, by proxy. The dialectical opposition which would be an obstacle to such identification is removed, and the playwright may involve his audience ever deeper with a character. The problems these plays express are of a moral rather than metaphysical nature, for the figure with whom the spectator is to identify must be entangled in the dilemma of social conflict. This need not suggest

4. P. Bürger, "Illusion und Wirklichkeit im *Saint-Genest* von Jean Rotrou," *Germanisch-romanische Monatschrift* XIV (1964), p. 267.

that the style of the earlier theater has become extinct—it survives in
the fantasies of Thomas Corneille and Quinault, for example—but it
has certainly been superseded by another style.

It is noteworthy that other forms of the theater evolved in a similar direction: the *ballet de cour* (see Appendix 2) is reduced from an
all-embracing, "total" theater to a stage spectacle; the old semi-im-
provised (and hence more intimate) farces disappear; the *commedia
dell'arte* is replaced by the more formal *comédie italienne;* and the
pièces à machines form a genre of their own as the regular theater
uses less and less scenery (indeed, after the Marais troupe was deci-
mated for the last time that theater had to produce these *pièces* almost exclusively to survive in competition with the Hôtel de Bourgogne, better equipped with acting talent).

The shift in emphasis, then, begins with a theater which involves
the spectator in a total dramatic situation, which forces him into
metaphysical preoccupations by loosening his grasp on reality; and
ends with a theater which makes him identify with the emotional
and moral problems of a single, recognizeable character. This shift,
of course, has other implications for the theater.

The French theater between 1625 and 1635 produced relatively
few simple tragedies. Indeed, the comedies and pastorals produced
during this period should be considered tragi-comedies, in view of
the definition applied to comedy a short time later.[5] The analysis I
have made of their style points toward a number of conclusions about
these theatrical genres; or at least adds some details to a continuous
debate.

What distinguishes this style is its lack of concentration on a single
center of interest, the constant flow of confidences from those on
stage to the audience, and, of course, the interplay of dramatic elements. These traits seem to reflect the inability of the writers of the
period to endorse any single view of the "human condition," or man's
relationship to his "destiny." This confusion is communicated to the
spectator by the fluctuating levels of illusion; the stage appears as a
kind of Bedlam, itself the symbol of an unbalanced world. Such an
approach to man (and to the stage) is distinctly anti-tragic.

Man can be guilty neither of hubris—he cannot flaunt "gods" of
whose existence he is unsure—nor of any kind of "personal" failure,

5. See Jacques Schérer, *La Dramaturgie classique en France* (Paris, 1962),
p. 459.

lacking as he does an absolute standard against which to measure that failure. He can be measured only against himself, in terms of an expected reaction to a given situation. The tragic sense proceeds from man's failure to exceed the limitations of his humanity. If a man comes up to an expected level, he is simply fulfilling his possibilities —and this fulfillment seems to constitute the *admirable* for Corneille. If he fails to do so, he is more likely to appear ridiculous than anything else.

Can the awareness of uncertainty itself be tragic? I would suggest that it cannot be, when that lack of certainty is seen as the basic mode of being. When awareness itself is a part of the uncertainty of the human condition rather than outside, it can only echo the condition; it cannot make a commentary upon it. The idea of tragedy involves consciousness, the adoption of a position, a self-testing. The uncertain awareness cannot then be tragic. Any attempt at tragedy in such circumstances will necessarily be a fraud. It will be the measuring of man against a false obstacle, and will become tragi-comic because it merely fools the spectator into believing momentarily that the obstacle is mightier than it is.

Corneille, in destroying the false language of preciosity, created a certain absolute, a phantom existing in the mind, but one that provided an ideal against which a man's power could in truth be tested. His own heroes are not usually tragic, because they do indeed measure up to this phantom, at the risk of seeming inhuman. Racine's characters, on the other hand, are always ambiguous: faced with a sublime passion which almost seems to represent the path to the absolute, their "obligations" as social beings prevent their accepting it. The opportunity to grasp all that this passion implies is overwhelming, and they are bound to fail.

The tragic situation seems to demand a stable view of the world, where a known quantity—man—can be pitted against another known, absolute quantity, such as an ideal born of the intellect, or the certainty of fate. The comic situation, on the other hand, seems to involve the pitting of man against man, or against society. This kind of tension may obviously become tragic, as when, for instance, the protagonists take on the attributes of an absolute or of something eternal. The form of the struggle is similar, but the level (and the language) is different. Even the elements compounding the tension may be virtually identical, as in *Macbeth* and *Ubu Roi*. If, as Bergson and others

have shown, comedy is a social phenomenon, then one may suppose
that the theater is always conducive to comedy, whereas tragedy
seems possible only when playwrights adopt a firm metaphysical
stance and endow their characters with a definite world view.

The hero in seventeenth-century French drama developed from a
creature who epitomized the *admirable* to a more tragic figure, who
aspired to the sublime. The *admirable* hero achieves whatever he is
capable of (however remarkable); the tragic hero's desires exceed his
capacities, and he fails. In comedy, a similar impulse toward the creation of strong character is reflected in Molière's works. Often a character seems to represent the essence of a particular kind of being;
this elimination of superfluous attributes defines the tragic hero as
well. In both cases, certain problems are focused, or crystallized, as
it were, in a single nucleus.

An unidentified critic (1667) of *Tartuffe* remarked that whatever
"manque extrêmement de raison" is ridiculous; anything contrary to
a predictable character reaction is absurd.[6] This criterion implies that
the comic is not at all far from the tragic, for both connote excess:
a view which may help explain such plays as *Dom Juan* and *Le Misanthrope.* These plays center on a figure of preposterous idealism, who
gains stature in juxtaposition with a mediocre humanity. Alceste's
righteous scorn for mankind becomes comic when he refuses even the
most elementary concession; his vehement responses are quite inap-
propriate to his "civilized" surroundings. Yet if he tempered his tone
to suit his milieu he would fall short of his ideal, and fail in his effort
to surpass himself: there is a significant gap between the ideal and the
situation in which it is expressed.

That comedy should move in this direction is implicit in the theater's progression from communion to individuality. Still, these comedies are virtually unique, for the good reason that the social action of
comedy necessitates an effort to bring the spectators into the confidence of those on stage. (Indeed, it is because one of the characters
in *Le Misanthrope* is practically in league with the spectators that they
can laugh at Alceste, and the same is true also of Dom Juan.) Early
comedy achieves this relationship by mocking the whole affair: the

6. See Molière, *Oeuvres,* éd. Eugène Despois et Paul Mesnard, 13 vols. (Paris,
1878), IV, 529-66. For further comments on this, see Will G. Moore, "Molière's
Theory of Comedy," *Esprit Créateur* VI, 3 (1966), 137-44.

stage devices which the action necessitates invariably destroy the illusion. Later, with the creation of stronger characters, the spectator is enabled to mock one person through his identification with another; and the object of this mockery may cease to be part of the illusion.

The change I have examined clearly favors the development of tragedy, and the preponderant success of the latter after 1640 (apart from the singular example of Molière) may be ascribed in large part to this change.

Appendix 1: The Dating of the *Comédies des comédiens* of Gougenot and Scudéry

Lancaster gives the date of the first performance of Scudéry's play as 1632 because it is mentioned in Chandeville's preface to Scudéry's *Le Trompeur puni,* whose *privilège* to Pierre Billaine is dated December 18, 1632, and whose *achevé d'imprimer* is January 4, 1633. Lancaster claims that this reference is to the play's appearance in print, not to its performance, and that it must therefore have been performed by the time the preface was written.[1] In fact, this part of Chandeville's preface reads as follows: "Voila quel est le sentiment touchant ce Poëme, que vous verrez bientost suiuy d'vn Vassal Genereux & d'vne Comedie aussi extraordinaire en son inuention, que reguliere." This "Comedie" must be the *Comédie des comédiens,* because in Scudéry's preface to *Arminius*[2] he says that play was composed after the *Vassal genereux.* The reference is to "un" *Vassal genereux,* not "le", which would seem to imply that it was not yet known, and would accordingly suggest that the preface is referring to performance. One should, then, date the play's first performance in 1633. This is confirmed by an *Epigramme* of Guerente published before *Le Trompeur puni,* which ends as follows:

> Poursuy de trauailler tousiours de mieux en mieux,
> Et bien que tous les deux soient dans vn poinct extreme,
> Acheuant ton VASSAL, fay dire aux enuieux,
> SCUDERY tous les ans se surpasse luy-mesme.[3]

Since the comedy was composed after the tragi-comedy, the reference to the incomplete state of the latter at this date would clearly include the comedy as well. Furthermore, if Gougenot's play had appeared before Chandeville wrote his preface, why had Scudéry not already named

1. Lancaster, *History,* I, 472, n. 4.
2. Georges de Scudéry, *Arminius, ou les frères ennemis, tragi-comédie* (Paris, 1644).
3. The two plays referred to in the second line are *Ligdamon et Lidias* and *Le Trompeur puni.*

his play by the same title, since when it appeared it was obviously intended to compete with Gougenot's? It seems probable that Gougenot's play did not, in fact, appear until 1633, the year suggested by the Frères Parfaict,[4] and that its swift publication in the same year (a swiftness which I assume to be the only reason for Lancaster's choice of 1631/32 as a date which would allow for a rather more normal period to elapse between performance and publication) was spurred by the almost simultaneous appearance of Scudéry's play. Perhaps Scudéry was working on a five-act play when Gougenot's was performed, and he simply combined what he had with notes for another play to make a schema similar to Gougenot's so that the Marais might have a rival play. (In 1634, the verse play *L'Amour caché par l'amour,* which forms the play within the play, was replaced, according to the *Gazette,* by Corneille's *Mélite,* so such a manufacturing of the play is not out of the question[5]). If this is indeed what occurred, then the play by Scudéry supports further what I suggest in Chapters 2 and 3: because it was not merely a simple emulation of Gougenot's play, it provides further evidence that dramatists of the time were bent on examining their theater.

---

4. See les frères Parfaict, *Histoire du théâtre françois depuis son origine jusqu'à présent,* 15 vols. (Paris, 1734-49), V, 62ff; and their *Dictionnaire des théâtres de Paris,* 7 vols. (Paris, 1756), II, 125.

5. Parfaict, *Histoire,* V, 73.

Appendix 2: The *Ballets de Cour*

The change I have described as taking place in the regular theater was echoed in the *ballets de cour*. That this should be so is significant, for the effect of the ballets depended almost entirely on movement, design, and machines, rather than on a text:

> On peut presque dire que la machine était le fond même du ballet de cour. Son rôle commençait quelquefois avant l'action, par la construction ou l'apparition subite de la salle, qui formait ainsi la première partie du spectacle.

Later in the same work, Fournel comments on the costumes:

> Les costumes rivalisèrent avec les machines: ils étalaient générale-ment d'une richesse surprenante. Un ballet était pour les courti-sans une occasion solonnelle de lutter d'éclat, tant par orgueil personnel que pour faire leur cour au roi, qui aimait le faste en toutes choses, principalement dans les habits, autour de lui comme sur sa personne.[1]

In a very real sense the ballet at the beginning of the seventeenth century was an *impromptu,* an entertainment of the court rather than the theater. Strictly speaking, of course, it was a highly organized affair, but to the "spectator", who had friends in the ballet or was a performer himself, it was a kind of game: the court itself presented in a slightly different guise. And the guise was never complete; a ballet often reproduced an actual situation. Fournel cites the example of two lovers who find themselves "remplissant des rôles où ils retrouvaient une image de leur passion réciproque."[2] The ballets of Benserade, and the earlier ones whose designs have survived, provide examples of verses with double meanings: a personal implication, almost always clearly comprehensible, either for the "character" speaking or for the one spoken to; and a meaning deriving from the plot of the ballet. Like certain plays of the period, such ballets come very near to reality.

1. Victor Fournel, éd., *Les Contemporains de Molière,* 3 vols. (Paris, 1863-75), II, 209 and 212.
2. Ibid., II, 192.

According to Henry Prunières,[3] the ballet originated in the more-or-less impromptu and disorganized *momeries* of the Middle Ages, and this spirit of improvisation characterized the later ballets as well. Beaujoyeulx's *Balet comique de la Royne* (1581) is much more organized than these *momeries* ever were, and the dancers have become noble, even royal; but the affair still has the air of a joyous party rather than a theatrical presentation. This particular ballet apparently ran from 10:00 P.M. to 3:30 A.M., by no means an unusually long performance. Usually each ballet was performed only once, which enhanced the atmosphere of freshness and informality. At one point in the *Balet comique*, a nobleman comes running from Circé's garden (the set) and begs the protection of the King (who was, of course, among the "spectators").[4] The audience could scarcely be more closely involved with the spectacle. In this particular ballet, as in not a few others, praise of the King, of his power and his court, was one of the central themes, and as such he and his court were involved in the action at every turn, including the final defeat of Circé.

Prunières suggests that the *ballet de cour* reached the height of its glory and development around 1620, before the death of De Luynes (1621), who arranged most of them; and that his death touched off a decline until the ballet *Prospérité des Armes de la France* in 1641.[5] This period of decline, of course, coincided with that period when the public, conventional theater in Paris was offering an experience similar to that sought by the earlier ballets.

At the beginning of the century, its moment of greatest achievement, the *ballet de cour* was indeed a "total" theater; one that incorporated the spectators as participants, a kind of organized seventeenth-century "happening" involving all those present in an experience different from, but not totally separate from, their everyday reality. Prunières has characterized the state of the "ballet-dramatique" at this time, as it has developed from an older "ballet-mascarade":

3. Henry Prunières, *Le Ballet de Cour en France avant Benserade et Lully* (Paris, 1914), pp. 3-9.
4. This ballet has recently been reprinted in facsimile: Baltasar de Beauioyeulx, *Balet comique de la Royne, 1582*, ed. Giacomo Alessandro Caula (Turin, 1962); see also the long examination by Ludovic Celler, *Les Origines de l'opéra et le "Ballet de la Reine" (1581)* (Paris, 1868).
5. Prunières, *Le Ballet de Cour*, pp. 121-24.

> Le genre nouveau, paré de toutes les grâces et de toutes les séduc-
> tions des fêtes de Cour antérieures emprunte au drame son intrigue
> suivie et son unité. La musique et la danse cessent d'interrompre
> l'action pour y participer. Récits, airs, ballets, pantomimes ont
> leur raison d'être au seul point de vue de l'expression dramatique.
> Nous sommes loin des mascarades italiennes ou françaises aux in-
> trigues rudimentaires; ici la poésie, la musique et la danse con-
> courrent également à l'effet scénique.[6]

And into this total effect is placed the spectator/participant, the
nobleman of the court.

However, between 1620 and 1641 an important change, already
underway, nearly completed its course: the raised stage became a
standard part of the theatrical event. Although in the apparently remarkable *Ballet de la Prospérité des Armes de la France,* which (together with *Mirame*) opened the Palais Cardinal in 1641, a bridge
linked the King with the stage, and although Benserade continued to
write the King and his courtiers into his ballets,[7] the very fact that a
bridge was needed seems to dramatize the widening gap between the
spectator and stage. Increasingly, the roles are taken by professional
actors, and the ballets are staged with the intention of creating an illusion. The same trend is reflected here as in Torelli's elaborate sets,
designed to convince the spectator of the play's reality.[8] The *Gazette*
described the astonishment of the spectators when Torelli staged
Rossi's *Orfeo* in 1647: "Les changements de décoration étaient sur-
prenants; les spectateurs doutaient s'ils ne changeaient pas eux-
mêmes de place."[9]

Classical dramaturgy makes empathy easier for the spectator, because the total illusion is placed before him on a single level. For this
kind of empathy to occur, the spectator cannot himself be physically
a part of the illusion. The apprehension of his own physical presence
in it prevents the spectator from accepting the illusion, at an intellectual or imaginative level, as a different temporal and spatial environ-
ment. Even for the actor, immersed in his character, the situations of

6. Ibid., p. 93.
7. See Charles Silin, *Benserade and his "Ballets de Cour"* (Baltimore, 1940).
8. See Bjurström, *Giacomo Torelli.*
9. Quoted by André Villiers, "Illusion dramatique," p. 5.

the play, and the motivations of other characters, self-forgetfulness
is rare indeed. His sharing in the action of the illusion, after all, is
based on a lack of belief in its reality. For a spectator to include himself, in terms of personal identification with a character, in the stage
illusion, his imagination must ignore the existence of his body. The
spectator sitting *before* the illusion may, if the staging is not intru-
sive, easily forget his own physical presence and accept the emotions
of the stage character: classical dramaturgy depends on this possibility. In the ballets, however, when a courtier would often be playing
himself as well as a character, surrounded by spectators in the absence of a raised stage, the concentrated identification achieved during later plays was quite impossible. Even the machinery, with all
its impressiveness, served an entirely different function in the earlier
ballets:

> Aux prouesses de Francini pour le *Ballet de la Delivrance de
> Renaud* [1617], la rapidité des changements avait fait pousser
> des cris d'étonnement à un public transporté par l'originalité, la
> variété, la nouveauté, la splendeur des décorations et des cos-
> tumes, la prolixité des effets de la machinerie. Mais alors la
> totalité du spectacle, malgré la scène du fond et ses perspectives,
> s'inclut encore dans les dispositions centrales du jeu et de l'au-
> dience—d'une audience qui se sait dans la même salle, les pieds
> sur le même plancher que les joueurs. Le spectacle ne se détache
> pas sur le 'plan du tableau', sur le plan du cadre de scène, comme
> l'*Orfeo* [1647] de Torelli, conforme au nouveau principe illusion-
> niste. Les climats de participation, les comportements perspectifs
> ne sont pas les mêmes.[10]

The *ballet de cour* clearly enjoyed a more considerable capacity than
the traditional theater to create a kind of total experience. In gradually turning its back on those possibilities and evolving towards *opéra*
and *pièces à machines* (whatever the precise connections), it reflects
the preoccupations central to the development of the regular theater.
The characteristics which permitted a total experience would obviously hinder its evolution in this direction, for it could never achieve com-

---

10. Ibid., p. 24.

plete *vraisemblance*.[11] Nonetheless, it went far enough to indicate that the development I have traced was not confined only to one level of the theater.[12]

11. See, for example, comments of Saint-Hubert in *La Manière de composer et de faire réussir les ballets* (Paris, 1641), p. 7, quoted by Prunières, *Les Ballets de Cour,* p. 132; those of the abbé Michel de Pure in *Idée des spectacles anciens et nouveaux* (Paris, 1668), II, 214; and those of the père Ménestrier in *Des Ballets anciens et modernes selon les règles du théâtre* (Paris, 1682), p. 176, both sources quoted by Fournel, *Contemporains,* II, 157 and 358.

12. Jean Rousset shows the same development by contrasting the *Ballet de Circé* (i.e. the *Balet comique de la Royne*) with the *Plaisirs de l'Ile enchantée,* a courtly *fête* enjoyed at Versailles in 1664 (*L'Intérieur et l'extérieur,* pp. 173-74).

Bibliography

The first part of this bibliography contains only those texts cited in the present volume; the second part contains, in addition to those actually cited in my text, other critical works which have been of some importance in its formulation.

PRIMARY SOURCES

Aubignac, François Hédelin, l'abbé d'. *La Pratique du théâtre,* éd. Pierre Martino. Alger: Carbonel; Paris. Champion, 1927.

––––. *La Pucelle d'Orléans, tragédie.* Paris: Anthoine de Sommaville & Augustin Courbé, 1642. [Probably versified by Isaac de Benserade.]

Auvray, Jean. *L'Innocence descouverte, tragi-comédie.* n.p., 1628. (This play [first published 1608] is probably the work of an earlier Jean Auvray than the following two plays.)

––––. *La Dorinde, tragi-comédie dédiée à la Reine.* Paris: Anthoine de Sommaville & André Soubron, 1631.

––––. *La Madonte, tragi-comédie dédiée à la Reine.* Paris: Anthoine de Sommaville, 1632.

Balzac, Jean-Louis Guez de. *Les Oeuvres, divisées en deux tomes.* Paris: Thomas Jolly, 1665.

––––. *Les Oeuvres diverses.* Paris: Toussaint Quinet, 1664.

Baro, Balthasar. *La Parthénie, dédiée à Mademoiselle.* Paris: Anthoine de Sommaville & Augustin Courbé, 1642.

––––. *Le Prince fugitif, poème dramatique.* Paris: Anthoine de Sommaville, 1649.

Beauioyeulx, Baltasar de. *Balet comique de la Royne, 1582.* ed. Giacomo Alessandro Caula. Facsimile edition. Turin: Bottega d'Erasmo, 1962.

Benserade, Isaac de. *Meleagre, tragédie.* Paris: Anthoine de Sommaville, 1641.

––––. *La Mort d'Achille, et la dispute de ses armes, tragédie.* Paris: Anthoine de Sommaville, 1636.

193

Beys, Charles. *Les Illustres Fous,* ed. Merle I. Protzman. The Johns
    Hopkins Studies in Romance Literatures and Languages XLII.
    Baltimore: Johns Hopkins Press, 1942.

Boileau-Despréaux, Nicolas. *Oeuvres complètes, précédées des
    oeuvres de Malherbe, et suivies des oeuvres poétiques de J.-B.
    Rousseau.* Paris: Lefèvre, 1835.

Bossuet, Jacques-Bénigne. *Oeuvres complètes,* éd. P. Lachat, 31 vols.
    Paris: Louis Vivès, 1862-66.

Brosse, N. de. *L'Aveugle clairvoyant, comédie. Representée sur le
    Theatre Royal devant leurs Majestez.* Paris: Toussaint Quinet,
    1650.

——. *Le Curieux impertinent, ou le jaloux, comédie.* Paris: Nicolas
    de Sercy, 1645.

——. *Les Innocens coupables, comédie.* Paris: Anthoine de Somma-
    ville, Augustin Courbé, Toussaint Quinet, et Nicolas de Sercy,
    1645.

——. *Les Songes des hommes esveillez, comédie.* Paris: vefve Nico-
    las de Sercy, 1646.

Chapelain, Jean. *Opuscules critiques,* éd. Alfred Hunter. Paris: Droz,
    1936.

Corneille, Pierre. *Oeuvres,* éd. Charles Marty-Laveaux, 12 vols. Paris:
    Hachette, 1862-68.

——. *Clitandre, tragi-comédie,* éd. R.-L. Wagner. Genève: Droz; Lille:
    Giard, 1949.

——. *L'Illusion comique, comédie,* éd. Robert Garapon. Paris: Didier,
    1957.

——. *Le Cid, tragi-comédie,* éd. Maurice Cauchie. Paris: Didier, 1946.

——. *Mélite, pièce comique,* éd. Mario Roques et Marion Lièvre.
    Genève: Droz; Lille: Giard, 1950.

——. *La Place royalle ou l'amoureux extravagant, comédie,* éd. Jean'
    Claude Brunon. Paris: Didier, 1962.

——. *La Veuve, comédie,* éd. Mario Roques et Marion Lièvre. Genève:
    Droz; Lille: Giard, 1954.

Corneille, Thomas. *Poëmes dramatiques.* Nouvelle édition, 5 vols. Paris:
    Nion fils, 1738.

Cyrano de Bergerac, Savinien. *Oeuvres comiques, galantes et littéraires,*
    éd. P. L. Jacob, 2 vols. Paris: Delahays, 1858. Vol. II.

Deroziers-Beaulieu, le sieur. *Le Galimatias, tragi-comédie,* in *Ancien
    théâtre français,* éd. Viollet-le-Duc, 10 vols. Paris: Jannet, 1856.
    Vol. IX, pp. 427-503.

Desfontaines, Nicolas. *L'Illustre Comédien ou le martyre de Sainct-Genest, tragédie.* Paris: Cardin Besongne, 1645.

Desmarets de Saint-Sorlin, Jean. *Les Visionnaires, comédie,* éd. Gaston Hall. Paris: Didier, 1963.

Durval, Jean Gillebert. *Les Travaux d'Ulysse, tragé-comédie tirée d'Homère, et dédiée à Monseigneur le Duc de Nemours.* Paris: Pierre Menard, [1631].

Du Ryer, Pierre. *Argenis et Poliarque ou Theocrine, tragi-comédie.* Paris: Nicolas Bessin, 1630.

——. *L'Argenis, tragi-comédie, derniere iournée.* Paris: la vefve Nicolas Bessin, 1631.

——. *Esther, tragédie.* Paris: Anthoine de Sommaville et Augustin Courbé, 1644.

——. *Les Vendanges de Suresne, comédie.* Paris: Anthoine de Sommaville, 1636.

Fournel, Victor, éd. *Les Contemporains de Molière. Recueil de comédies, rares ou peu connues, jouées de 1650 à 1680,* 3 vols. Paris: Firmin-Didot, 1863-75.

Fournier, Edouard, éd. *Le Théâtre français au xvie et au xviie siècle ou choix de comédies les plus remarquables antérieures à Molière,* 2 vols. Paris: Garnier, n.d.

Garnier, Robert. *Oeuvres complètes (Théâtre et poésies),* éd. Lucien Pinvert, 2 vols. Paris: Garnier, 1923.

Gaultier Garguille [Hugues Guéru, dit]. *Chansons,* éd. Edouard Fournier. Paris: Jannet, 1858.

Gill, Austin, éd. *Les Ramonneurs, comédie anonyme en prose.* Paris: Didier, 1957.

Gombauld, Jean Ogier de. *L'Amaranthe, pastorale.* Paris: François Pomeray, Anthoine de Sommaville et André Soubron, 1631.

Gougenot, le sieur. *La Comédie des comédiens, tragi-comédie,* in *Ancien théâtre français,* éd. Viollet-le-Duc, 10 vols. Paris: Jannet, 1856. Vol. IX, pp. 303-426.

Grévin, Jacques. *Théâtre complet et poésies choisies,* éd. Lucien Pinvert. Paris: Garnier, 1922.

Hardy, Alexandre. *Les Chastes et loyalles amours de Theagene et Cariclee, reduites du Grec de l'Histoire d'Heliodore en huict poëmes dragmatiques, ou theatres conseccutifs.* Paris: Jacques Quesnel, 1623.

——. *Le Théâtre,* ed. E. Stengel, 5 vols. Marburg: Elwert; Paris: Le Soudier, 1883.

Jodelle, Etienne. *Oeuvres complètes,* éd. Enea Balmas, 2 vols. Paris: Gallimard, 1965 and 1968. Vol. II.

La Calprenède, Gauthier de. *La Mort de Mithridate, tragédie.* Paris: Anthoine de Sommaville, 1637.

La Croix, C. S. de. *La Climene, tragi-comédie pastorale.* Paris: Jean Corrozet, 1631.

La Mesnardière, Hippolyte-Jules de. *La Poetique.* Paris: Anthoine de Sommaville, 1640.

La Taille, Jean de. *Saül le Furieux; La Famine ou les Gabéonites, tragédies,* éd. Elliott Forsyth. Paris: Didier, 1968.

Mairet, Jean. *L'Athenaïs, tragi-comédie.* Paris: Jonas de Brequigny, 1642.

——. *Chryséide et Arimand, tragi-comédie (1625),* éd. Henry Carrington Lancaster. The Johns Hopkins Studies in Romance Literatures and Languages V. Baltimore: Johns Hopkins Press; Paris: Presses Universitaires de France, 1925.

——. *Les Galanteries du Duc d'Ossone,* in *Le Théâtre français au xvie et au xviie siècle,* éd. Edouard Fournier, 2 vols. Paris: Garnier, n. d. Vol. II, pp. 217-79.

——. *L'Illustre Corsaire, tragi-comédie.* Paris: Augustin Courbé, 1640.

——. *La Sophonisbe,* éd. Charles Dédéyan. Paris: Droz, 1945.

——. *Sylvanire,* ed. Richard Otto. Bamberg: Buchner, 1890.

——. *Sylvie, tragi-comédie pastorale,* éd. Jules Marsan. Paris: Droz, 1932.

Mareschal, André. *La Cour bergère, ou l'Arcadie de Messire Philippes Sidney, tragi-comédie.* Paris: Toussaint Quinet, 1640.

——. *Les Railleries de la Cour ou le railleur, comédie,* in *Le Théâtre français au xvie et au xviie siècle,* éd. Edouard Fournier, 2 vols. Paris: Garnier, n.d. Vol. II, pp. 146-208.

Le Mémoire de Mahelot, Laurent et d'autres décorateurs de l'Hôtel de Bourgogne et de la Comédie Française au xviie siècle, éd. Henry Carrington Lancaster. Paris: Champion, 1920.

Molière [Jean-Baptiste Poquelin, dit]. *Oeuvres,* éd. Eugène Despois et Paul Mesnard, 13 vols. Paris: Hachette, 1873-1900. Vol. 4.

Monléon, de. *L'Amphytrite. Dediée à Monseigneur le marquis Deffiat.* Paris: la veufve M. Guillemot et Mattieu Guillemot, 1630.

Montchrestien, Antoine de. *Les Tragédies. Nouvelle édition d'après l'édition de 1604,* éd. Louis Petit de Julleville. Paris: Plon, 1891.

Ouville, Antoine le Metel, sieur d'. *Les Morts vivants, tragi-comédie*. Paris: Cardin Besongne, 1646.

Pichou. *Les Folies de Cardenio, tragi-comédie*, in *Le Théâtre français au xvie et au xviie siècle*, éd. Edouard Fournier, 2 vols. Paris: Garnier, n.d. Vol. II, pp. 3-67.

Prade, Jean le Royer, sieur de. *Annibal, tragi-comédie*. Paris: Nicolas et Jean de la Coste, 1649.

Racan, Honorat de Bueil, marquis de. *Les Bergeries et autres poésies lyriques*, éd. Pierre Camo. Paris: Garnier, 1929.

Rapin, le père René. *Réflexions sur la poetique d'Aristote, et sur les ouvrages des poetes anciens et modernes*. Paris: François Muguet, 1674.

Richelet, Pierre. *Dictionnaire françois. Nouvelle édition*. Amsterdam: Elzevir, 1706.

Rotrou, Jean. *Oeuvres*, éd. Viollet-le-Duc, 5 vols. Paris: Desoer, 1820.

Sabbattini, Nicola. *Pratique pour fabriquer scenes et machines de théâtre*, translated by Maria and Renée Canavaggia and Louis Jouvet. Neuchâtel: Ides et Calendes, 1942.

Saint-Evremond, Charles de. *Oeuvres melées*, éd. Charles Giraud, 3 vols. Paris: Techener, 1865.

Sarasin, Jean-François. *Oeuvres*, éd. Paul Festugière. Paris: Champion, 1926.

Scarron, Paul. *Le Romant comique*, in *Romanciers du xviie siècle*, éd. Antoine Adam. Paris: Gallimard, 1962.

Schélandre, Jean de. *Tyr et Sidon ou les funestes amours de Belcar et Meliane, tragédie*, éd. Jules Haraszti. Paris: Cornély, 1908.

_____. *Tyr et Sidon, tragi-comédie*, in *Ancien théâtre français*, éd. Viollet-le-Duc, 10 vols. Paris: Jannet, 1856. Vol. VIII, pp. 5-225.

Scudéry, Georges de. *Andromire, tragi-comédie*. Paris: Anthoine de Sommaville, 1641.

_____. *L'Apologie du théâtre*. Paris: Augustin Courbé, 1639.

_____. *Arminius, ou les frères ennemis, tragi-comédie*. Paris: Toussaint Quinet & Nicolas de Sercy, 1644.

_____. *La Comédie des comédiens. Poeme de nouvelle invention*. Paris: Augustin Courbé, 1635.

_____. *Ligdamon et Lidias, ou la ressemblance, tragi-comédie*. Paris: François Targa, 1631.

_____. *La Mort de César, tragédie*. Paris: Augustin Courbé, 1636.

_____. *Le Prince déguisé, tragi-comédie*. Paris: Augustin Courbé, 1636.

———. *Le Trompeur puny, ou l'histoire septentrionale, tragi-comédie.* Paris: Anthoine de Sommaville, 1633.

———. *Le Vassal genereux, poeme tragi-comique.* Paris: Augustin Courbé, 1636.

Tallemant des Réaux, Gédéon. *Les Historiettes,* éd. Georges Mongrédien, 8 vols. Paris: Garnier, n.d.

Théâtre françois ou recueil des meilleures pièces du théâtre, 12 vols. Paris: P. Gandouin et al, 1737.

Théophile de Viau. *Les Amours tragiques de Pyrame et Thisbé, tragédie,* in *Oeuvres complètes,* éd. Maurice Alléaume, 2 vols. Paris: Jannet, 1855. Vol. II, pp. 95-142.

Tristan l'Hermite, François. *La Mariane, tragédie,* éd. Jacques Madeleine. Paris: Hachette, 1919.

———. *Osmon, tragédie,* éd. Edmond Girard. Paris: La Maison des Poètes, 1906.

———. *Panthée, tragédie,* in *Théâtre françois,* 12 vols. Paris: Gandouin et al, 1737. Vol. II, pp. 446-548.

Trotterel, Pierre, sieur d'Avès. *La Tragédie de Sainte Agnès. Publiée sur l'imprimé de David du Petit Val (Rouen, 1615).* Paris: Librairie des Bibliophiles, 1879.

Viollet-le-Duc, éd. *Ancien théâtre français,* 10 vols. Paris: Jannet, 1856.

SECONDARY SOURCES

Abraham, Claude K. *The Strangers: The Tragic World of Tristan l'Hermite.* University of Florida Monographs. Humanities XXIII. Gainesville: University of Florida Press, 1966.

Adam, Antoine. *Histoire de la littérature française au xviie siècle,* 5 vols. Paris: Del Duca, 1962-68.

Aristotle. *Poetics,* trans. and ed. Ingram Bywater. Oxford: Clarendon Press, 1909.

Arnaud, Charles. *Les Théories dramatiques au xviie siècle. Etude sur la vie et les oeuvres de l'abbé d'Aubignac.* Paris: Picard, 1888.

Artaud, Antonin. *Le Théâtre et son double.* Paris: Gallimard, 1964.

Attinger, Gustave. *L'Esprit de la commedia dell'arte dans le théâtre français.* Paris: Librairie Théâtrale; Neuchâtel: La Baconnière, 1950.

Baldwin, Charles Sears. *Renaissance Literary Theory and Practice.*
    Gloucester, Mass.: Smith, 1959.
Barrault, Jean-Louis. *Réflexions sur le théâtre.* Paris: Vautrain, 1949.
Baty, Gaston. *Rideau baissé.* Paris: Bordas, 1949.
——, et Chavance, René. *Vie de l'art théâtral des origines à nos jours.*
    Paris: Plon, 1952.
Beaumarchais, Pierre-Augustin Caron de. *Théâtre,* éd. Georges Girard.
    Paris: Firmin Didot, 1928.
Bénichou, Paul. *Morales du grand siècle.* Paris: Gallimard, 1948.
Bergson, Henri. *Le Rire. Essai sur la signification du comique.* Paris:
    Alcan, 1938.
Bernardin, Napoléon-Maurice. *Un Précurseur de Racine: Tristan
    l'Hermite, sieur du Solier (1601-1655). Sa famille, sa vie, ses
    oeuvres.* Paris: Picard, 1895.
Bizos, Gaston. *Etude sur la vie et les oeuvres de Jean de Mairet.* Paris:
    Thorin, 1877.
Bjurström, Per. *Giacomo Torelli and Baroque Stage Design.* Stock-
    holm: Almqvist & Wiksell, 1961.
Boorsch, Jean. "Remarques sur la technique dramatique de Corneille."
    In *Studies by Members of the French Department of Yale Uni-
    versity,* ed. Albert Feuillerat. Yale Romanic Studies XVIII. New
    Haven: Yale University Press, 1941.
Borgerhoff, E. B. O. *The Evolution of Liberal Theory and Practice in
    the French Theater 1680-1757.* Princeton: Princeton University
    Press, 1936.
Bray, René. *La Formation de la doctrine classique en France.* Paris:
    Hachette, 1927.
Büdel, Oscar. "Contemporary Theater and Aesthetic Distance,"
    PMLA LXXVI, 3 (1961), pp. 277-91.
Bullough, Edward. " 'Psychical distance' as a Factor in Art and an
    Esthetic Principle," *British Journal of Psychology* V (1913), pp.
    87-118.
Buffum, Imbrie. *Studies in the Baroque from Montaigne to Rotrou.*
    Yale Romanic Studies, Second Series IV. New Haven: Yale
    University Press; Paris: Presses Universitaires de France, 1957.
Bürger, P. "Illusion und Wirklichkeit im *Saint-Genest* von Jean Rotrou,"
    Germanisch-romanische Monatschrift XIV (1964), pp. 241-67.
Castor, Grahame. *Pléiade Poetics. A Study in Sixteenth Century
    Thought and Terminology.* Cambridge: Cambridge University
    Press, 1964.

Celler, Ludovic. *Les Origines de l'opéra et le "Ballet de la Reine" (1581).* Paris: Didier, 1868.

Clements, Robert J. *Critical Theory and Practice of the Pléiade.* Harvard Studies in Romance Languages XVIII. Cambridge, Mass.: Harvard University Press, 1942.

Cohen, Gustave. *Histoire de la mise en scène dans le théâtre religieux français du Moyen Age.* 3rd ed. Paris: Champion, 1951.

———. *Le Théâtre en France au Moyen Age,* 2 vols. Paris: Rieder, 1928 and 1931.

Dabney, Lancaster E. *French Dramatic Literature in the Reign of Henri IV. A Study of the Extant Plays Composed in French between 1589 and 1610.* Austin, Texas: The University Cooperative Society, 1952.

Dalla Valle, Daniela. *Il Teatro di Tristan l'Hermite. Saggio storico e critico.* Università di Torino, Pubblicazioni della Facoltà di Lettere e Filosofia XV, 2. Turin: Giappichelli, 1964.

Deierkauf-Holsboer, S. Wilma. *Le Théâtre du Marais,* 2 vols. Paris: Nizet, 1954 and 1958.

———. *L'Histoire de la mise en scène dans le théâtre français à Paris de 1600 à 1673.* Paris: Nizet, 1960.

———. "Vie d'Alexandre Hardy. Poète du Roi," *Proceedings of the American Philosophical Society* XCIV, 4 (1947), pp. 328-404.

Descotes, Maurice. *Le Public du théâtre et son histoire.* Paris: Presses Universitaires de France, 1964.

Diderot, Denis. *Oeuvres esthétiques,* éd. Paul Vernières. Paris: Garnier, 1965.

Doat, Jan. *Entrée du public. La Psychologie collective et le théâtre.* Paris: Flore, 1947.

Doubrovsky, Serge. *Corneille et la dialectique du héros.* Paris: Gallimard, 1962.

Duvignaud, Jean. *Sociologie du théâtre. Essai sur les ombres collectives.* Paris: Presses Universitaires de France, 1965.

Faguet, Emile. *La Tragédie française au xvie siècle.* Paris: Fontemoing, 1912.

Forsyth, Elliott. *La Tragédie française de Jodelle à Corneille (1553-1640). Le thème de la vengeance.* Paris: Nizet, 1962.

Foucault, Michel. *Folie et déraison: histoire de la folie à l'âge classique.* Paris: Plon, 1961.

Fries, Wilhelm. *Der Stil der Theaterstücke Rotrous. Eine Untersuchung über Formprobleme des barocken Vorstadiums der französischen Literatur des Klassizismus.* Würzburg: Richard Mayr, 1933.

Gaiffe, Félix. *Le Rire et la scène française.* Paris: Boivin, 1931.

Garapon, Robert. *La Fantaisie verbale et le comique dans le théâtre français du Moyen Age à la fin du xviie siècle.* Paris: Armand Colin, 1957.

Ghéon, Henri. *L'Art du théâtre.* Montréal: Serge, 1944.

Gouhier, Henri. *L'Essence du théâtre.* Paris: Plon, 1943.

_____. "Tragique et transcendance: Introduction à un débat général." In *Le Théâtre tragique,* éd. Jean Jacquot. Paris: Centre Nationale de la Recherche Scientifique, 1962.

Grossvogel, David I. *The Self-Conscious Stage in Modern French Drama.* New York: Columbia University Press, 1958.

Guicharnaud, Jacques. "Beware of Happiness: Mairet's *Sophonisbe,*" *Yale French Studies* XXXVIII *(The Classical Line),* pp. 205-21.

Harvey, Lawrence E. "The Denouement of *Mélite* and the Role of the Nourrice," *Modern Language Notes* LXXI, 3 (1956), pp. 200-03.

Hubert, Judd David. *Essai d'exégèse racinienne: les secrets témoins.* Paris: Nizet, 1956.

_____. *Molière and the Comedy of Intellect.* Berkeley & Los Angeles: University of California Press, 1962.

_____. "Les Funestes Amours de Belcar et Meliane," *Revue d'Histoire Littéraire* LVIII, 1 (1958), pp. 16-34.

_____. "Le Réel et l'illusoire dans le théâtre de Corneille et dans celui de Rotrou," *Revue des Sciences Humaines* XCI, n.s. (1958), pp. 333-50.

Jacquot, Jean, éd. *Le Lieu théâtral à la Renaissance.* Paris: Centre Nationale de la Recherche Scientifique, 1964.

_____, éd. *Réalisme et poésie au théâtre.* Paris: Centre Nationale de la Recherche Scientifique, 1960.

_____, éd. *Le Théâtre tragique.* Centre Nationale de la Recherche Scientifique, 1962.

Jouvet, Louis. *Témoignages sur le théâtre.* Paris: Flammarion, 1952.

_____. *Réflexions du comédien.* Paris: Librairie Théâtrale, 1952.

Kernodle, George R. *From Art to Theatre. Form and Convention in the Renaissance.* Chicago: University of Chicago Press, 1944.

Knutson, Harold C. *The Comic Game: A Study of Rotrou's Comic Theater.* University of California Publications in Modern Philology LXXIX. Berkeley & Los Angeles: University of California Press, 1966.

Lancaster, Henry Carrington. *The French Tragi-Comedy. Its Origin and Development from 1552-1628.* Baltimore: Furst, 1907.

———. *A History of French Dramatic Literature in the Seventeenth Century,* 5 parts in 9 vols. Baltimore: Johns Hopkins Press, 1929-42.

Lanson, Gustave. *Esquisse d'une histoire de la tragédie française.* New York: Columbia University Press, 1920.

Lawrenson, Thomas E. *The French Stage in the Seventeenth Century: A Study in the Advent of the Italian Order.* Manchester: Manchester University Press, 1957.

———; Roy, Donald; and Southern, Richard. "Le *Mémoire* de Mahelot et l'*Agarite* de Durval: vers une réconstitution pratique." In *Le Lieu théâtral à la Renaissance,* éd. Jean Jacquot. Paris: Centre Nationale de la Recherche Scientifique, 1964.

Lebègue, Raymond. *La Tragédie française de la Renaissance.* Bruxelles: Office de Publicité, 1954.

———. *La Tragédie réligieuse en France. Les Débuts (1514-1573).* Paris: Champion, 1929.

———. "De la Renaissance au classicisme. Le théâtre baroque en France," *Bibliothèque d'Humanisme et Renaissance.* Travaux et documents II (1942), pp. 161-84.

———. "Quelques survivances de la mise en scène médiévale." In *Mélanges d'histoire du théâtre du Moyen Age et de la Renaissance, offerts à Gustave Cohen.* Paris: Nizet, 1950.

———. "Le Répertoire d'une troupe française à la fin du xvie siècle," *Revue d'Histoire du Théâtre* I-II (1948), pp. 9-24.

———. "Unité et pluralité de lieu dans le théâtre français (1450-1600)." In *Le Lieu théâtral à la Renaissance,* éd. Jean Jacquot. Paris: Centre Nationale de la Recherche Scientifique, 1964.

———. "La Vie dramatique en province au xviie siècle," *XVIIe Siècle* XXXIX (1958), pp. 125-37.

Lough, John. *Paris Theatre Audiences in the Seventeenth and Eighteenth Centuries.* London: Oxford University Press, 1957.

Loukovitch, Kosta. *L'Evolution de la tragédie réligieuse classique en France.* Paris: Droz, 1933.

Marsan, Jules. *La Pastorale dramatique en France à la fin du xvie et au commencement du xviie siècle.* Paris: Hachette, 1905.

May, Georges. *Tragédie cornélienne, tragedie racinienne. Etude sur les sources de l'intérêt dramatique.* Illinois Studies in Language and Literature XXXII, 4. Urbana, Illinois: University of Illinois Press, 1948.

Mélèse, Pierre. *Le Théâtre et le public à Paris sous Louis XIV, 1659-1715.* Paris: Droz, 1934.

_____. *Répertoire analytique des documents contemporains d'information et de critique concernant le théâtre à Paris sous Louis XIV, 1659-1715.* Paris. Droz, 1935.

_____. "Les Conditions matérielles du théâtre à Paris sous Louis XIV," *XVIIe Siècle* XXXIX (1958), pp. 104-24.

Michelis, P. A. "Aesthetic Distance and the Charm of Contemporary Art," *Journal of Aesthetics and Art Criticism* XXVIII, 1 (Sept. 1959), pp. 1-45.

Moore, Will G. *Molière: A New Criticism.* Oxford: Clarendon Press, 1949.

_____. "Molière's Theory of Comedy," *Esprit Créateur* VI, 3 (1966), pp. 137-44.

Mongrédien, Georges. *Dictionnaire biographique des comédiens français au xviie siècle.* Paris: Centre Nationale de la Recherche Scientifique, 1961.

_____. *Les Grands Comédiens du xviie siècle.* Paris: Le Livre, 1927.

Morel, Jacques. *Jean Rotrou, dramaturge de l'ambiguité.* Paris: Armand Colin, 1968.

_____. "La Présentation scénique du songe dans les tragédies françaises au xviie siècle," *Revue d'Histoire du Théâtre* II (1951), pp. 153-63.

Moynet, M. J. *L'Envers du théâtre, machines et décorations.* Paris: Hachette, 1888.

Nadal, Octave. *Le Sentiment de l'amour dans l'oeuvre de Pierre Corneille.* Paris: Gallimard, 1948.

_____. "La Scène française d'Alexandre Hardy à Corneille." In *Le Préclassicisme français,* éd. Jean Tortel. Paris: Cahiers du Sud, 1952.

Nelson, Robert J. *Corneille: His Heroes and Their Worlds.* Philadelphia: University of Pennsylvania Press, 1963.

——. *Play Within a Play. The Dramatist's Conception of his Art: Shakespeare to Anouilh.* Yale Romanic Studies, Second Series V. New Haven: Yale University Press, 1958.

Orlando, Francesco. *Rotrou dalla tragicommedia alla tragedia.* Turin: Bottega d'Erasmo, 1963.

——. "Il sogno di Erode e i motiva della Mariane," *Saggi e Ricerche di Letteratura Francese* II (1961), pp. 31-79.

Parfaict, Claude et François, les frères. *Dictionnaire des théâtres de Paris,* 7 vols. Paris: Lambert, 1756.

——. *Histoire du théâtre françois depuis son origine jusqu'à présent,* 15 vols. Paris: Morin et al, 1734-49.

Petit de Julleville, Louis. *Les Mystères,* 2 vols. Paris: Hachette, 1880.

Prunières, Henry. *Le Ballet de cour en France avant Benserade et Lully, suivi du "Ballet de la délivrance de Renaud."* Paris: Laurens, 1914.

Raymond, Marcel. *Baroque et Renaissance poétique.* Paris: Corti, 1955.

Reese, Helen Reese. *La Mesnardière's "Poétique" (1639): Sources and Dramatic Theories.* The Johns Hopkins Studies in Romance Literatures and Languages XXVIII. Baltimore: Johns Hopkins Press, 1937.

Rigal, Eugène. *Alexandre Hardy et le théâtre français à la fin du xvie et au commencement du xviie siècle.* Paris: Hachette, 1889.

Rivaille, Louis. *Les Débuts de P. Corneille.* Paris: Boivin, 1936.

Rousset, Jean. *L'Intérieur et l'extérieur: Essais sur la poésie et sur le théâtre au xviie siècle.* Paris: Corti, 1968.

——. *La Littérature de l'âge baroque en France: Circé et le paon.* Paris: Corti, 1954.

Roy, Donald H. "La Scène de l'Hôtel de Bourgogne," *Revue d'Histoire du Théâtre* (1962), pp. 227-35.

Sakharoff, Micheline. *Le Héros, sa liberté et son efficacité de Garnier à Rotrou.* Paris: Nizet, 1967.

Sartre, Jean-Paul. "Forgers of Myths: The Young Playwrights of France," *Theatre Arts* XXX, 6 (1946), pp. 324-35.

Schérer, Jacques. *La Dramaturgie classique en France.* Paris: Nizet, 1962.

Schüler, Gerda. *Die Rezeption der spanischen Comedia in Frankreich in der ersten Hälfte des 17. Jahrhunderts: Lope de Vega und Jean Rotrou.* Cologne: Walter Kleikamp, 1966.

Schwartz, I. A. *The Commedia dell'Arte and its Influence on French Comedy in the Seventeenth Century*. New York: New York University, 1931.

Silin, Charles I. *Benserade and his "Ballets de cour."* Baltimore: Johns Hopkins Press, 1940.

Sorel, Charles. *Histoire comique de Francion*. In *Romanciers du XVIIᵉ siècle*, éd. Antoine Adam. Paris: Gallimard, 1958.

Spingarn, J. E. *A History of Literary Criticism in the Renaissance*. New York and London: Columbia University Press, 1908.

Starobinski, Jean. *Jean-Jacques Rousseau: la transparence et l'obstacle*. Paris: Plon, 1957.

Stendhal [Marie Henri Beyle, dit]. *Racine et Shakespeare*, in *Oeuvres complètes*, éd. Georges Eudes, 25 vols. Paris: Pierre Larrive, 1946-56. Vol. XVI.

Sutcliffe, F. E. *Guez de Balzac et son temps: Littérature et politique*. Paris: Nizet, 1959.

Touchard, Pierre-Aymé. *Dionysos: Apologie pour le théâtre*. Paris: Seuil, 1949.

Valle Abad, Federico del. *Influencia española sobre la literatura francesa: Juan Rotrou (1609-1650). Ensayo critico*. Avila: Senén Martín, 1946.

Vanuxem, Jacques. "Le Décor de théâtre sous Louis XIV," *XVIIᵉ Siècle* XXXIX (1958), pp. 196-217.

Van Baelen, Jacqueline. *Rotrou: le héros tragique et la révolte*. Paris: Nizet, 1965.

Van Roosbroeck, Gustave L. "A Commonplace in Corneille's *Mélite:* the Madness of Eraste," *Modern Philology* XVII, 3 (July 1919), pp. 29-37.

——. "Preciosity in Corneille's Early Plays," *Philological Quarterly* VI, 1 (1927), pp. 19-31.

Védier, Georges. *Origine et évolution de la dramaturgie néo-classique*. Paris: Presses Universitaires de France, 1955.

Vilar, Jean. *De La Tradition théâtrale*. Paris: Gallimard, 1963 (first published 1955).

Villiers, André. "Illusion dramatique et dramaturgie classique," *XVIIᵉ Siècle* LXXIII (1966), pp. 3-35.

Vinaver, Eugène. *Racine et la poésie tragique, essai*. 2ⁿᵈ ed. Paris: Nizet, 1963.

Voltaire, François-Marie Arouet de. *Oeuvres complètes,* 40 vols.
    [Genève: Cramer], 1775. Vols. II-X.
Weinberg, Bernard. *A History of Criticism in the Italian Renaissance,*
    2 vols. Chicago and London: University of Chicago Press, 1961.
√ Wiley, W. L. *The Early Public Theatre in France.* Cambridge, Mass.:
    Harvard University Press, 1960.

Index